T0132703

Big Bang Being

Developing the Sustainability Mindset

A fascinating book that uncovers and deeply explores a question we've all pondered: why we do what we do. Isabel Rimanoczy walks us through carefully researched case studies to uncover the intriguing similarities – and differences – between people who dedicate their lives to the greater good. Immensely enjoyable and effortless to read, the author gets to the heart of the essential issue of how we can instill altruistic values to the next generation of leaders – and how they can do even better than us.

Jeffrey Hollender, Founder, Jeffrey Hollender Partners; Co-founder, Seventh Generation

Anybody who has worked in the sustainability field for as long as I have has often asked themselves a key question, which Isabel Rimanoczy also poses in *Big Bang Being*: Why is the pace of change so glacial? And a key part of the answer, as she explains, is that we are dealing not just with vested interests but with vested emotions, vested behaviours, vested psychology and vested cultures. Changing all of these will be an intergenerational task, but important clues on how it can best be done can be found within.

John Elkington, Executive Chairman, Volans; Co-founder, SustainAbility; author of *The Zeronauts: Breaking the Sustainability Barrier*

This is an ambitious and admirable book. Our challenge is to *be* as well as to *do*; and, as Dr Rimanoczy emphasizes, that *being* is a critical foundation for doing meaningful innovative things. Carl Jung emphasized that integration of all parts of us, particularly the unconscious, is the great challenge of maturity; and I would add that it is what gives true leaders the "mass" they need to really make a difference. This book focuses on how to both become and do: the inner as well as outward journey.

Harry Strachan, Former Professor at INCAE and Harvard Business School; Director Emeritus, Bain & Co.

In *Big Bang Being*, Isabel Rimanoczy knocks the reader out of her comfort zone and questions Western society's core beliefs. *Big Bang Being* contraposes our traditional values of economic growth, achievement, comfort and independence with far more sustaining concepts – interdependence, collaboration, humility, and balance. Read and act on this fundamental wisdom.

Rick Schnieders, Chairman and CEO (Retired), Sysco Corporation

It is clear to any serious scholar of business that not all's right with the world, as Browning wrote. The problem is not the unceasing drive for more efficiency and more profits; the problem is that business is no longer aligned with the worldly context in which it operates. One might say that business, if it ever had a soul, has now lost it, but it cannot recover it by following the myriad of green, sustainable, or socially responsible pathways being taught at now virtually all schools of business and management. The problem lies not in that metaphorical soul of an organization, but in the souls of those leaders and managers riding the wave of these new programs.

Isabel Rimanoczy's *Big Bang Being: Developing the Sustainability Mindset* comes from her understanding that how business executives picture themselves far beyond the next quarter's results is critical in determining whether the business will break out of the pack. Whether conscious of it or not, their underlying philosophy shapes these executives' aspirations and ways of operating. It drives them to create fair trade organizations that would look irrational in a class on supply chain management.

The world-view's underlying management education and practice is focused almost entirely on the left brain's notions of rationality and order.

The way we look at the world shapes our reality, making us partners in a creative process. If we see ourselves living in a fragmented, mechanistic, and "rational" world, if we experience at the same time extreme optimism and feelings of emptiness and paranoia, we may be subject to too much of a left hemisphere and too little of the balancing act contributed by the right hemisphere.

True sustainability that encompasses the historical aspirations of all human beings lies outside of the definitions and metrics that business uses. Mangers have to escape these definition and metrics, but that will take a change in the way they think, exercising their right brains. Rimanoczy spends much of the book showing us how to do this. She is informed in this by the 16 leaders she interviewed as well as a wide range of spiritual and philosophical domains. One key that emerges is that executives concerned about their legacy are able to transcend the standard values that drive business: Economic growth, Achievement, Control, Wealth, Comfort, Independence, Competition, Knowledge, and Speed. She has included many practices she uses as a "legacy coach", doing just what she has written about.

People who intend to leave a better world after they has finished their life work do this by being the change they picture. Gandhi is most remembered by these words, "You must be the change you want to see in the world." The key to this lies in the word be. The title of the book refers to this kind of being in an exaggerated manner to show how far away from it most of us are today. Although business schools may find this message hard to swallow, it is critical to their and to our futures. If the state of the world continues to deteriorate, sooner or later the finger of blame will point directly at business. Management schools would do well to consider putting the lessons in this book into their present curriculum on an equal or raised footing with everything else.

John Ehrenfeld, Executive Director, International Society for Industrial Ecology; Former Director, MIT Program on Technology, Business, and Environment; author of *Sustainability by Design*

In revisiting some of my favorite philosophical sayings recently, I was struck again by the comment of the philosopher José Ortega y Gasset, who said, "I am both a man and my environment. And in order to save myself, I must save it as well." A few days later I received this book by Isabel Rimanoczy, who in a refreshing, thought-provoking way sheds new light on the Spanish philosopher's thought.

Big Bang Being is a book so readable and accessible that it might almost appear self-evident. However, all her statements, reflections, and conclusions result from a thorough, passionate, and responsible intellect.

The book illustrates, suggests, and inspires the reader to take on a task that is demanded by the times in which we live: to develop to its fullest our humanity, our intellectual capacity, and our way of being. And to do it for ourselves and for others, so as to safeguard life on this wonderful planet. Ultimately, the task is to help save our environment, which is the only one we have, and in so doing, to save ourselves.

Silvia Zimmermann del Castillo, Argentine thinker and author; Director, Argentine Chapter, Club de Roma

I appreciate the way Rimanoczy distills lessons from the stories of the leaders she interviews. Instead of imposing theory she finds the common threads. Sixteen people's lives offer insights into leadership that are useful for all of us.

Hal Hamilton, Founder and Co-director, Sustainable Food Lab

A stimulating and provocative guide for developing the sustainability mindset that we all need to acquire. Creative, serious, playful, and fun to read. Highly recommended.

James A.F. Stoner, Professor of Management Systems and chairholder, James A.F. Stoner Chair in Global Sustainability, Fordham University; author and co-author of *Management* **(Prentice Hall)**

Isabel describes her wonderful journey of addressing the environmental challenges facing our society, and she does it by emphasizing self-awareness and focusing on the meaningful experiences of certain business leaders. What motivates us to help? What do we expect from ourselves in the process? Why is it that we can achieve self-realization in this area more

than anywhere else? This book is a good starting point in beginning to reflect and then step into action to achieve, sustainability.
Marcelo Fumasoni, Vice President, Human Resources, Region Latin America and Canada, Novartis

A sound review of why business leaders and others find it difficult to embrace sustainability actions. But it provides clear suggestions on why and how they should act with the emphasis on personal values and ideas. It also shows why change will involve a huge struggle, and therefore time, but which can be hastened if those with the power to influence take quality time to reflect and pause. A core message is that beyond our addiction to speed, there is the need to be informed and stop the denial.
Chandran Nair, Founder and Executive Director, Global Institute for Tomorrow; author of *Consumptionomics*

In this book, Isabel Rimanoczy manages to both describe and to discover the essence of modern leadership. A resource that, in these times, seems to be in short supply. Precisely because of this absence, we are immersed in a social, institutional and, in many cases, economic labyrinth, from which we struggle constantly to find our way out.

However, as Isabel describes the research findings into the sustainability mindset, she highlights the keys to the challenge we face as we redefine the paradigm for a model of sustainability. The author challenges everyone to develop a strong bond with their environment, because humans are the only beings capable of making the needed change. Every decision we make is meaningful, and it is the combination of our actions that will create the proper environment in which positive change will take place.
Aleandra Scafati, Founder, Ecomujeres.com.ar; Director, Post Graduate Program for the Environment and Sustainable Development, Pontificia Universidad Católica Argentina

The magic of a great storyteller is to take truths from the personal to a circle of friends and fellow travelers to the tableau of society, commerce, mindsets, and the world we live in. Isabel Rimanoczy's poignant stories, evocative questions, and quirky illustrations point to new ways of living and leading. Her *Big Bang Being* threads this journey with lessons from ancient wisdom and modern science, and speaks deeply and intelligently to the ties that bind us to nature and to one another. Food for the mind, the heart, and a better future.
Philip H. Mirvis, PhD, Senior Fellow, Global Network on Corporate Citizenship; co-author of *Beyond Good Company*

Rimanoczy is passionate about fostering an awareness in us of the importance of creating an environmental sustainability mindset. This book will help readers realize how to leave a personal legacy by committing to start their personal journey to make a difference in the world for future generations.

Nancy Zentis, PhD, CEO/Founder, Institute of Organization Development; Founder, South Florida OD Network

We need more "big bang beings" to truly win the fight for sustainable development. This informative and engaging book tells you how you can become one.

Oliver Laasch, Founder and Director, Center for Responsible Management Education (CRME); author and editor, *Principles of Responsible Management: Sustainability, Responsibility, Ethics* (forthcoming, September 2013)

Big Bang Being could no be more timely nor relevant. The street gladly believes that business leaders do not care for the environment as much as they care for their profitability and share price. I believe the two cannot be separated anymore. This book brings the point across with wonderful examples to emulate. A recommended read for all in the boardroom and top management.

Fernando Paiz, former chairman, Wal-Mart Central America

Other books by Isabel Rimanoczy:

Action Reflection Learning

Minervas Circles of Dialogue

BIG BANG BEING

Developing the Sustainability Mindset

Isabel Rimanoczy

Routledge
Taylor & Francis Group

LONDON AND NEW YORK

First published 2013 by Greenleaf Publishing

Published 2017 by Routledge
2 Park Square, Milton Park, Abingdon, Oxon OX14 4RN
711 Third Avenue, New York, NY 10017, USA

Routledge is an imprint of the Taylor & Francis Group, an informa business

Copyright © 2013 Taylor & Francis

British Library Cataloguing in Publication Data:
   A catalogue record for this book is available from the British Library.

   ISBN-13: 978-1-906093-87-7 (pbk)

Cover: Matías Fernández Beltrami
Art and illustrations: Mirah
Back cover photograph: Mariam Tamborenea

To my parents, and my grandparents,

for what they stood for.

Contents

Foreword
Ervin Laszlo

Isabel Rimanoczy fills an important hiatus in our attempt to think out the strategy that is most likely to bring about an acceptable level of sustainability in our crisis-prone world. We know that the current economic political and even ecological and social system is not sustainable as it now functions, and we know that the change required for making it sustainable must be fundamental. But we are still not clear just what that change involves. Most of all, where to begin? It is here that this book offers truly invaluable information.

The classical thinking is that change must happen at the top; the political leaders must change their strategies. They must lead in a fundamentally different and better way. But the more recent thinking is that the leaders are not capable of making the necessary shift: they are too locked into their current position, being dependent for their power on popular favor in the electorate and, above all, for the support of the major lobbies that provide the influence and the funds for them to be elected, and, once elected, to stay in power. Thus the emerging wisdom is to concentrate on civil society – on the new-thinking alternative cultures, where sustainability is seen as a basic value. But here the evidence suggests that, here, if not the will, then the power to effect the necessary change is lacking. Civil society groups are as yet dispersed and do not possess the necessary clout to change economic and political systems – even if they are making important changes in the civic domain.

It would appear that we are locked into a hopeless situation. The requirement for change is growing, as both the economic-social-financial system and the associated ecological system are moving toward thresholds of irreversibility. The status quo is not tenable, and is fraught with danger. If a major "tipping point" occurs before we are prepared for it, effecting the necessary change could be both extremely costly and high-risk. It may not be possible in practice. Do we then sit still and wait for disaster to occur? Or hope for a miraculous shift in the balances of power that decide our future? No, Isabel Rimanoczy tells us, we can turn our attention to an element in the decision-making structure of our time that we had not sufficiently exploited. This is business leadership.

Of course, attention has focused on business managers in regard to exercising responsible leadership, but the assumption has been, and still largely is, that they exercise such leadership if it's in their own interest. Being responsible is good for business, so let's make our businesses responsible – within the limits where it makes good profit. This is perceived as advanced thinking in business circles. The problem with acting on it is that what is good for business in the short term may not be good for society in the long. If what we need is fundamental change, serving the existing interests in the system is only to reinforce that system and make it more resistant to change. We need business people not as "facilitators" and "stabilizers" but as "catalysts" and "transformers." But would that not ask business people to have the courage to go against their perceived interests? Would any business leader be willing to do that? Would he or she not undermine his or her own position and decision-making base if he or she does?

Asking this level of social altruism of business leaders seems far-fetched. But Isabel Rimanoczy shows us that it is not. There are business leaders who are motivated to "do good" even at the risk of not "doing all that well," at least in the short-run. We had known that there are such people in the world, but they were believed to be mainly, or perhaps entirely, in the ranks of retired people, with a business background but no actual business engagement. They are well-meaning and possibly intellectually influential people, but not effective power-holders: important but not sufficient elements to effect real change. Business people must act as powerful business leaders on the job, exercising power with a transformative mindset.

It was not clear whether such people exist. Reading this book, we realize that they do. And we know something even more than that: we also know what makes them tick. What the critical factors are that shift a profit- and power-oriented manager into a sustainability-oriented transformative leader.

And here is where another door opens: one that shows us that the transformation begins in our heart, in our mindfulness, in the values that lie behind our actions. Our Western, materialistic and consumption-based model has brought us collectively to a breaking point. As the visionary study of *The Limits to Growth*, back in the '70s, tried to show us, there is something that cannot continue the way it goes, and it's up to us to lead the change. The path to the urgent transformative change lies, however, not so much in the technical innovations, but foremost in the paradigm shift. We need, for once, to understand the interconnectedness of all that is; the systemic interrelationships; that human beings are part of Nature not above it; and that the experience of deep, spiritual "being" comes before any doing. If we can tap into this ancestral wisdom, which is seen in these business leaders but is also in every one of us, we may not be too late to build a bridge over the cliff we're heading for. This is what Rimanoczy suggests with the "big bang being."

It is of course always risky to generalize from particular instances. But in this case the risk is worth taking; it's an opportunity we cannot let go by. What we get here is extremely useful information. We could use it in addressing the business community, catalyzing the transformative mindset in key individuals who can become change accelerators. We need them, and we all can become one of them.

Ervin Laszlo

Preface

CEOs making a difference: why wait for retirement?

One glorious morning a few years ago I was sipping coffee and reading a magazine story about a corporate CEO who was about to retire and who was talking passionately about his next project – working in a philanthropic cause.

Yet another CEO retiree engaging in philanthropy, I mused. What is it about these retired leaders engaging in causes for the common good? Is it a fashion? Has it always been so and journalists just didn't report on it? I could imagine that after a busy corporate life, there may be a need to continue to be active, and maybe retirement is the perfect time to start thinking of leaving a legacy, but don't we all shape a legacy, daily, with the decisions we make and the interactions we have?

And, I asked myself, what about these leaders who are in the news every day? Were they aware of the impact that their daily decisions were having on the environment? On communities? Because multinational corporations, whose business strategies, processes, value systems and personnel traverse geographic borders, definitely do impact the lives of people across the entire globe! To engage, as a retired person, in causes to benefit society, is great, but I wondered what would be the effect on the world if leaders were to assess the impact of their decisions *while they were still in power*, and if they were to be mindful of this influence throughout their careers.

How would it shape their thinking? How would it inform their decisions? And I even posed myself an ironic question: If we all would consider the potential impact of the products we design, the services we launch, the materials we use, or the communications we spread, and let that thinking guide our actions – would we still need philanthropy to such an extent?

It was shortly after this, that I first heard about how Howard Schultz, CEO of Starbucks, had championed an unusual initiative. I learned that he had launched a program that required the African processors and suppliers of coffee beans in his company, as a condition for them to continue selling to Starbucks, to provide access to education and medical care to the coffee bean farmers. I was amazed by this news. The company didn't need to do this for business or political reasons, especially since it was not advertised as part of a PR campaign. As evidence of this, I had a difficult time even finding this story in the news. At the same time, the lives of people who Schultz himself might never meet were impacted by this decision, and I was struck by the innovative use of purchasing power to support a community. Why was Schultz doing it? I did some research and found that Schultz, having experienced the health struggles of his family and its difficulties in affording required treatments, was especially sensitive to the need for workers to have access to health care.

I was thrilled with this story, and wondered if there were other leaders who actually used their decision-making power and influence to make a difference while they were still in a leadership role. If this were the case, I wondered if we could understand what propelled them to do something that was not "business as usual." It seemed that if we could identify the knowledge, skills, experiences, attitudes, or mindset that had guided these people, then perhaps we would be able to intentionally develop these competencies in the next generation of leaders!

Thus it was that I began my journey. I made the focus of my doctoral research at Columbia University to study what I found to be the unexplored phenomenon of leaders who champion initiatives with the aim of having a positive impact on the environment or the community.

The first challenge was to find them. Where were these leaders who were engaging in projects that made a difference, projects that were not at heart philanthropic endeavors, but instead were part of the business strategy? Who were these people taking these actions even though the latter were not part of their expected role? I was particularly interested in studying leaders who were not hired for their interest or expertise in CSR, because I thought we could surface more valuable information, applicable to all kind of leaders, if we studied the non-experts. So I didn't look for the corporations' PR professionals, or Corporate Responsibility Officers. I was looking for business leaders who were not in charge of corporate donations to philanthropy, but were personally and innovatively fostering a different type of initiative.

I soon found myself immersed in a new world. My mailbox became filled weekly with books about sustainability, corporate social responsibility, profits with purpose, and leaders leaving legacies. I felt I was learning a new language, reading with amazement data describing the environmental conditions of the planet's resources, the CO_2 emissions and the distinction between the different greenhouse gases, the contributions of industrial practices and consumption, the social impact of our "Western" way of living, the dismaying projected impact of these forces in the future. I underlined paragraphs, made notes, drew faces of shock and fury in the margins, and at times put down the book because I was overwhelmed, and had to cry. I felt the urge to share what I was learning with others, yet this was not easy. I could barely understand this new language, and while I knew it was very serious and urgent to communicate, I didn't yet have the vocabulary. And when I talked about the "S" word, sustainability, I got a lot of blank faces. What, people seemed to say, was I talking about? Some looked at me with compassion and tolerance, others with blunt indifference, and some appeared to wonder how someone could be interested in such a tangential, distant, irrelevant topic. It is hard to imagine that this was, indeed, happening in the U.S.A. only six years ago. People just didn't talk about sustainability or the environment. Today, there is constant environment-related news in the media. Weather conditions make headlines every single day. The film documentary *An Inconvenient Truth* brought heightened awareness to many people, and Al Gore received a Nobel Prize. Some people later questioned its data, but it still drew great attention to the topic. CSR became an official "must" for large multinational organizations, and initiatives have been launched that have begun to change the ethical landscape within corporations. Chief among these are Principles for Responsible Investment;[1] Reporting Principles Initiative;[2] Principles for Responsible Management Education;[3] The Oath Project;[4] to name a few.

In my quest for understanding, I began to explore different questions and assumptions. Why were corporations engaging in initiatives that were not required by the business strategy, yet were making an impact on the world? Who was behind those initiatives? The books provided me with stories and descriptions of technical innovations, yet nothing about the individuals leading the revolutionary efforts – the people who were, however, precisely at the center of my quest. Who were they and why where they doing it? Was it part of their need to leave a legacy? Were they aware of the potential impact they could have due to their role and status? Were they motivated by a sense of personal mission? Were they spiritual, maybe religious, people? Had they been traumatized by some personal experience and were they trying to convert the trauma into something positive? Was it a political tactic, a defensive PR strategy? Was it something related to how they grew up, or where they were raised? Perhaps mentors and teachers played a role? Were they inspired by what competitors were doing? Was it related to age, to guilt, to altruistic values? Was it a personality issue? I knew that we would not be able to replicate the environment in which they were raised, nor the traumatic experiences with other leaders. But, I reasoned, if there *was* something that adult educators could distill, influence, articulate, inspire, and aim at, we might have the keys to unlocking a different generation of leaders. It was worth the exploration.

In addition, I had questions about how they had gone about implementing their initiatives, how they "sold it" to their colleagues, Board, shareholders, and employees. What obstacles had they faced, and what had they found helpful in their journey that might inspire and help other leaders shorten their learning curve? What attitudes were essential? What mindset was critical?

I realized that books and published stories would not give me those answers. They featured initiatives but not the personal journey behind them. I found nothing about why some business leaders acted in a "business as *un*usual" way. A 2009 study by researchers Laura Quinn and Maxine Dalton[5] suggested there was a "need for leadership theorists to better understand the factors prompting certain leaders to adopt a focus on sustainability." Unable to find any academic research studies that addressed these questions, I made the decision to conduct my own research. For that, I had first to find these exceptional leaders. It was not easy, but I found them.[i]

---

[i] Of course there were certainly many more than the 16 leaders portrayed in my study, and many more emerging every day; I just stopped at this number for the purpose of my research.

I met with them, and our conversations were profound, intimate, moving, and of an unimaginable richness. "You are asking interesting questions," and "No one ever asked me these questions before," were typical of responses I received. There were moments of silence, moments of joyful memories, moments of pain, expressions of bliss. There were dreamy eyes, even teary eyes.[i]

The experience I had throughout these two years of interviews was one of the richest of my life. It has been a journey that transformed me profoundly. The interviews with these 16 leaders became the springboard for the broader exploration of the values and mindsets of our civilization that forms the bulk of this book. The interviews opened the door to a revision of what is holding us back in our progress towards sustainability. It was something so close to us that we would barely notice it. And at the same time, the key to a more sustainable world was also closer than we would imagine, right there in our souls. I discovered that it was personal, and also about people.

I would very much like to share my journey with you.

---

[i] Because of the nature of their stories' contents, all names are changed and the identity of the individuals and their organizations has been carefully protected.

Acknowledgments

Sitting down to write the Acknowledgments page made me pause and ask myself: Where did this book start? A 2003 workshop in Fort Lauderdale, at which Lynn Gray introduced an exercise called *The Amazing Achievement Award* came to mind. We had to write an acceptance speech for an award we were to receive in 2010. That was a turning point for me, as I suddenly realized that while I had a happy life, there was nothing I could think of that would deserve a special prize. In a short lapse of 60 minutes, I had the dramatic experience that my life was perfectly happy and … meaningless! In a desperate attempt to overcome the shocking discovery, I crafted a dream: The amazing achievement award would be given to me because I coached leaders who decided to make a difference in the world, and they did great things as a result. Laying out the road to get there, I envisioned I could go back to school, start a doctoral study, write a book, and find a place to teach where I could meet those "leaders." Thank you, Lynn! That event marked the beginning of a journey of self-discovery, personal development, spirituality, and growth.

When I found the right program at Teachers College, Columbia University, I had the support of my family and friends. On deciding to study business leaders making a difference, Professors Victoria Marsick, Lyle Yorks, and my special mentor, Jeanne Bitterman, encouraged me all along the way. Ernie Turner, my life partner, suggested a name for my dream: "You can be a Legacy Coach, to work with people who want to make a difference." Joe Laur and my colleagues at the AEGIS program cheered me up with this idea and helped me with their ideas and contacts.

Then came the numerous leaders, who are behind the many lessons shared in this book. To each of them goes my deepest gratitude for having believed in this project, for their generosity, for the gift of their precious time, and for their willingness to pause and reflect, and candidly share their very personal stories. I realize

I was asking unusual questions, more interested as I was in your transformational journeys than in business stories and accomplishments. You became the real anchors of the ideas of a better world that is, yes, possible and within our reach.

Another milestone was laid by Professor Aixa Ritz, Director of Graduate Studies at the School of Hospitality and Tourism Management at Fairleigh Dickinson University. She attended my session at the Transformational Learning Conference in Bermuda, where I presented the preliminary findings of my research. As I finished my session, she approached me excitedly and said: "This is fabulous! Do you have a course to teach how to develop the sustainability mindset?" I hesitated, because in my dream I had it, but in the real world I didn't. After a pause, I said: "I can have it." So I worked on the design of the program, which I continued refining and teaching in the years that followed. Then came my friend Doug Cohen, insisting I needed to meet Prof. James (Jim) Stoner, at Fordham, and introduced us. Prof. Stoner was intrigued by my course and decided we should champion it together for the university's MBA students. To him and the students of both schools goes my gratitude as well: We learned from and with them.

This book started several times over the span of the last three years. As happened to me before, I decided to put on paper "what I had to share," and ended up learning so much in the process that the contents became different and richer – and even surprising to myself.

Yet what made me pick up the project every time I had dropped it was the encouragement of my dear friends and colleagues. I have to thank my friend Clara Arrocain who asked me "when do you start the next?" when I was still writing my previous book. And Prof. Jeanne Bitterman, who warned me: "Don't wait! Time runs." And Silvia Leon, who boosted my self-confidence, and Prof. Jim Stoner, who kept asking: "How are you doing with your book?" and suggesting we use it as class material in our jointly taught class at Fordham.

To the readers of my chapters: Boris Drizin, Jim Stoner, Paul Roberts, Maria Nathan, Martha Driemer (my mom!), Ernie Turner, Jim Young, a big thank you for your wonderful critique, feedback, suggestions, and encouragement. And my special gratitude to Tony Pearson, who developed infinite patience converting my sometimes "too Spanish" English into real English.

To Mariam Tamborenea, my soul mate in so many projects, I have to thank for inviting me to bring art and poems into the book, and for suggesting this powerful title, that, as she said, "you cannot say it out loud without feeling the energy, it makes you zummm!" I am thankful for Matias Fernandez's great design for covers and to Chris Murray's careful and professional editing – the third time he is part of my writing journey! My gratitude goes also to my friend Hector Legrand, who worked hard in the production of this book; his rigorous and playful attitude made our interactions so enjoyable.

I cannot finish this list without thanking my friends, Veronica, Maica, Silvia, Jonelle, the Manzanitas, Jorge, Stephanie, the Minervas, and my family who nurture my heart with unconditional love, as well as my life partner Ernie, the sponsor of my dreams, and who helps me jump over any obstacle by providing his ideas, his visions, and his simple (and powerful!) two words: Why not?

To all of you, and to the many wise people whose thinking triggered and inspired my own thinking, on the shoulders of which we're standing today, my deep gratitude and my humble commitment to keep working to make this world a better place.

~

So what is the Big Bang Being? As with the cosmological model, this Big Bang starts in singularity, within each individual … at our core, when we glimpse the little something that we had lost track of. For a short moment we see it, we have a fleeting experience, yet we recognize it, it is something very familiar. We have no names for it, no precise words to describe it. A feeling? We may be left with the desire to experience it again, whatever the "it" was. Perhaps, we get to that place again, sometime. As we spend more time lingering in that bizarre yet deeply familiar feeling, we begin to emanate a different energy into our environment. For a moment, or more frequently, we radiate something that we're not controlling, yet it is noticed by others. In the cosmic Big Bang, the Universe started as singular energy converted into particles and expanded. It happened rapidly.

The Big Bang of humanity follows the same pattern and structure. We're part of Nature, and so this shouldn't come as a surprise. Starting with a thought, a quiet minute, a moment of peace, a smile with no reason. Wavelike energy spreads and touches others. From person to person, even when we're not physically close. This doesn't matter, the same way it doesn't matter where the Twitter that may cause a revolution is written. Viral spread of light-ness. When we want to trace it back, we can no longer find where it started. Because it happens in so many beings at the same time.

We all are ready for the experience, because of the invisible thread that connects us to the Universe. You will know when you see it. Stay alert, you're a key part of the Big Bang Being.

Introduction
Lieben und Arbeiten – Love and Work

When asked for the definition of mental health and fulfillment, Sigmund Freud, the father of psychoanalysis, had two words: *Lieben und Arbeiten*, love and work. In this book we will find how 16 business leaders brought together their compassion, their caring for others and the world, with their work.

True, only on rare occasions are we able to meet the person behind initiatives that made a positive impact on the world, even less have an in-depth view into their feelings, concerns, hesitations, doubts, and most intimate thoughts. What is seen publicly is the initiative, the impact on the bottom line and the community, or sometimes on the environment. Yet it is their *personal* stories that can be most inspirational, since they draw our attention to the fact that amazing achievements start in simple ways, with just the thinking of one individual. And when we find out that the "exemplary individuals" have many very "human' aspects that we identify with and find in ourselves, it brings us closer; and particularly, it may even trigger in us the question: If she could do it … I wonder what could *I* do?

This book has been written for the many people I have met who are feeling some kind of unmet need to "do something" meaningful, something that provides them with a deep purpose, a profound (spiritual?) satisfaction. They sometimes seek it; sometimes they carry the unmet need alongside "business as usual," occasionally having a moment where they realize that something is still missing in their life. By sharing with the reader the richness of the personal interviews I was privileged to conduct with a group of business leaders who made an impact on the world, I hope to build that bridge from their innermost soul to the soul of the reader, the other seeker. And the shortest distance between any two people, no matter how far apart they may seem from each other, is the one between their souls.

The interviews, however, were only the beginning of the journey. The lessons of the interviews made it possible to identify how we can all develop a sustainability mindset, in other words, the thinking and the being that can take us from breakdown to breakthrough on this planet. Each one of us can play a part in leading the change; actually we are already playing a part – we are just not necessarily aware if that is the part we would like to play, or aware that we choose the change we are contributing to unfold. In this book, I invite readers to explore their own thinking and being dimensions, and uncover dimensions that lead to a fuller life not only for self, but for our collective.

Through my research, I was also able to name the values that are holding us back and the alternatives that we have, at our fingertips – and "mindtips." Who wouldn't want to shed values that are keeping us trapped in a lifestyle that is stressful to exhaustion, demands so much of us, and still leaves us with a feeling of emptiness, after fleeting moments of satisfaction? The good news is that we have all we need to change that situation, with a paradigm change to start tomorrow morning.

But most of all, I realize I wrote this book to inspire, to develop awareness of what is possible, of the personal opportunity that each one of us has to contribute to making this a better world. This statement that sounds ambitious and grandiose – is actually very simple, and it starts with a meeting with oneself. I put on my Legacy Coach hat and provide some hints and guidance for this throughout the pages of the book.

How is this book organized?

Part I presents the 16 leaders, including a summary of their story and their initiatives. You will find the factors and circumstances that created in this group the readiness to consider doing something for the "greater good," and the lessons learned in the challenging process of championing a sustainability initiative in organizations that had not seen such a thing before. I identify and discuss the five leadership roles that played a key role in the journey of these leaders.

Part II goes a little deeper, as you will find two dimensions that were not obvious but which underlay the way these business leaders championed the initiatives: the Thinking and the Being.

These less visible dimensions became fundamentally important to the development of a sustainability mindset.

In the dimension of Thinking, you will find the two thinking structures that lead to the sustainability mindset: Innovative Thinking, describing the key role played by out-of-the box perspectives in addressing the complex challenges of the new world, and Systemic Thinking, with its six components of the systemic perspective (Both/and; Interconnectedness; Long-Term View; Cyclical Flow; Complexity; and Cooperation).

In the dimension of Being, I present examples of the being orientation: through personal transformation and development of consciousness, and through the spiritual organization, showing the flow from the personal sphere to the world. The being orientation constitutes the central and most surprising component, anchoring the real paradigm shift and transforming the view on business.

Part III explores why sustainability change is so slow, and addresses the "elephant in the room": the values and beliefs that anchor our Western *Weltanschauung*, or worldview, which are at the foundation of our collective identity, and which may be impeding individuals from making a faster switch into sustainable practices. I address the values of Economic growth, Achievement, Control, Wealth, Comfort, Independence, Competition, Knowledge, and Speed. These values are reinforced by other important forces, which I call the "enablers": Science and technology, Media that connect us, and Globalization.

After exploring why certain values are so important to our identity – and in what ways they played an important role in the problems we are facing, creating a sort of unconscious self-inflicted damage – you will find that things don't have to be the way they are. While our planet is rapidly changing, we also have the opportunity to change ourselves and begin making a different imprint.

Taking a closer look, the values that are part of our problem can be grouped into different categories: those that need to be redefined and reshaped; those that invite us to develop our whole brain; and those that are an opportunity to evolve as human beings into a higher level of development.

Part IV addresses the alternatives that we have to convert the unsustainable values into opportunities that will permit humanity to thrive and to break through the obstructions that prevent us from stasis.

Finally, Part V takes us beyond the tipping point, and presents us with an opportunity to evolve as humans developing a new way of thinking and being on this planet. This transformation is so radical and significant, that I called it the *Big Bang Being*. Here you will find details about how the possibilities to make a difference lie in our very core: it's something personal, and it's about people.

Interspersed throughout the book, I included legacy-coaching interventions for the readers who wonder "So what?" "Now what?" and "What is in it for me?" You will find questions and exercises that I would use in a Legacy Coaching session. The questions may trigger your reflection, and may lead to you coming up with your answers, but you don't have to. It's also good enough to just acknowledge the questions, ponder them, linger on them, and let them stay with you. Sometimes, just staying with a question is a better road to wisdom than finding an answer.

And to honor the right brain hemisphere that guides me so much, I gave it a voice too. You will find that voice in the images and poems that are distributed throughout the text.

Eric Fromm wrote that there are two ways to read a book: the first, as an act of consumption, trying to "get it all" through the end, in what he calls the "having" mode; the second, in a participatory way, getting involved by the words and the meaning between the lines. When we read a book by plunging into it, we flow with it, we let it challenge and transform our thinking, we pause to let it act on us. We live it and we come out different. He calls this the "being" mode. This book invites you to read it from within your being.

You just saw the issues that I plan to address. But what are *your* questions? Why did you pick up this book?
What are the issues that so concern you that you plan to spend time reading about them?

PART I
EXPLORING THE ICEBERG

So who are these leaders? In the following pages you will meet the 16 exemplary leaders I interviewed and who helped me understand why and how they championed meaningful initiatives that made a difference in the world. You will get to know them, and learn about their special initiatives. Given the level of personal disclosure and sharing of their particular journeys, the identity of the leaders and their corporations has been protected using pseudonyms.

Chapter 1

Sixteen Leaders

Carl (75)[i]

Carl is the founder and Chairman of a successful mid-size U.S. multinational corporation in the floor treatment business. Armed with a degree in engineering, he joined a corporation in this field, and was inspired by the owners to start his own company – thus showing his entrepreneurial spirit, a characteristic that defines not only his current business, but also his sustainability journey.

In the mid-1990s, clients began to ask what the company was doing for the environment, and one of his managers was eager to set up a task force to address the situation. Carl initially was not particularly interested, but at his manager's insistence he finally agreed. However, when he was asked to give an inaugural speech to this task force, he realized he didn't know what to say. "We're complying with all regulations! What else should we do!?" he wondered. Then one of his salespersons gave him the book, *The Ecology of Commerce*, by environmentalist Paul Hawken. As he began to read it, he felt very emotional; he describes his reaction as being "like a spear in the chest." The author described how species were becoming extinct as a result of human behavior, and how industries were playing an important role in this process that was destroying the planet. "I would read passages in bed at night to my wife, and we would weep together over the plight of the Earth, and I was part of the problem. I was part of this industrial system that's destroying the biosphere."

Carl decided to bring this new awareness into his business, and began talking to the leaders in his organization about "restorative behaviors." These behaviors referred to not only stopping doing harm to the environment, but also helping to restore lost resources. They meant influencing other industries so that

---

[i] For a chart with the demographics of the 16 leaders, see the Appendix.

6

other leaders could step up to this challenge, too. Today his company has become an international best-practice case, one that sets an example of what is possible and how a business can be both restorative to the environment and profitable at the same time.

Evan (53)

Evan is the Director of Quality in an organization in the apparel industry that advertises its commitment to environmental responsibility. His education is in botany and plant physiology, although it didn't lead him to become interested in environmental causes. He indicates, "You might think that that would lead me to wanting to do something about the environment. But what the education tended to provide me with, was just an inability to look at anything and not understand how complex it was." He does, however, trace back to his education the mindset and perspective that he has carried into his different jobs and his real passion to see the whole system. He is a very rational, analytical person, who talks about sustainability as a result, not a goal.

He cites as a positive aspect of his organization's culture its "grassroots approach," which encourages individuals to come up with innovative ideas to improve the business and then to seek resources to execute them. This stance, he believes, has helped him implement his ideas. On the other hand, this same organizational culture led for a while to some organizational incoherence, because the individual initiatives were fostered without ensuring that they fit under one strategic umbrella. Recognizing this, the CEO gathered the leaders of the projects and invited them to develop a unified strategy. Evan took this opportunity to champion a strategy that would aim at a higher operational efficiency, because "not being efficient is to be wasteful."

In 1995–96, he proposed a more integrated business approach, one that required synchronization of effective operational, financial, and environmental plans leading to business success. He formed a group called Environmental Quality Development and converted the company into a leading recycling business. It now takes polyester and nylon garments, recycles them, turns them back into yarn, and manufactures new polyester garments out of them. No other company in the world, he indicates, has accomplished that yet.

He decided, further, to take on a teaching role in the organization, and he has talked to different internal audiences, written papers that provide a vision of how efficiency could be achieved, and shown the opportunities for attaining it. He is always looking at the bigger picture, and is well known for challenging assumptions, exploring the wider range of cause-effect connections, and assessing the impacts of decisions.

Paul (47)

Paul is a social entrepreneur, and is currently the President and Founder of a cooperative – a fair trade coffee business that he started in 1997 with the purpose of using the business to tell the story about coffee farmers, and their poverty level living conditions that "the 55 percent of American people that drink coffee are not aware of."

He grew up in a small town, in a very religious middle-class family. His educational background is business administration, and he started his career working in the banking system. However, he was always an inquisitive and curious person, and early on he began to question what he really wanted to do, and what his purpose in life was. Opening his mind to new possibilities, he was curious to find out about alternate life styles, and he interviewed people who had chosen very different ways of organizing their lives.

One significant encounter was with a European biker who came "for a few weeks" to the U.S. but instead stayed several years, biking around the country, meeting new people from diverse backgrounds and a variety of interests. He did it to show that people were intrinsically good and not threatening as the media, which is known to portray only dramatic and violent stories, would warn. By doing this, he was planting seeds of peace. Inspired by this man's experiences, Paul quit his position in the family business and went on a bike ride himself to educate himself about how other people lived, and how they dealt with their challenges. It was on his first trip to Africa that he had the opportunity to experience poverty from close up. "I had just seen what two-thirds, three-fourths of the world's population live like, and I had never experienced this in my country." This trip moved him profoundly and made him realize how many people in the world live in poverty – an awareness that he had not had in his hometown and country.

This experience ignited in him the desire to do something to reduce inequity. He began to volunteer at Habitat for Humanity, traveled to Africa again and stayed several years there, deepening his understanding and personal connections with local cultures.

It was one trip to Guatemala that prompted him to take concrete action to deal with poverty. He decided to set up a business that supported local coffee farmers, one that would pay them a better price by selling the coffee in the U.S. He still very much enjoys this connection with the farmers, and describes it as the most rewarding part of his job. His personal mission is to use the business as an instrument to make people aware of the reality of coffee farmers' existence.

Pam (53)

Pam is a former executive in a multinational corporation in the apparel industry, where she had a successful career at the Director level in the area of product design. She grew up as a bit of a "rebel" in a middle-class family with many siblings. She trained for many years in competitive sports, and her own professional career was marked by a strong need to compete and excel. However, this changed radically in her early 40s, when she had a number of transformational experiences and shifted her competitive attitude into a more collaborative one, which as we will see later is an important characteristic for championing sustainability initiatives.

A significant event in her life that changed her awareness about social injustice occurred on one trip to Asia in the early 1990s when she experienced discrimination; she felt she was not listened to, "not recognized as a person." Another impact she relates came two years later, also in Asia, as she witnessed the awful working conditions, especially the toxic vapors in which people worked at one of her company's manufacturing site. She felt the urge to do something, realizing that while technically progressive, the way the company was operating was not good enough. She began to ask herself if the corporation understood the implications of what it was doing. This was a "slow awakening," she observes.

Then a critical incident happened in the mid-1990s, as she had another of several miscarriages and her husband was diagnosed with cancer. She read about the effects of a drug that was sold several decades ago to prevent miscarriages, effects that could be passed on the daughters. She found out that her mother had indeed taken that medication (later banned). In addition, her husband had been exposed to DDT and his cancer was connected to that chemical. These two discoveries made her wonder, "What else are we doing and NOT seeing the impacts?"

She began to wonder if the corporation understood the environmental and health implications of the materials it was using. She searched for experts in sustainability and learned about its demands and its benefits. She realized that the corporation had to become more strategic in terms of sustainability, that it was not enough to just have a CSR department that dealt with policies. She played a leading role in incorporating a systems perspective into the business, starting in the product design area but ultimately impacting the whole organization.

Willie (70)

Willie is a retired executive in a U.S.-based corporation in the technology area, where, with his background in engineering, he was VP of Product Development. He grew up in the countryside, very close to Nature, which is something that has had a profound impact on him. He is a critical thinker with an inquisitive attitude and tends to identify with the underdog. "When I was a kid we played cowboys and Indians and I wanted to be the Indian." He likes high-energy "mission impossible" tasks.

Willie led a product development initiative in the early 1990s that was revolutionary, because it paid attention to the materials and components that went into the product, where they came from, and how they would be disposed. Although this was a very new practice in the industry, he thought of it as "common sense," and determined to instill this attitude among his colleagues. He asked questions such as, "What is the purpose of my life? What am I here for?" to a group of product designers who had a very deep and transforming experience as a result. These people were simply not used to spending time reflecting on their life purpose, but as they did so, the experience changed their perspective about their roles, their contributions to the environment and society, and ultimately impacted their designs of new products. The team that worked with him for several years in the design of this breakthrough product was personally engaged and passionate about its task, which made it fun. The team members got the "big picture," and once one does that, he indicates, one cannot go back. Our conscience tells us what needs to be done.

He feels a great urgency to accomplish what he has in mind and has a lot of hope in the younger generation, because they are proactive, imaginative, and have good values. He is currently teaching at a university.

Suzanne (39)

Suzanne, who grew up in an upper-class family, has a background in science, and is a VP in R&D for a multinational corporation in the food industry and agribusiness. As a teenager and college student, her desire was to find meaningful work, perhaps to do social work; she originally thought of being a doctor or working with health issues as a way of contributing to the greater good. However, she married and started her corporate life, and didn't think of those values again. She feels badly now about having put them on the "backburner of her mind."

A couple of years before our interview, her boss asked her to take his place at a meeting where other corporations would be represented, to discuss sustainability initiatives. She realized she didn't know anything about the topic and so did some research before going. Once she was at the meeting, she noticed that no one actually knew much about the topic, and she felt she could contribute in a valuable way even though she was not an expert. At that point, her dormant values and socially oriented interests were revived in her and she determined to pursue them anew. She asked her boss if she could attend those meetings regularly, and she began to participate actively since she saw this as an opportunity to give back to the community.

By participating in the meetings she came up with ideas on how to spread the understanding of sustainability both inside her corporation and among its customers. She became an advocate and started talking to others in her organization, providing them with information, and educating the leaders of her corporation by means of presentations on sustainability. She noticed that while the organization was in fact doing quite a bit in this arena, the efforts were not well communicated and coordinated. As a result, she created a cross-functional task force where key stakeholders would participate in, and work on, common projects. The goal was to embed the concept of sustainability from concept to manufacturing and finished products – basically into all areas of the organization, as opposed to sustainability being a topic of reflection once the products were already developed.

She thinks her passion for sustainability began as an opportunistic means to instill hope at a time when the corporation was undergoing stress, restructuring, and job uncertainty. It also became, for the organization, a competitive advantage valued by its clients. And soon it took a value on its own: something that started as a means of taking the employees' minds off their stress or gaining respect from clients was picked up by the employees as a valuable cause in itself. The company organized large training events, and developed materials to inform and prepare the sales force on how to use the company's application of sustainability principles as a selling point, and accompanied them when they visited key clients. Furthermore, the sustainability task force trained the corporation's leaders and invited them to cascade the learning throughout their organizations. The challenge was to embed it deeply enough, so that even in tough times people didn't abandon them.

Robert (53)

Robert has a degree in engineering and is in charge of plant operations at a large multinational pharmaceutical company. His sensitivity towards issues of social justice and community action originated in his childhood when he was a member of an economically challenged family with many siblings and a working mother.

As an adult, he reflected on how he might use his role in the organization to influence his co-workers to take advantage of the multiple opportunities available to them in the area of sustainability. He is a self-learner and studied the issues and challenges of sustainability for a year, learning facts about the impact on the world of global warming, pollution, and social issues. The more he learned, the more he felt the need to share his learning so that he might educate his friends, colleagues, staff, and employees.

As an engineer, he worked on projects designed to improve efficiency or reduce costs, and he felt that the projects offered him and his workers good opportunities to do that by incorporating effective sustainable practices. To this end, he implemented a reward system for people who contributed innovative suggestions, and while this generated some good ideas, he felt he still did not have the level of engagement he would like. He persuaded the organization to measure and keep track of these initiatives, and to put together a manual of practices that could be used in other sites, and thus effect a transfer of "know how" throughout the organization. His management has given him its full support, and has agreed that his staff should implement the proposed changes. He wants his legacy to be that he was part of a generation that tried to make a difference. What started as an intellectual exercise has become a passion, and he says that he "would feel embarrassed not doing something."

Daniel (56)

Daniel is the Director of Corporate Awareness in an innovative medium-sized corporation that produces green household products. He grew up in a wealthy upper-class family of "born-again Christians"; however, he couldn't "take that"; he felt a narrowness in the religious interpretation, and states that from an early age he developed a rebellious attitude towards authority. As an example, Daniel demonstrated against the war in Vietnam even though his grandfather owned a company that supplied materials for the war effort. Interestingly, it was the family business that inadvertently led to Daniel's attraction to environmentalism. In the late 1980's, when the family business was cited for using practices that were inimical to the environment, the event gave rise to Daniel's conviction that it is critical to educate corporate America, and to embody concern for the environment into the very fabric of corporate strategy. This conviction, in turn, resulted in him helping establish and grow an environmental management-consulting firm that helped Fortune 500 companies design business "to do more with less."

He has a Masters degree in Ethics and Environment Ethic, earned at Divinity School, where he developed a sense of pluralism and the coming together of all religions. He also has a strong philosophical foundation that he developed over the years through extensive reading, participating in learning communities, and incorporating systems thinking as a worldview.

He is particularly concerned and critical about the current role of business. "Business delivers stuff; is a machine. It reduces the humanity in the person. We need to design a place differently, with love, sharing, wellbeing," he indicates. He thinks that it is necessary to change people's mindset. "The world is machine-minded. We don't see systems thinking. In every deliberation we have to think of the impact seven generations ahead." He is an active promoter of a holistic perspective, and comments that "We have to consider Earth and humanity. Everyone should understand the workers involved, the water impact, the chemistry." He is able to do this because of his unique position in charge of the organization's Corporate Awareness philosophy, and he has the full support of the founder of the corporation, who created a supportive organizational culture, a value-based business.

Daniel goes after big dreams. He wants to cooperate in creating a regenerative economy, giving back to the Earth more than we take out of it, making people and the Earth healthier. His passion is helping people in organizations develop a different framework in their thinking. He says "there is a point in the crumbling where some need to be in the creation of the new. In the next five years, there will be much more havoc. Global warming is real; the stimulation package is not enough; water and land are not healthy." In the fight to save the planet, he considers himself as one of "the new knights," and wants to see business as a provider of goods that serve humanity's basic needs, rather than "indulgence consumption," and would like to tap into the essence of the person – help them find their purpose, their core, and their values.

Diego (56)

Diego is the President and Founder of a small coffee roasting company that buys organic and fair trade coffee beans from indigenous communities in different locations of the world. He describes himself not as a businessman who does social good, but as a social activist who runs a business. He grew up in a middle-class Jewish family, headed by a stepfather who was psychologically abusive to him. The effect was, he feels, that his voice was "silenced." As a consequence he developed the desire to help others to have their voices heard; for example, he worked with indigenous groups, helping them to defend their rights; he also participated in anti-nuclear activism and against pollution. As a teenager, a demonstration against the Vietnam War showed him the power of lawyers, and that inspired him to become a lawyer. His success in this field led to his friends joking that he would be the first Jewish president of the U.S.A. in the year 2000. He thinks his social activism originates in the community service heritage of Judaism, and the need to do good that is promoted in that religion.

He was always curious about languages and other cultures and religions, so he traveled and lived in Japan, Burma, Thailand, Indonesia, and Iran for several years. In those countries, he studied Judo, Zen Buddhism, and Sufism; read; and met people and learned from them with both the "eye and the heart." He comments that a big influence in his life was the study of Buddhism and Hinduism, plus, in the Jewish tradition, the concept of "intentionality: When you engage your whole being, energetic and physical being in an activity, things then happen automatically for the better." He does yoga and meditation to this day.

Addressing his wish to help others, he concluded that charitable giving seldom generated real social change, and decided to become a businessman so he could really have an impact, since in his opinion business is the engine of change. His idea was to have a company based on social, ecological, environmental, and cultural principles, not based on profits. This idea materialized as the coffee roasting company he now leads, an organization for which he travels around the world and personally establishes relationships with disadvantaged communities, such as indigenous tribes, and native farmers in third-world countries. He has developed organic self-developing farming communities in Ethiopia, Kenya, Peru, Colombia, Guatemala, El Salvador, Nicaragua, Sumatra, and Papua New Guinea.

Craig (37)

Craig is the youngest person interviewed, and he was recommended to the researcher by another interviewee, because of his exceptional spirit and initiative. With a background in finance, Craig is in charge of Investor Relations in a large food corporation, where he has worked for a couple of years.

This corporation has very altruistic values expressed in their mission and vision statements, values that are a reflection of the personal characteristics of its founder. Although the founder is no longer with the company, the values are maintained and are visible in its environmental consciousness, in the ecologically designed buildings, in the respect and concern for the welfare of the employees and the level of support and appreciation for them. This organizational culture, he indicates, in addition to the exemplary role model of the president, provided powerful and inspiring influences to Craig as he pursued his initiative.

The initiative he describes was integrating and organizing all the current sustainability related efforts currently under way. He noticed that in different areas of the organization people were carrying out valuable sustainability related initiatives, but there was no full awareness of the value of these actions among employees, and in fact were not necessarily seen as part of the corporate citizenship. As a consequence employees, customers, investors or community were simply not aware of all that was being done. To his mind, due to this lack of awareness, the organization was missing the opportunity to inspire others, and to reinforce the good behaviors that were already in place. As a result, he decided to identify and then organize all the current initiatives, and he created a process and a system to educate the whole organization about the extent of the sustainability efforts and to expand its impact.

It was clear to him that somebody simply had to take action to reinforce the message, and he felt it may just as well be him. He describes himself as always having been interested in doing good, and felt personal satisfaction from such action. He received generous help from many quarters following the problematic birth of his daughter and he decided to become involved in philanthropic causes after that experience. He wants to leave the world in a better place than he found it and this is an important driving force in his life, both inside the organization and outside. He learned from people he met, plus family and friends, that satisfaction comes from providing a service to others. "It'll sound soft, but I believe it to be true. The personal reward from contributing to these issues is far greater than any type of other reward, whether it is financial or a job opportunity. If you participate in these areas and you know that you are making a positive impact in the community in which you live or in the business in which you interact or the fields out in the California valley, that you may not even see on a daily basis sitting here, but you know the decisions you're making and the work you're doing is improving those things – those personal rewards as part of having a more positive life are tremendous."

Harry (60)

Harry grew up in a solidly middle-class family, in which his grand-father was a farmer and his father a city planner. He defines himself as a farmer, and early in life he was deeply involved with the local community of farmers, helping them organize as they struggled through an economic crisis. With a tendency to identify with the underdog, he has always been a social activist and a community organizer who gained experience bridging interests and forming alliances between different stakeholders. Having grown up in a family that believed in a world full of well-meaning people and continuous progress, Harry lived through the Vietnam War as a teenager, and had his first shock as that reality challenged his assumptions and beliefs.

He started his sustainability journey when he joined Donella Meadows, the main author of the Club de Rome report "Limits to Growth," at the Sustainability Institute, and when she passed away he was invited to take her position. It was Peter Senge, an American scientist and director of the Center for Organizational Learning at the MIT Sloan School of Management, who suggested in 2004 that he create an organization that would bring together corporations, not-for-profit, and governmental organizations to address big global problems. Harry met this suggestion with conflicted feelings, since his political beliefs didn't place much faith in the corporate world. On the other hand, he had seen enough criticism emanating from the NGOs' side about industry's impact on the environment, and realized that without business involvement these significant problems were probably not solvable.

This motivated him to found an association which has the purpose of creating a space where leaders from the three main stakeholder sectors (government, NGOs, and corporations) can analyze problems, seek solutions, and share lessons. Above all, his aim was that this space would foster dialogue to integrate diverse points of view on the global problems of hunger, pollution, and poverty.

He believes in the power of open conversations where people are motivated, despite their differences, to seek common goals and shared strategies. He talks about tapping into each person's passion, about the need to bring one's self fully into the room so as to unleash huge power and energy. In addition, he believes that facilitating experiential sessions, where people journal, reflect, dialogue, and exchange insights from each other, is enormously effective. "It's important to learn to see through the others' eyes," he says.

Harry has a deep sense of responsibility for doing good, and acknowledges that it pains him to witness the hurt, the oppression, and the damage being done to the world by social inequality and uncaring organizations. He feels a connection to the Earth, and has at a gut level a commitment to people less privileged than himself. The biggest satisfaction, he says, comes from helping these people to find their voices, to connect their work with their own values, and to seeing the enthusiasm this generates.

He comes from a religious background, initially Protestant and later Quaker, and has tried out different meditative practices. Today he defines his religion as being open to energy fields, in touch with the divine, being grounded on the Earth, and connected with Nature. He sees his work as his life mission. He wants to use all his available resources to make the biggest impact possible and feels an urgency to do so because of his age.

Patrick (66)

Patrick, whose educational background is technical, is the retired CEO of a mid-size corporation in the high-tech area. It was, though, his complex family upbringing that formed the basis of his abiding interest in the sustainability movement. As an orphan, he was raised in a number of foster homes mostly on the farm, where he learned the "subsistence model" of living: a model in which thrift was the byword, and where the family sought to make use of all food and every item. It was at times a very traumatic upbringing, where he experienced verbal abuse and life-threatening experiences, but where he also learned how to be a survivor, and to appreciate that happy people are more successful than sad ones.

Material things and appearances never mattered to him. He acted in non-conventional ways from a very young age, and was used to challenging authority, power, and wealth, as well as to standing up for himself and speaking up for what he believed in.

He was environmentally active by the time he was in high school, and he learned much from one of his foster fathers who was very conscious of taking care of the land. From this man and others, he acquired a sense of "what is right and what is wrong" at a very early age. It was this learning that prompted him, when he worked in a large corporation, to challenge the company's decision to canalize a river, because it was damaging the environment. He always felt the need to protect Nature, and was convinced that progress and Nature don't have to be mutually exclusive.

He believes that people should be able to evolve emotionally, spiritually, intellectually, and psychologically in the business world, rather than living a frustrated life where their potential is seldom realized. Workers should be able to learn to know themselves and to develop. This belief system has led him to a different concept of business. In his role as CEO, he took it as a personal task to speak to the employees and educate them to see the larger picture, to think systemically, and to pay attention to the environment. His goal was that everybody understood what role they individually were playing within the larger whole, and he provided a new vision in that corporation which impacted many lives in a transformative way.

Patrick believes his motivations to act emanate from a combination of anger and hope. He is upset with the notion that human beings are superior to Nature, instead of being a part of it, and he traces this idea back to his underprivileged upbringing when he developed the need and skill to speak for those who had no voice.

He has a holistic sense of what business should be, and believes that individual growth is as important as profits and customer satisfaction. It was this that informed the growth and effectiveness of his informal teaching role, and he is as proud of this role as he is of "running the business" in his role as CEO. He loves to see people bestir themselves as they become more self-aware and then go on to influence others to behave in more positive ways.

He wants to make an impact now in a way that has the highest leverage. He is not sure yet how or where, but he feels a sense of urgency, knowing that he doesn't have a lot of time left. He has, he says, a "deep fire in my belly, a profound anger at how foolish human beings are as a whole."

Michael (60)

Michael is the CEO of a large food corporation, from which he is retiring after having worked there for several decades. He grew up in a very small town in a rural area, where his father had a grocery store and he feels a close connection with soil, Nature, and growing food. He grew up in a religious Christian family and he now practices Buddhism, and does daily meditation practices, which he says provide him calmness and a connection to Nature and humankind.

It was Michael who introduced organic field greens as a product in the mid-1980s, which was very early in the sustainability movement's history. He mentions it was not easy to bring his ideas into the corporation, since the prevailing paradigm was that business had nothing to do with sustainability, and he had to proceed slowly in an almost "subversive" and quiet way. In presenting his yearly goals, he deliberately included wording about sustainability, and he sent articles on the topic to the management and the board to read. He recognized the need for patience and persistence, but he realized, too, that his journey felt very lonely, and that it was important to meet some like-minded people. He planted seeds in one-on-one conversations and he talked to small groups about his ideas, following up with those who showed signs of interest, and encouraging them to become champions of their ideas.

It was obvious to him how persuasive his ideas would be if he were to meet his business goals and to show increased sales and profitability. This he was able to do, since the market for organics grew, and it has been easy to convince young people, he observes, since they are operating with a different worldview and can see the importance of sustainability more clearly.

He mentions that it has been particularly encouraging for him to see how the seeds he planted have grown; almost the entire organization has adopted sustainability practices and mindset, and he admits to being surprised to discover that "people really care!" Michael considers this as his personal mission.

Ronald (53)

Ronald has been engaged in sustainability initiatives for over twenty years. With an educational background in accounting and business, he worked for more than ten years in the area of warehousing and logistics for a packaging supplier of a large fast food chain. He was raised in a very religious family and his parents had been strict in instructing him in what they considered the right and wrong behaviors. He mentions that as a child and teenager he greatly admired and was inspired by President John Kennedy, especially his creation of the U.S. Peace Corps with its invitation to

Americans to make a difference in their world. After college, he immersed himself in finding a job, building a family, and earning money, and he found that those higher motivations remained "latent."

In the late 1980s, the fast food chain that was the main client of the packaging company where he worked began to receive strong criticism from different environmentalist organizations about the chain's practices. This happened at a time when several other issues impacted his life. He was in his mid-30s and it began to occur to him that that his work had become a bit mechanical. In addition, around that time he went through a very traumatic experience with the violent deaths of his brother and pregnant sister-in-law. This unexpected event made him reflect on the fragility of life, and the possibility that his own life could end at any moment. This made him review what he wanted out of his life. He therefore welcomed the opportunity to do something that resonated with his values and his dreams to make a difference, and took it on as a project.

In 1989, sustainability was not a common concept in society, and there were very few experiences to learn from in terms of how to reduce a company's ecological footprint. He decided to remedy this and invited experts in sustainability to give talks to his co-workers; he, too, began talking to different audiences internally, bringing awareness, information, and education on the impact his corporation was having on the environment.

He considers this work his personal mission. He realizes that the beliefs and the thinking of the corporate world were quite different from the perspective of NGOs working to protect the environment. He found himself understanding very easily the alternate perspective. "I'm an activist; somehow I'm like an internal NGO representative."

Mark (45)

Mark is an entrepreneur who was previously the CEO of a restaurant chain, where he introduced significant changes to make it "green" in the early 1990s. His background is business – he is himself the son of an entrepreneurial father, and grew up in a family that owned a number of restaurants. He was in a European country that has strong beliefs in the notion of social responsibility. For many years he has been involved in projects related to the promotion of non-violence and health issues, motivated by the loss of his only sibling to a chronic disease. He mentions that the loss of his sister was a traumatic experience that resulted in him feeling a combination of survivor guilt and an absence of real meaning in his life.

When he took over the family restaurant business, it had many problems, and people were critical of the company's environmental behavior. He was curious to establish "the truth" of the criticism, and thus he invited in an expert who had developed a framework for organizational sustainability. That person made a presentation assessing the problem and the possible solutions, which Mark found painted a very depressing picture. "I wanted to shoot myself, it was so depressing; I was suicidal!" he says, until the expert showed how the problem could be addressed.

Together he and the consultant worked for 15 years educating the employees, giving speeches, and creating awareness throughout the organization. He found that many of the employees he trained became very excited, and wanted to take immediate action, and he had to calm them down "because it's impossible to change a whole business at once." Since then he has succeeded in making his business "green," which has also made his business grow and thrive.

Mark seeks a more human form of capitalism and considers that his life mission is to convince people that there is a way of doing business where all the stakeholders benefit. This is for him long-term sustainable capitalism, where corporations are great places to work, and where everyone – employees, community, environment, shareholders – can benefit. He wants his legacy to be that his efforts have meant something to many people. He wants to be like "Warren Buffet meets Mother Teresa": creating companies where customers love to shop and employees have fulfilling work experiences – companies that make both money and meaning.

Connie (50)

Connie is a corporate lawyer in a large multinational corporation in the retail sector. She feels lucky to have a very supportive organizational culture that encourages employees to pioneer personal initiatives and to figure out how to bring them to life.

Connie is a reflective person who has been meditating for 16 years, but she is quick to assert that she wasn't always like this. In her early 30s, she is not proud to admit, she was a typical "yuppie," with very shallow interests, and a tendency of not thinking too deeply about life. Then her brother suffered a violent death and this traumatic event became her catalyst for change. She began a spiritual journey, pondering on who is God, and "not putting myself first, but understanding we're all part of a larger being." At that time she was an attorney in a law firm, where she was deeply unhappy; she didn't care for what she was doing; it had no meaning; it was not fulfilling. So she consulted a career counselor, who helped her reflect on what she would like to do with her life. But, she says, "It's actually about who I am, because after developing one's spiritual side the other answers follow. Once we identify what our place is in the world, it's easier to find what we like to do, because intuitively we know our gifts and unique talents." She indicated that the question, "Who am I?" was with her for a long time. She felt a yearning that she needed more than what she was doing; she didn't feel whole.

As a side job to her current position, she has been undertaking several initiatives that have had a big impact on the communities and the environment. One was to re-write the code of ethics of the company, involving all the suppliers of the value chain, educating and informing them on the footprint they were collectively making. She persuaded them to take responsibility for acting in a sustainable way, as well as to understand the consequences of not acting. As a result, this large company was able to spread awareness and involve its whole global supply chain; this has had a huge environmental and social impact. It's the side job "that keeps me going," she says.

She thinks about her purpose, what she can do, and must not fail to do, and thinks this is triggered by prayer and contemplation that makes her "more open to tugs." She mentions feeling "a hole in the heart" that needs to be filled, and that we all have that. Community service, pulling together people who are very different but who have a common goal, is her way to fill that hole. She wonders if her role may be to help people find their purpose through sessions of dialogue and consciousness-raising. Along those lines, she identifies with the concept of servant leadership.

She has found it challenging to bring a spiritual dimension into the business world; people react saying "this is not the UN," or calling it "Kumbaya." However, she thinks of the "disjointed mess" she has experienced at work because people don't talk about spiritual topics. She has been persistent and has organized some safe spaces where people have a chance to talk to each other about what they really believe, and it is a big success.

She has large dreams for herself: she would like to act on a global scale to reduce poverty, because this is working for peace. "I may be planting the seeds."

Chapter 2

Something Prepared Them for Their Journey

The first question that I was curious to explore centered on what allowed the exemplary leaders to be ready to take the first steps in an unknown journey. What were the events that contributed towards preparing them for championing an initiative aimed at the greater good? I was hoping that understanding their personal journeys would provide insights into how we could intentionally develop that readiness in others. What I found was an extensive number of insights, which I have grouped under two umbrella concepts: Personal Mission and Social Sensitivity.

Personal mission

I use the term "personal mission" to refer to a sense of an inner calling, a strong urge to take action, the need to make a personal contribution to the world. I found that this was an important aspect for these exemplary leaders: 14 immediately resonated with the question on what prepared them for their journey, talking about mission and thoughts of making a contribution. "No doubt, definitely," said Paul. "My work is my personal mission" Ronald indicated, and Daniel was blunt in his determination to succeed, stating that he didn't feel "overwhelmed by the idea to change the Earth." Mark explained that he always looked at his "life's mission to convince people that there's a way of doing business where all the stakeholders actually benefit," a very unusual concept in light of how we typically look at business.

There is little doubt that the need to find meaning and purpose, and to demonstrate value-based behavior is connected with spirituality. This word requires definition, since *spirituality* is a broad concept that can have multiple interpretations, and can be used in many different ways. I define spirituality as thoughts people have about being connected to a higher order, and the consequences of this connection on one's life and behavior, such as the need to find purpose, to make a contribution, or to commit to actions for the greater good of our society.

It was surprising to find how important the concept of spirituality was for the leaders. Thirteen of the 16 recognized in one way or another that spirituality had a connection to their initiatives. However, it is important to point out that their individual interpretations of the word were varied and idiosyncratic. This is understandable, since "spirituality" and "business" are two words that don't always fit easily together.[i] In Western society, the working environment has been kept secular, and has focused on its separation from an employee's religious or spiritual life.[6] As André Delbecq puts it,[7] "Speaking of God, transcendence, or spirituality in the context of work was out of bounds." The topic of ethics – that is, the values behind leaders' decisions – was not an openly discussed topic in the workplace until a series of corporate scandals became known. In that context, learning how to speak from a spiritual mindset remains, to this day, an important yet difficult life skill.[8] Martin Rutte, founder and board member of the Centre for Spirituality and Workplace at Sobey School of Business, in Halifax, Nova Scotia, indicates that people have not developed a language to talk about spiritual themes, especially outside of religious settings.[9] This may explain the discomfort with which several respondents reacted to one term or another used by me in attempting to describe the motivation; these included "a higher being," a "calling," a "spiritual motivation," or a "religious inspiration." For example, Patrick indicated:

> (Laughing) I don't really subscribe to the fact that I particularly have any big goal in life, that there's something out there that's truly what I need to do. I subscribe to the fact that when I'm doing something that resonates with my body, my whole being … that's right. I don't think that there's somebody out there that says, "Let's see now. Patrick, we're gonna program you to go and save the

---

[i] Increasingly, business schools are incorporating courses and seminars about business and spirituality in the workplace. In this connection, the work of Mary Gentile, "Giving voice to values," has been an extremely valuable contribution to bring a different perspective to the "business as usual" attitude.

people in Ethiopia. Once you find that that's your mission in life, you'll be happy and fulfilled."

Yet regardless of whether or not they subscribed to the idea of a calling or a mission, participants related to the deeply felt need to act. "I have to do this, there is no way *not* to do this" (Robert) "I've a big sense that there's a lot more that I'd like to be doing to give back to the community" (Suzanne). Some felt it as a way of being of service to the world, instead of focusing only on self (Pam). Some viewed it as a sort of social mission: "This needed to be done for the business and ... for the environment and ... for the society" (Michael). "How do I intentionally act ... such that more women can come along behind me and start to break those barriers?" (Pam). For six participants it was part of a life dream.

> The mission is more so to leave it better than I found it, to be sure that I give back ... it's just part of what's inside me to want to ensure that we all leave this place better than we found it ... that's part of my fabric and I just have a general desire to do that. (Craig)

It was also interesting that eight participants mentioned the idea of leaving a positive legacy. "Because part of that whole legacy conversation is really about what will you be remembered for ... You'd like them to remember you for something...that you tried to do something" (Robert). "So what are we leaving to our children?" (Willie).

Have you ever wondered if your talents and personal gifts were given to you for a larger purpose than you are using them for?

If so, what would that larger purpose be?

For some, the mission was connected with being aware of certain personal gifts and talents. Five individuals mentioned that they wanted to give back to others. "I happen to believe that you're put on this world to do something and to mean something, and to take your gifts and your talents and actually be of service to the world. I think that is your job." (Mark). Patrick phrased it this way: "I want to help, take the gifts that I have and use them in a way that's more than just benefiting me." Suzanne, who initially wanted to be a medical doctor, described her current struggle which was to

> ... take all the skills that I've learned in business and take some organization that could really do something, whether it's in medical research or whether it's poverty reduction or whatever that is, and to be able to apply that and have that be how you make your living. I think that would be really, really rewarding. But that's not the life I have right now.

While 14 leaders mentioned the concept of a mission, a calling, leaving a legacy, or an urge to act, only in three cases was such a mission or calling an element that had featured consciously in their minds *prior* to starting the initiative. Their commitment to their new purpose was reinforced by the awareness of the personal contribution that they were making, not by the desire to make a difference. This is a very interesting finding. On one hand, it indicates that within the sample of 16 leaders studied, only a few were motivated by a conscious need to accomplish a clarified personal mission. For most of the others, the sense of mission evolved over time, and became clarified as they embarked on their initiatives. Their motivation evolved as the initiatives progressed, and as they witnessed the impact of the initiatives, and peoples' reactions to them. This impact reinforced them in their growing sense that this was maybe something they "had to do." This insight has led me to think that the prospects are good for the development of a generation of leaders more oriented towards the "greater good." Perhaps we don't have to wait for people to come with a fully formed sense of calling, but can hope that the motivation develops as we invite individuals to take on projects or initiatives that they feel passionate about.

Have you ever thought about having a
particular mission?
If so, what would it be connected to?
Is there anything you feel you *need* to do,
something that you could not live *without*
doing?

Social sensitivity

The sense of having a personal mission was an important finding in assessing what prepared the leaders, but it was not just their need to make a difference that was key. I found that their engagement in projects that impacted the greater good was rooted in a heightened social sensitivity. Through different circumstances they all developed a consciousness and sensitivity towards social issues such as poverty, inequity, injustice, and human suffering, and these played an essential role in inspiring them to take action. Some of them developed their social sensitivity early in their lives, as a result of their upbringing. Teachers who had discussed world politics and the current events with them were especially influential in shaping their critical thinking, and so were mentors who became role models to them in their younger years. This reinforces the important role that educators can play, the influence they can have when they foster critical thinking in students, especially exploring deeper meaning in seemingly mundane daily events.

In a recent email exchange with the author after a class offered at the MBA program of Fordham University, students commented:

> We as future leaders have the power to take the steps necessary to bring about a change. I believe that education is the best way to ignite that gut feeling and I think lectures of the similar nature should be given more often, and not only in business schools but also in undergraduate schools and high schools. (Andra)

Another student expressed the sudden heightening of awareness:

> I was surprised by the fact that there were so many things happening every day, directly or indirectly, influencing global sustainability. But why I was never aware of them before? Is there any other thing I have been overlooking but I have to keep an eye on? Since now I have noticed them, what should I do next? Your speech aroused many questions in my mind. Though I have no clear answer to them but I know I have to do something beneficial to our environment. (Caren)

Yet not everyone in my study was inspired by teachers in their earlier years. For nine of the leaders, they were adults before they encountered events that triggered their awakening in this arena. For some, it came in the course of travel and for Pam, Diego, and Paul it was eye-opening experiences they had as they met people in other countries living and working in deplorable conditions. Paul recalled:

> And I met some basket weavers and I met some weavers of cloth and some potters – and some sculptors in Zimbabwe, and they were all making these beautiful things that I knew sold for a lot of money in the States and they were getting hardly any money for what they were doing. ... I just thought: I can do that and I can pay them a lot more than what they're making. And I was gonna use business to do good.

Being in an unfamiliar context is always a powerful experience[10], since being exposed to a different way of living or thinking heightens awareness of our own habits and worldviews. We are so used to being "ourselves," to living and operating in our familiar environment, that we naturally take our customs and assumptions as "reality." Nothing gives the lie more to that attitude than finding oneself in an unfamiliar environment. Paul shared a deep-felt memory:

> ... the moment from that trip that made me start thinking is ... that they take you out to see a Masai village out in the Serengeti, and the driver paid the chief for the group to be able to walk through the village and see people who were living in a way that I had never seen humans living, and it was obvious that they were very poor and that the chief just made a lotta money off the driver and wasn't gonna share it with anyone, and it was just a horrible situation. I felt like ... the cameras that we were carrying and everybody was taking pictures of people and not asking permission and that our cameras were worth more than their annual income. And so I was on this amazing trip where we saw many things in Kenya, but that moment stuck with me and that I had just seen what two-thirds, three-fourths of the world's population lives like, and I had never experienced that in my country ...

Pam came in touch with disturbing information while witnessing the poor working conditions of women in Asia:

> I noticed the smell; I mean, the chemicals that are used when you stick things together ... they're very toxic. ... It was hot and there was this one woman on the line working with this chemical, visibly pregnant. I asked my interpreter to ask her whether or not the smell bothered her. And her answer sticks with me to this day. She said only on Sundays, which is the one day they don't work. That was the day she would have headaches ... a wake-up call that there is such huge disparity in the world. I think that's when I really started

to be extremely active and vocal around diversity and inclusion and equity.

For both these people, being brutally confronted by information that was new for them became a key trigger for awakening their social sensitivity. For others, information reached them through a variety of channels. For Carl, it was Paul Hawken's book *The Ecology of Commerce* that caused him to review his own contribution to the problems of society. For Mark, it was listening to an expert who made a presentation on the environmental consequences of our industrial era; for Suzanne, it was when she began surfing the Internet for information. Information in all cases generated a strong reaction, and pushed them to act.

Are you aware of your current personal contribution to the problems of our world? How do you think you are contributing to the problems? What are the thoughts and actions that give rise to your contribution?

Learning about opportunities to act served as a stimulus for others. Evan and Craig saw that their respective organizations were not maximizing the opportunities at hand to make a positive impact on sustainability, and decided to act. Suzanne thought that engaging employees in working on community projects might offset the stress and uncertainty they were experiencing as a result of the turmoil the organization was in. She thought that if people are unhappy and the organizational climate is distressed, the opportunity to focus on a community project could act as a distraction, ease their discomfort, and instill hope. It could, further, bring a positive image to the corporation and be viewed as a competitive advantage by their clients.

There is growing acceptance that sustainability efforts can positively impact the bottom line, that companies "can do well by doing good." Interestingly, in all the cases when an initiative started as a "convenience," or a rational decision to take advantage of an opportunity, or a means to an end – profit, savings, or a better working atmosphere – it soon became a goal in itself, as the leaders championing the initiative couldn't help but develop an authentic passion for the topic. The emotion became the fuel.

There is an adage that posits when the student is ready the master appears, and I am struck by the fact that when the opportunities for change presented themselves, these individuals were ready to pick up on the chance. For some, parenting was a critical experience that shaped their thinking. Robert reflected that if "trying to make life better for your kids is part of your responsibility, then making a world that those kids are going to live in better is also, from a selfish perspective, something you should be doing." Willie felt something similar, aware of the vulnerability of his own children, and wondered, "I'm going to ignore everybody else's children but my own? So what are we leaving to our children?" For Carl, his awakening came when he was in his mid-sixties. As he learned about the problems caused by industry in the environment, he recognized his own contribution to that problem, and how this would impact his grandchildren, who represented the next generation: "I was part of this industrial system that's destroying the biosphere! The living systems and the life support systems of Earth are in decline partially because of me, and by this time, I had grandchildren."

We all are part of the system that is destroying the biosphere. Jump ahead a few years, when the children born today are entering their teenage years. One of them, who is particularly close to you, asks you why your generation allowed the damage to happen; if you were aware of what was happening; and what you did to change.
How would you answer them?

For some, one factor that created a fertile ground for change was the experience of living a fragmented life, feeling a disconnect between the different aspects of one's self. Suzanne, who had wanted to be a doctor but was working in a food corporation, reflected, "It kind of took me further and further away from that path of maybe doing something meaningful for people other than selling food." Connie described it in no uncertain terms.

> I would really get physically these feelings of ... such unhappiness, and I just didn't care for my work, it didn't have any meaning for me ... and then I get a hole, this feeling in my heart that I'm not complete, that my life is not complete right now or I'm not doing what I need to do.

Substantive life changes are frequently triggered by traumatic events, and this was certainly the case for a few individuals who had had transformational experiences. Pam shares her personal saga:

> I think when I was absolutely hit over the head and where my life took a 180 degree turn was in '97 and '98. I had just had another miscarriage and my husband was diagnosed with cancer five months later. And while he was in chemotherapy I read a book called *Living Downstream*. And she [the author] talked in there about the effect of chemicals in our environment in our day-to-day life.

Pam connected both her miscarriages and her husband's cancer with the exposure to certain chemicals at different points of their lives. In her case, it was a pharmaceutical product that her mother had taken, and which later was established to have affected the reproductive capacity of the next generation. As for her husband, his lung cancer was found to be connected to his exposure as a child to DDT, a chemical then used as an insect repellent and later banned.

For Daniel it was learning to interact with his autistic son as he became aware of the unexpected vulnerabilities of life. For Mark it was the loss of his only sibling to a slow disease. Connie describes her traumatic event:

> I was a family of just two kids, and my brother was killed. And it was, you know, it was a violent death. ... And at that time, that's when I really took a new, you know, what's the meaning of life-type thing. ... And I think, at that time, it was an opportunity to start a new way of thinking, a new way of life ...

Ronald also relates the violent loss of his brother and pregnant sister-in-law. This unexpected tragedy was a shock that caused him to review how we was living his own life, which, he felt, could also end any moment before he could make any positive contribution.

The common outcomes of these traumatic events are that they led the individuals to pause, take a closer look at how they were living their lives and reflect on their priorities. As I think back and relive the many emotion-laden moments of the interviews, I find myself asking, "Do we need tragedies to occur, in order for us to pause, take stock, and ponder what we are doing with our life, our one life?"

If you were to learn that you have just one more year to live, would you make any changes in the way you're living?

What would those changes be?

The role played by feelings

Feelings, feelings ... They constituted the fuel that motivated these leaders to champion their initiatives. The interviewees cited the intense feelings that were generated among them as they learned about environmental problems, as they reflected on their own contribution to the problems, as they realized that corporate practices were creating health hazards, fostering unintended injustice, and contributing to social inequity. The distressing events that destiny presented to some individuals resulted in profoundly moving emotions that caused them to review their lives from a different perspective. The triggers may have differed, but they all led to intense repercussions and forever altered lives.

Seven leaders talked about pain, sadness, despair, and depression. Diego mentioned he would go out into the woods and cry and yell, a practice he learned from Native Americans to assuage grief. Carl described it in violent terms: "as a spear in the chest, the point of that spear touched my soul ..., it's your conscience ripped out of your heart." Connie talked about a hole in the heart that she didn't know how to fill. Mark described his reaction after listening to an expert, who talked about the environmental situation of the planet:

> I'll never forget as long as I live the feeling I had after his first two hours because I was ready to shoot myself. I mean, I was literally – I've never been more suicidal in my life. It was so depressing what he told me that I was literally distraught.

Others described being shocked, deeply concerned, or afraid:

> I'm extremely frightened about our future. … I think there has been just irreparable damage. I think we're going to hit another point in time where it'll be a cataclysmic turning point in terms of how we look at the system within which we're living. I just think there's something out in front of us that is going to, once again, reframe all of our questions and how we look at what used to be. (Pam)

Diego expressed a similar viewpoint: "we're heading closer and closer to a place where we won't be able to turn back." Harry talked about the sense of urgency brought about by his being 60 years old and by the urgency to address climate change, while Patrick was "appalled" that only one person in the corporation had ever heard the word "sustainability." Paul couldn't believe a farmer would rather keep a small coffee plant than have a new house built on that land if to do so would mean he would lose the plant. The starkness implicit in this choice caused him a turmoil of confusion, amazement, and disbelief.

Guilt and debt were other emotions mentioned. Carl would read passages of Hawken's book at night to his wife, and they would cry together over the crisis of the planet, realizing that he was part of the problem since he had created an industry that, along with others, was contributing to the destruction of the biosphere. Mark felt guilty following the death of his sister. Why had he been spared and not her? Her death galvanized him to determine that he should at least make the most out of his life, do something meaningful with it. Evan was part of a group with "organizational, cultural guilt," since his company manufactures outdoor products and the employees are outdoor loving people, but are not being environmentally responsible in their operations. Guilt was a strong factor in Suzanne's sudden awakening:

> I'd always kind of known that we were out there doing things, but it was, I was probably just busy doing my day job, and I didn't worry too much about it … it's sort of embarrassing when I look back to

think how little energy I sort of put into it. ... I think if anything I feel guilty sometimes because I don't do enough...

Anger served as the spark that kindled fire in six individuals who expressed feelings of rage, rebelliousness, and a sense that something was "driving them crazy." Their language was very passionate, very vivid. Willie talked about "what blows my mind"; Patrick mentioned "a deep fire in my belly and deep anger about just how foolish human beings are in the aggregate." Daniel and Diego described themselves as rebels, and several expressed how much they tended to identify with the "underdog" in society. Even Evan, one of the most rational and least emotional individuals, was motivated by the logic of how things had to be, and described how he got passionate about his initiative, as a sense of personal achievement: "It was like "Wow! If I can get an idea across or this project done, then I will have actually *done something*."

It is interesting to note the role that feelings played in motivating these leaders to action, particularly since feelings are seldom considered as trustworthy counselors in corporate decision-making. Indeed, business is typically conducted in a rational, logical manner, with decisions based on objective thinking. Any emotional components are expected to be identified and, if possible, neutralized to get the "best possible decisions." This, we are taught, comes more easily to men, who are culturally shaped to be disconnected from their feelings. Women, conversely, from an early age have the cultural "permission" to connect with their feelings while men are encouraged to put their feelings aside especially in corporate environments, where "being emotional" is not helpful for career, or for earning respect.

This finding opens a new perspective with significant implications in the way we develop the next generation of leaders, and I will come back to this in a moment. But first, let me share with you an interesting turn: how the leaders' feelings connected with the awareness that they could have a positive impact, if they just decided to act.

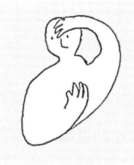

What do *you* feel when you read about environmental or social problems in the world?

What can I do?

What happens when we learn about a problem, when learning about it creates intense feelings in us? We may become overwhelmed, paralyzed, feel helpless, resigned, or depressed. Or we may convert the emotional turmoil into actions. As the leaders became increasing informed about the problems and opportunities, they also connected, because of their leadership role, with a sense of responsibility to take action. "So only industry has the power to change all of that!" reflected Carl, while Willie thought that the only option he could see was to design products that would never end up in a landfill. Michael saw the business opportunity to make a difference but also felt a responsibility to the community, and so did Craig, who expressed the personal need to leave this place better than he found it: "Just to educate people and educate the world and educate our customers, our suppliers, and anyone else that's interested, it felt like we have a responsibility to do that." Daniel thought about the wisdom of the Iroquois: "In every deliberation we have to think of the impact seven generations ahead." Connie, who works in a large multinational corporation in the retail industry, used these compelling words to describe her insights:

> ... it was everything. I mean it was – it's everything that was happening, [...] the war and poverty, you know, all over, different wars all over. The global, you know, obviously climate change. I mean just [...] knowing what's going on and being aware of the greater role ... that we can play, I mean that was everything. It was all of a sudden just showing people we can't be isolated. We are the solution, because we are such a major global player. I mean you could do all these things at, you know, a cottage industry, beautiful,

you know, make your Vermont cheese in a little tiny village in Upstate Vermont or New Hampshire, and [...] do a sustainable and artisan cheese, maybe part of the slow food movement, and have a really cool thing. But are you going to have an impact on a global scale?

Robert, working in a multinational pharmaceutical corporation had a similar reaction:

I believe that we all have an opportunity to create positive energy and impact people around us. Once that light went on that way, then I started to say: 'Well, how big can this be? How far should you go? How far can you influence people?'

The leadership role holds an inherent power, and several were aware of that potential. "We signed up for this call to action, we need to do something. We need to make this meaningful in our organization" (Suzanne). Connie reflected on her role, saying, "Maybe my job is to lift the veil to everybody, and have them open and see." Patrick described how he took his role and gave it an educational spin:

I said that we were going to become a learning organization and [...] a cornerstone would be that we would learn about sustainability, and that I would take everyone through this education process.

Being in a corporation meant, for some, acknowledging that beyond their individual influence, the organization also had resources available that could be used. Connie was asking herself and others: "Are you doing the best you can, given the opportunity that you have right now?"

It was interesting to observe how knowledge can become a burden, almost a hot potato that needs to be passed on to others. 15 leaders realized that they now knew something that their colleagues, peers, or employees didn't, and they felt the *urge* to do something, and this something was to start spreading the knowledge. Carl, who later made public speaking about the achievements of his exemplary corporation an almost full-time occupation, described what sharing the information meant for him.

... everybody's doing the best they can, given their level of awareness. All of this journey that we're on is about raising levels of awareness, and there's always a higher level of awareness for anybody. ... How do you put back more than you take? This is how we do it, by influencing others.

Connie indicated how she thinks about what she knows. "[We all] have a tremendous amount of responsibility. And that's what I'm trying to teach people." Mark described it this way: "So having seen all of that, I just looked inside of me, and I said, 'What can I do?'" [i] As I applied my findings in other settings, I encountered similar reactions to those of the leaders of my study. One setting was with college students who were exposed to stories and information that made them more aware of the impact we are collectively making on our planet. A student of the Masters program in Hospitality and Tourism reflected:

> I believe a little nudge, awareness, example, or reflection can help start movements/actions/decisions in being responsible producers and consumers. Without realizing it, many will support projects like what we started. (Jacqueline, Philippines)

And another described how she experienced a need to act:

> There was a voice whispered to my ear most of the time that I'd better do something which relates to what I am learning from the Sustainability Course. There's no one to push or force me to do that thing or this thing, I'm just willing to do it on my own, and it happened!" (Tram, Vietnam)

Do you feel a sense of responsibility when you reflect on the current problems?

If so, what do you do about them? What would you like to do?

After a brief two-hour class, Rich, an MBA student, reflected: "I realize that each of us should now look within ourselves and

---

[i] Personally, as I was writing down my research reflections at the end of my journey, I noticed that I had gone through a very similar process: the more I learned, the more I knew, the stronger my need to share that information with others, or else what was the purpose of just knowing it!? Me, too, I needed to act.

figure out how we can contribute to the environment in order to make the world a better place."

So let me share with you how the leaders in my study went about converting their need to do something, into action.

Chapter 3

Against the Odds

"What can I do?" was the question that spontaneously came up for several leaders, as they sought to convert their feelings into actions. Each one in their own particular way had learned about the planetary emergency, about the shortcomings of the industrialized world in taking care of natural resources, about educating our children, about protecting their health, about living happy and balanced lives and existing in peace with each other. What can I do?, was the insistent question they asked themselves, and I was curious to hear their answers. I found them most instructive.

The context

Independently of when and how they began their transformational journey, they shared a common trait: They all were championing a perspective hitherto unheard of within their corporate culture. They were all seeing, for the first time, something that their peers, bosses, or employees had not seen before, something that had never been part of the business agenda. They were seeing something that had gone astray in the world, and they were beginning to get a glimpse of the role their own organization was playing, and the role their organization could play in addressing the problems. Interestingly, this is a characteristic that this group has in common with visionary entrepreneurs and leaders. They both find themselves in situations where they see something that others don't, and they both realize that the role and scope of the business agenda has been expanded.

Mark described the difficulty he encountered as he introduced something that was new in every sense: a new awareness of the problems, as well as a need for innovative solutions. Both, he realized, were contrary to the concept of business as defined by Milton Friedman: that the business of business is business. Mark acknowledged to himself that business *actually plays a role in the environment*, that it has a civil responsibility to be what he called "profit with purpose." But not many saw it his way:

> Because the thing that frustrates me about this topic is that I meet so many great CEOs who are really good at what they do, meaning running a big company. That's a hard thing to do. ... It requires a lot of stamina and patience and fortitude and qualities. And the vast majority of CEOs in the world are really good people. I mean, I meet them. I see their families. They're good people. They're not – they don't steal. They don't cheat. They don't lie. They're honest. They're hard working. They have high integrity. They make almost all the right decisions. And then on Sundays often – or Thursday nights – they do phenomenal things. They are involved and they lead whole church missions through Africa, and they're active people. They do stuff, and they spend an inordinate amount of their free time helping the world. They have their own private foundations– but somehow there's this self-erected fence between what they do at work and what they do at home, and my goal has been to knock down that wall and bring that compassion and that kind of care for the world into their CEO-ship. I'm not suggesting that they don't care, but they don't – it's not as visible – in fact, some CEOs are opposite. They can be opposites. You can hear them make decisions at work, and you go like, "I just heard you on Sunday talking to this charity over there." I mean, is this the same guy?

Leading up to 1996, I had really created a platform about this topic – call it social responsibility, or whatever you call it – and I was speaking about it. I was traveling around the country and inviting people to speak and talk about it, and I felt increasingly lonely in my peer group. There were no CEOs – I tried to get CEOs to care about this, and they always said, "Mark, we love you, but this is crazy. This is your thing. Go do it, but we don't care."

Mark was not the exception. Eight of the leaders mentioned how lonely it felt to be pioneering something so radically different, so different that there was not yet a "language" to talk about it. In this sense we are more fortunate today since the media has helped to expand environmental literacy and we are globally more aware of the problems; we have a common vocabulary to refer to sustainability, climate change, and social impact.

On the other hand, there is still so much we have not scrutinized in the way we produce and consume, so little we have studied concerning the impact of our actions. In a recent class with MBA students, I randomly distributed pages of a newspaper, and asked each student to find something that was "unsustainable," and circle it in pen. After a while they began to laugh and exchange comments, since no matter what section of the paper they had in front of them, there was barely anything that should NOT be circled. This brings us closer to the experience of Pam, who was increasingly concerned with the lack of understanding of the potential effects of the chemical components used in her industry. "What else is in our world around us that we're working with today that we don't even know the impact of?" was her troubled question.[i]

All the leaders started on a journey in which they had to find their own answers and their own way. For most of them it was the pre-Google, pre-Facebook era (something difficult to imagine today!) which posed an additional challenge to their quest for understanding. *How do you find who else on this planet is thinking something like me, worried about something like me, developing ideas or experiments about this?* wondered Mark. But whether with or without Internet searches, they were walking in unexplored terrain, and uncertainty was the name of the game. They set out to find books and articles, and sought out experts as they engaged in

---

[i] As of February 2012, a report was presented by the UN Panel on Global Sustainability that addresses the global sustainability problem (finally!) from an integrated, systemic perspective. Among their 56 recommendations, they ask governments to develop better labeling policies that allow consumers to read and understand the components and origins of the products they consume. www.un.org/gsp/report

their "self-directed learning approach." This approach is now within reach of practically everyone with access to the Internet, and the ready availability of knowledge opens us to information on topics that we were just not aware of. For instance, we have access to previously hidden data, and can discover, to our consternation, that a habit we never noticed is totally unsustainable. Take eating, for example. In many parts of the Western world, (and the U.S.A. especially) we take for granted that we can cook with tomatoes in winter, or can buy kiwis from New Zealand anytime. But we seldom ask ourselves what is the personal carbon footprint resulting from making a simple dinner. A few years ago it was said that ingredients for the average American dinner "traveled" 2,000 miles to the dinner table, but this number is considerably higher these days. Try it for yourself. If you live in the Eastern United States, perhaps the wine came from South Africa (12,000 miles); the lamb from New Zealand (17,000 miles); the vegetables from California (3,000); the oranges from Israel (8,000); and the gelato from Italy (5,000). What is the real cost of that meal? It's up to us to figure out how we might change the way we think and act.

The leaders in the study searched out experiences they could replicate, copy, and learn from – but they couldn't find much guidance. Evan reached out to his company's suppliers to learn from their processes.

Our suppliers – because we only design product in here. We don't actually *make* anything. So other people make it. And we can suppose what they do and how they do it, but we don't really know. And so we say, "Well, let's ask them." And we pulled together a conference. This was one of the steps during this phase, because we just didn't have any examples back in 1997. Well, it was really interesting. We found out there were very few examples out there – that people coming to these kinds of conferences were seeking advice from us, and us from them, and I think we figured out that we were very, very much on the forefront of a new idea. It was kind of shocking because, gosh, that's kind of depressing, too.

It can be depressing – or it can be an exciting opportunity – to explore and create things anew. We may be inclined to think that fortunately times have changed, and that what was a challenge back in the mid-1990s is no longer the same challenge due to multiple communication vehicles, social media, and a more expanded awareness of climate change and social issues. Yet with growing awareness comes the realization of the substantial scope of what we need to change. There may be more individuals to collaborate with, and learn from, yet the dimension of our challenge is growing. Or perhaps we are just learning to see and notice the dimensions of the challenge, since we are bound to "see" only what we know; and until we are able to understand new perspectives, we walk among hypotheses, intuitive observations, hunches, scientific tests, unchecked assumptions, opinions, and draft theories. Increasingly, we realize the challenge is larger than imagined, and we cannot grasp the total implications because of the systemic conditions with reinforcing loops and tipping points that rapidly change the landscape. This means we all today carry a similar uncertainty to the one experienced by the business leaders of the study. Like them, we collectively need to figure out what should be done to address our challenges.

The leaders in my study consulted with others, questioned friends and colleagues, and talked about their concerns wherever they could, trying to exchange resources and ideas in what was a form of "social learning",[11] a real accelerator of knowledge creation that happens when we connect with others. The Society for Organizational Learning created a Sustainability Consortium, inviting a dozen corporate executives to meet and discuss their concerns, and offering them a space for deep and candid conversations. Pam recalls how important that consortium was for her:

I don't know what I'm talking about, but I know this needs to be done. What's the language? Are there any case studies? Do you guys have any examples of how this? And so we were in this exploration, this journey together because we were all pretty much at the same stage. We were still trying to define what it meant at the corporate level.

Many things are easier when done with others. Who is one person that you would consider when brainstorming ideas of what you'd like to do?

They experimented, used a trial-and-error approach, and learned as they received feedback from their own actions. They accepted the fact that no one had all the answers. In fact, no one even had all the questions, and no one knew very much. Still, within this challenging context, I found that they unknowingly played five distinctive leadership roles.

The five leadership roles

At this point I want to share some assumptions that I carried into my research. The first is my assumption that the individuals I would interview had had some kind of "aha" moment that launched a transformative experience. I imagined they awakened, decided what they wanted to do, and did it. What I found, however, was not like that at all. Traditional linear thinking can make us feel comfortable and offer a logical way to consider a challenge. It provides us a road map to follow, but it is not how reality works.

My interviews served as an impetus for the leaders to convert their lived experience into a story, and when we tell a story our mind organizes events and facts into a sequence, creates cause and effect connections, and paints before-and-after relationships. But reality is not linear. Instead it is complex and messy: We progress in spiraling movements, learning as we go, repeating, correcting, forgetting, and most of the time not taking the time to reflect and extract meaning from our experiences.

Yet, throughout the narratives of these 16 leaders I was able to recognize five distinctive leadership roles: these leaders were Inspiring, Communicating, Engaging, Implementing and Disseminating.

Inspiring

No one said, "I decided to inspire others." Yet their "fire in the belly," their passionate convictions, led them to seek ways to share that fire with others.

For several, it was about making a point to connect the benefits of their particular initiative with the operations of the corporation. Evan, for example, framed the situation as the company being an ecosystem within the natural ecosystem, and that the success of the company was as dependent on a healthy environment as it was on a good financial plan. Patrick met with all employees in groups of 50 for nearly two hours, and he told them:

> Look, we're in the clean energy business; we need to understand this in the context of sustainability in order to understand how to position ourselves. If you're here for other reasons than that, I'm gonna try to explain to you why this is the most important reason.

Some shared big visions; for example, seven indicated they talked about leading a movement. In Carl's words:

> ... so that became sort of the vision coming out of that task force meeting, the vision of leading the industrial world towards sustainability ... going from sustainable to restorative. ...You can't tell people how to think or what to think. You can only show them a vision and urge them to follow me, you know...

Connie exhorted the employees: "Come on, we've gotta go. We've gotta change." Paul saw his corporation as an example:

> We're actually trying to build this organization where it can be modeled and where others can use some of the things that we've learned just by making ... as much as we can transparent and post it on our website, or you know, be willing to have conversations with other people that have similar ideas.

Another way of inspiring others was through using self as example, through sharing their personal experiences. Carl wrote a speech entitled "The Eco-odyssey of a CEO," and Robert said that in order to be respected in teaching sustainability it was necessary to be perceived as "walking the talk." "So you need to be able to say, 'Hey, this is what I'm doing.'" Interestingly, I observed a similar behavior among the students of a Sustainability Mindset course at the Hospitality and Tourism program at Fairleigh Dickinson University. Towards the end of the course, several students observed that, as a result of the course, one of their areas of personal transformation was that they had changed their behaviors and were trying to be an example to their roommates, family and friends, by acting in more environmentally responsible ways. In the same course taught at an MBA program hosted by Fordham University, some students established as a personal evaluation criterion, the desire to assess their accomplishments, to "change my habits in my personal life and at work" in order to "inspire others" to change.

Some of the leaders found that a successful strategy to inspire others was to face the audience, "forcing people to think about things" (Evan), challenging their paradigms, or showing the flaws in the way we tend to understand the world. Pam had a straightforward approach to the leaders of her organization: "This is our role; these are choices that we make. What do we want to do differently? And do we really understand?" Others found success in replicating their own transformational experience; they would take people on trips to see different cultures and have personal encounters with a diverse environment. Willie relates how, over time, he and his team took 450 executives to a series of retreats held in a wilderness area, in what became a life-shaping experience for most of them. These real-life encounters and challenges made strong imprints on the hearts and the minds of the people who had faced new ways of being, and acting, together.

Communicating

There was, the group found, something unbearable about keeping what they had learned to themselves. Twelve leaders explained how they began teaching, speaking, and writing about what they knew, and how eager they were to transmit their new information to others. Harry made it part of his job to organize conferences, meetings, learning journeys, trips to the field, and small thematic seminars. This reaction of wanting to share their newfound perspectives with others was also reflected, I noticed, in two students of the MBA program, who decided to champion a project to educate children in sustainability, and to thereby seek to shape a different worldview starting in the young people's formative years. Another student suggested to a group of busy class colleagues that they create a "No Impact Week"[12] at their school, which was something that required a large amount of dedication and extra effort in a very short and busy term. Surprisingly, students who didn't have the time to complete all the readings or to write all the papers suddenly jumped at this idea, and in less than a week, 15 were enthusiastically exchanging numerous daily emails, and dividing the large project between several sub-task managers. The common goal? To share what they had now learned with others in the school – with every student and faculty and graduate, if possible!

As pragmatic business people, the leaders in my study were particularly focused on the importance of showing facts and hard data. "When I'm presented with facts that are compelling, I just surrender. I just say, 'Okay, great. Let's now do something about it,'" said Mark, who after extensively listening to the first expert talking about the planetary emergency called in his whole leadership team so they would have the same experience. Pam knew that she had to talk in a language that her organization understood. Thus, she went to find data to make her case:

> So, for example, if we create product the way we currently create it, we are producing x pounds of material waste every year, approximately that translated into almost U.S.$700 million of waste annually in our business unit alone. Seven hundred million dollars. So now you're coming at their pocketbook.

Yet these leaders also realized that what had profoundly moved them was not data alone – it was something that touched their hearts. Carl was told many times he had a compelling speaking style, and he never hesitated to bring emotion into his speech. People would tell him "You touched my brain and my heart." Paul shares how he organized meetings between farmers and corporate individuals:

> When the personal connections are made, then a lot of objections fall by the wayside or a lot of hesitancy falls by the wayside, especially when a coffee roaster meets the child of a coffee farmer.

They used storytelling, they created metaphors, taking for example the image of a mountain, called "Mount Sustainability," that all would jointly escalate, and with the summit symbolizing the zero footprint. Another strategy used was a geological perspective of where we are today, a presentation that demonstrated the swift, brutal impact of our industrial behaviors on the Earth, compared with the millions of years the planet needed to develop all species. They took care, moreover, as they argued their point, to acknowledge the opposite view, and to address contrary perspectives, objections, and doubts.

It was clear that successful communication would have an impact on behaviors and decisions. Evan explained it with these words:

> So once you get that through education it's really hard to let go of. It's something you see in everything you look at. Every time you see a problem in the company you're able to say, "Wow! It's simply that we're not really looking at the big picture," and it just comes up over and over and over again.

They used all the resources they could think of to pass on a message that was too important to be kept to themselves alone.

Engaging

Have you ever washed a rental car? For most of these leaders, it became clear that if they wanted people to care and to take action, they had to create ownership of the challenge among others through participative engagement. The few leaders who overlooked the importance of developing ownership, and who used only authority and communication skills in the attempt to persuade, had an uphill battle. "Maybe I would have reached out more and included the people who were fighting me and brought them in and gave them a piece of the action," said Willie reflecting with 20/20 hindsight.

Mark cited this good leadership insight. "The people support what they help create, and you can't tell people anything. They have to experience it. They have to share – there has to be a shared story." To create engagement, 11 individuals out of the 16 sought to create a team that could champion the cause and multiply the impact of their effort, as Evan explained:

> We pulled together a group of some people who had been working really hard. You have to pull together a much more team-based approach right from the beginning. You won't be successful if you try and push ...

Several leaders indicated the importance of organizing sustainability-related meetings where people could get together to talk and share ideas, sometimes in small groups. This helped to develop spontaneous advocates, and when the host found a high level of interest in somebody, he or she would personally foster it. They also created engagement by getting people to work on community projects, such as helping clean up a river and teaching disadvantaged children. Two individuals tried to create interest by offering monetary rewards. "The invitation was for employees to make a suggestion how to lower our carbon footprint or to save natural resources, and the corporation will pay you a reward." Perhaps surprisingly, this strategy failed to gain traction. Employees looked at it with little interest, viewing it as just another corporate initiative that didn't engage them. However, when the reward was nothing more than the ability to lower the environmental footprint, people seemed to participate more eagerly. This challenged their assumption about the importance of monetary rewards to promote CSR-related initiatives. Others found that emotional empathy and social sensitivity were more powerful motivators, and that personal fulfillment, and the satisfaction brought by doing good for others, acted as strong reinforcements.

Implementing

While motivation is important, implementation is the real test of the best ideas and innovative initiatives. For seven individuals, it was key to begin creating a concrete business case. Said Evan, "A lot of people (here) don't want the theory. They want the proof ... and so we needed examples." Several had to create new metrics to assess results and to learn how to present them. We can make a change, they stated, but how do we measure how much we are saving in resources? What is the saving in wasted materials, energy, water, or even employee time? Actively seeking feedback from others about what they were trying to do (and practicing listening skills to really hear it) were other helpful strategies. Thirteen individuals commented on the importance of paying attention to the reactions of colleagues, employees, and board members, because that allowed them to adjust and correct their actions. Interestingly 10 leaders talked about a new element, which was the joy and satisfaction they felt when they heard something back from those beneficiaries and colleagues who had bought into their ideas. This became a powerful reinforcement of their work. In Paul's words:

> ... every single day we do get to have some kind of interaction with the farmers that we feel like we represent here. So I'm fortunate in that I come into work every day knowing these are the guys that we work for. We represent them here. We want to treat them fairly ... we're honored to be working with them and that gets me out of bed.

One lesson about implementation, which came from two individuals, was the need to advance carefully, since as with other organizational change processes, people resist changing what or how they do things. In addition, sustainability is connected with the big problems facing our planet – climate change, pollution, depletion of resources, and social inequity, to name a few – and the very size of these problems can overwhelm and make people feel helpless. Robert said: "Forget about global warming! Let's just make our operations more sustainable from an environmental degradation viewpoint!" Seven individuals indicated that they were able to identify the opportunities that their organizational culture, sometimes unwittingly, had provided them. For Suzanne, it was a series of reorganizations that negatively impacted the morale of the employees; in addressing that issue, she said, "it was nice to have something very positive to talk about and to engage people." For Willie, it was the awareness his company had around health and safety matters, which was a culture fostered by the founder; Willie used this to determine that, as part of the design criteria, the product they would design would not contain any component that might end up in a landfill. Craig, who at that time had been at the company for only a couple of years, soon realized that there was a strong tradition of ethics that went back to the founder, who felt that employees should be "all interested in doing good things, and it's really important, [knowing that] it's not always the cheapest thing, it's not always the easiest ... the quickest thing ... It's an organization that has that as part of the culture."

A comment that seven individuals made was related to the importance of simply "starting where you are," and for several, this came as a lesson learned the hard way. Carl, who became a world role model in transforming an industry, recalls saying:

> Well, let's just do something, anything. Let's just *do something*. How do we take where we are, how do we start where we are, not where we wish we were but where we are, and evolve this thing toward what we want it to be?

Suzanne said "use what you have, don't make it a big resource intensive thing because that's when things get killed." Craig had a similar perspective:

> So, we are not changing the culture, we're not doing any kind of night and day, you know, big shifts here, all we're doing is just taking this foundation and just better organizing it and highlighting certain areas more so than we did in the past ... but it's all there ...

Evan warned: Make it work within the culture, and in the process you will change the culture. "But if you go into it thinking you are going to change the culture ... you'll be wrong." Connie said at first she "was making it way too hard." She went back to the mission statement of the company and found the necessary values already there. By building on existing values, she was no longer telling people they were doing everything wrong, and was no longer asking them to adopt a whole new way of thinking or doing everything. In sum, she framed the changes in terms of the company growing and evolving – not changing dramatically.

Thirteen participants were surprised by way of the reaction of their workforces, which taught them a valuable lesson about implementing CSR initiatives. While they expected an uphill battle of advocacy to persuade the corporation into doing something in a "business unusual" way, the employees unexpectedly leaped to embrace the opportunity. Carl shared a highlight of his journey, which was when the most critical executive in his company stood up in front of a large audience and publicly declared, "You know, all my working life, I've made compromises. Here's the chance to undo some of the damage I've done." As a result, a group came together and indicated they thought they understood sustainability and what that might mean for them – and they thought they could achieve sustainability in six years. Carl recalls that emotional moment: "They had no idea, such naïveté, you know, but people are galvanized around this shared higher purpose." Harry noted:

> If the people involved can tap their own, not just their minds but also their own passions and find inspiration, bring themselves

more fully into the room and connect with one another on a sort of values and meaning and purpose level, and not just a cognitive level, then all sorts of power gets unleashed.

Mark indicated he always had one hundred percent of his people say "Let's go!" and eager to get going because the argument was so compelling. In fact, this happened so much that he had to ask them to calm down and to accept that organizational change cannot happen all at once. Suzanne had a similar experience: "Everyone wanted to be part of the new council of sustainability, because they saw an opportunity to build something." Connie was equally surprised and said, "There's a lot of people who have tapped into parts of them that have not been filled, that they're jazzed about it, so they get a lot of ideas." In Patrick's experience, people had not been happy, but when they began to get turned on to something that was not only useful at work but also at home and in their personal lives, it allowed the employees to grow and derive real satisfaction working on a project which he likened to "building cathedrals." Willie commented that a product design team had worked on a zero-landfill product six days a week for six years; no one was paid for working on a Saturday, yet the parking lot was filled.

What is this all telling us? It shows an interesting paradox, and it uncovers a widely accepted myth. This myth is that business is driven solely by numbers, and that decisions based on a clear financial, ROI-based rationale are the right decisions. This myth also maintains that emotions and feeling-based decisions are not appropriate. The group of business leaders unconsciously accepted this myth, and presented their peers in the organization with the "best" business case they could build, in order to gain their acceptance and buy-in. However, and this is the paradox, with one exception, none of the leaders in this study bought into the notion of sustainability because of a rational, no-nonsense, set of data. They were pulled into it because something grabbed their heart, because they felt pain, guilt, empathy, and a sense of being overwhelmed. They experienced something that touched their soul, and triggered their actions. Interesting disconnect between their own motivations, and how they felt others should be motivated.

Disseminating

The efforts of implementation didn't end with engaging the audience. Once the train of change was moving down the track, the need to spread and disseminate the new perspectives became a deeply felt necessity. As evolutionary author Andrew Cohen[13] describes it, it is at the core of all livings to tend towards "becoming" something else, towards continuous expansion. The leaders worked upstream, which meant involving and educating their company's different vendors and suppliers. In Pam's words "I had to go out and start engaging some of our key suppliers, the big ones, and say, 'Here are our goals. We use your materials. We can't reach our goals unless you're in the game with us.'" She championed an educational initiative in her corporation that drove the effort to cascade the knowledge:

> We mobilized a one-year learning journey for 100 champions around the company, and exposed them to all the current thinking on sustainability – such that we could plant the seeds so they could go back into whatever part of the organization and start to mobilize around this.

Five indicated the importance of having a strategy to disseminate the new perspectives throughout the organization. Suzanne described it this way:

> … we needed to have that representation. We wanted someone from marketing, and particularly channel marketing, someone who understood the customer and what the customer might need. So we invited one of our directors. We wanted someone from supply chain …

This was not always an easy task, as Patrick indicates:

> Some people really liked it, some people discounted it, some people were disruptive, but everybody went through it. It was very nourishing and satisfying to see people wake up and suddenly start being self-generative and finding themselves becoming so self-aware that they were in fact influencing and affecting others in a positive way.

Paul discovered the importance of building bridges and developing alliances, and he saw this as a key part of his role:

> … to help different people see what they have in common, keeping this group pointed in the same direction even though, you know, there were a lot of individual personalities and sometimes there may be clashes.

Are you in an organization that needs some awareness-raising? An organization that you feel needs to identify a greater purpose in its daily work?
What is one thing you could do to start a conversation among your colleagues?

Something more

Inspiring, communicating, engaging, implementing, and disseminating were the key leadership roles observed in fostering sustainability initiatives in a corporation, and there is a large number of lessons to be drawn from the strategies that were tried out, both those that worked and those that (so far) didn't.

How different is this from the experience of entrepreneurs and leaders who drive large organizational change initiatives? There are many similarities. Entrepreneurs, like the sustainability pioneering business leaders, deal with something new.[14] They use trial and error to learn as they go, getting feedback from their own actions. They, as well as change leaders, have to navigate in uncertainty; they are aware that they don't have the full knowledge, never have all the information that would be desirable to make decisions, and yet are urged to move. They have to inspire, communicate a vision, and foster participation and collaborative action.

But another dimension emerged in the study, one that made the journey of these sustainability champions different than the typical journey of entrepreneurs and change leaders. It was more than information, knowledge, and change management skills. Something was happening under the surface, and it marked the tipping point between breakdown and breakthrough. What was happening was connected to the thinking and the being. There was something essentially different about these leaders' mindset. I called it the sustainability mindset.

PART II
UNDER THE SURFACE

An extensive literature review on the topic of business leaders championing sustainability initiatives indicates that there is still inadequate attention paid to the motivations, personal reasons, and psychological make-up of those individuals who make an active attempt to better our planet by using their own business as a vehicle.[15]

While I was curious to understand how these exemplary leaders felt and acted, I soon noticed that there was something else underlying their behaviors. It was not "what" they thought and did, but "how" they thought. For lack of a better term, I labeled it their *mindset*, meaning the way of processing information, which is based on paradigms formed by emotions, and tacit and explicit knowledge.

That sustainability touches more than the intellect had been observed before. In a study of 11 female graduate students learning about global future threats, scholar M. E. Rogers[16] observed that what she thought would be a cognitive experience, ended up being a holistic learning one, engaging emotions and spiritual dimensions. It was not just about acquiring information; it also involved a particular way of *processing* information. In a similar way, Emotional Intelligence researcher David Goleman[17] observed that intelligence was more than just a collection of cognitive aspects. It required in addition a number of emotional drivers in order to fully manifest itself in intelligent actions.

I grouped the findings related to mindset into two dimensions: the *Thinking* (both innovative and systemic) and the *Being*. This is partially in line with what Organizational Systems Professor John Adams[18] described as mental models related to sustainability, which he developed after asking 158 managers and consultants from the United States, Canada, the United Kingdom, the Netherlands, and India, to use adjectives to describe "how people think around here." He found six consistent themes, each of which he set up on a separate continuum:

- Time orientation: from short term to long term
- Scope of attention: from local to global
- Prevailing logic: from either/or to both/and
- Focus of response: from reactive to creative
- Problem consideration: from accountability and blame to learning
- Life orientation: from doing and having to being

The first three (time orientation, scope of attention, and prevailing logic) fall within what I classified as the *systems thinking* framework. Focus of response corresponds to *innovative thinking*, and life orientation corresponds to *being* orientation.[i]

---

[i] I didn't find in my study indications of problem consideration (blame versus learning), yet I found a sense of accountability, an awareness of the responsibility they had for contributing to the problems, which I analyzed in the previous section.

Chapter 4

The Dimension of Thinking

In analyzing my interviews, I found that the dimension of Thinking presented two distinct categories, Innovative Thinking and Systems Thinking.

Innovative thinking

What roles does creativity play for business leaders engaging in sustainability related initiatives? While they don't specifically connect creative thinking with sustainability, empirical studies in the area of entrepreneurship do point to the importance of innovation and creativity in scanning the environment for new opportunities and valuing new ideas.[19]

There are also non-academic reports that cite numerous data about an association between the two aspects, innovation and creativity.

Ben Cohen and Jerry Greenfield, creators of the ice cream brand Ben & Jerry's, authored an autobiographical book[20] where they detailed an account of the progressive steps in their journey from a small ice-cream shop connecting with the neighbors through special events to a full grown national business, replete with far-reaching and exemplary CSR practices. The practices cover areas such as: workplace and employee relations; accounting; product development using natural and organic ingredients; procurement; respecting diversity and partnering with social entrepreneurs like Greyston, a bakery in inner-city Yonkers, New York, which trained and employed economically disenfranchised people and funded low income housing at the same time; strategic location decisions (deciding where to build a plant is given special attention, because of the impact of a business in their community); ethical practices and compliance; investments; environmental packaging; transportation to minimize the carbon footprint; waste treatment; emissions control; marketing campaigns (i.e. instead of advertising, which they did not consider value-adding, they provided service to the communities organizing music festivals, opening "partnershops" that benefited nonprofit groups, etc.); educational events; social audit and reporting; and community projects among others. Each initiative is described by the authors as resulting from innovative thinking, from creative ideas emerging from team brainstorming sessions, or from Cohen's creative mind. They describe these initiatives as representing a radical shift from how business was practiced at that time: a shift that thus demanded the development of ingenious solutions and approaches.

We can find the need for innovative thinking also in the green building industry[21], where sustainability depends on invention and experimentation.[22] Another example of ingenuity is found in retail. Some years ago, Dan Henkle, Gap Inc.'s senior vice president for social responsibility, launched the campaign titled RED, which was one of the first initiatives of its kind. In this campaign companies funneled 50 percent of the profit from specific "red products" to The Global Fund, to fight AIDS in Africa.[23] While corporations have been contributing to philanthropic causes for decades, this was one of the first cases where a large campaign used advertising to boldly show the public their new commitment, and also to invite other organizations to participate in developing "red" products.

In some way, these pioneers were creating the foundation for a "virtuous circle," where competitors didn't want to be seen as "the one who is doing nothing," and where "nothing" could, in the eyes of the public, be viewed as unacceptably uncaring behavior.

Because of the efforts of these corporate change leaders, the number of companies launching creative sustainability initiatives has increased substantially, with some of them playing an exemplary role, and setting new standards for their industry. Such is the case of the outdoor apparel company Patagonia, which developed a program that recycles garments returned by customers, together with recycled soda bottles, to make new polyester fiber, which is then used in a new line of underwear.[24] In perhaps their boldest move, Patagonia invites clients through its advertising and website to think twice before shopping, stating "don't buy what you don't need." They declare their commitment to long lasting merchandise, but if something needs to be fixed, they either do it, or help find tailors in different locations to fix the garments. They take back used garments, explaining their philosophy: "Nothing wearable should be hoarded; useful things should be in circulation. Reuse what you no longer need, whether you've given up climbing or no longer wear brown. Donate unused clothes to a charity or sell them through the Patagonia Common Threads Initiative site on eBay or on our website (where you can also buy used rather than new)."

The pioneering sustainability initiatives of Interface, the manufacturer of business and residential carpeting are well known. Led by their late founder Ray Anderson, the company decided that instead of replacing whole carpet rolls that created huge waste, they would offer a tile-pattern system for carpets where carpet owners need only to replace single squares, thus reducing the use of energy and materials – not to mention generating savings for the customer. Since then, Interface has taken the lead in reducing its environmental footprint through innovations in the areas of energy, waste, facilities design, and transportation; in product design and manufacturing processes; and in the creation of an organizational culture of engaged employees who have taken the mission beyond the company and into the communities where they do business. They, too, are intentionally redefining how responsible business can be conducted.

Following an invitation of retail giant Wal-Mart to address the energy consumption of refrigerators, GE first developed a light bulb for refrigerators based on a computer screen light, which is a low-energy consumption feature. Over the past five years, the company has converted creativity and betterment of the planet into a core aspect of their business, adopting the by-line "Imagination at work." They describe themselves with these words: "We're determined to solve the world's biggest problems. By putting our collective imagination to work for a better future, we might get there yet. Is it possible to change the world? At GE we are doing it, one idea at a time. Imagination = innovation."

These few organizations are fine exemplars of responsible sustainability, and the good news is that the list has no end. Innovation and creativity are considered not only important factors to address problems, but also opportunities for profitable business.[25] When I read CSR reports with innovations such as these or find press releases in our inbox, I get excited and filled with hope at everything that is happening. Still, when I walk on the street, read a newspaper or go into a store, I see how much has yet to change.

What is behind the initiatives, which results in their implementation? What are the thoughts and strategies in the leaders' minds that ensure successful execution of the objectives? Is there anything that can be learned? What might we learn that we can employ to do more often, faster, and more successfully?

Twelve individuals in my study mentioned examples of how they had to think "out of the box," to be creative, to find solutions, and to explore ideas that could change the current processes and traditional operations. For a variety of reasons, they all felt the urge to act in a more responsible way towards the environment or the community, but found themselves shackled by a lack of precedents and experiences that could guide them as they went about implementing their ideas. What was clear to them was that inventiveness had to become integral to their *modus operandi*. Diego's business model (of supporting the creation of self-sustaining communities at the same time converting them into his vendors) was unique and had never been tried before. To Willie what was clear was the importance of "breaking the rules, not living by meaningless bureaucratic rules." Persistence was key: The desire to develop a solution that combined a reduction in cost with an improved impact on the environment was a motivation that could endure for several years:

> We've been testing for about eight or nine years now fuel cell batteries for forklifts; in our warehouses we have thousands of forklifts, almost all driven by these huge batteries that have to be charged every night. We worked with the supplier several years to develop a fuel cell battery that uses liquid hydrogen, so they get fuel once a week. The time savings are incredible and it has zero emissions. (Michael)

In some cases the innovation became a new standard, as Mark observes: "We had trucks running on French-fry oil, which now actually they do all over Europe, but, you know, 15 years later than us."

These examples portray the powerful impact of innovation as an (unintended) seed for change that goes beyond the innovative corporation. When we change something in our behavior or decisions, we are changing the "way of doing things" – and not only in our personal or corporate sphere. This impact can be represented with the image of a stone thrown into the water, and with the expanding circles reaching shores we cannot see or even imagine. How aware are we of the impact of our decisions? Does this awareness end in feelings of helplessness when we are confronted by the planetary crisis? How can we become more conscious of the impact of our actions so that we can be intentional and accountable for them on a larger impact level?

Do you ever think what impact that a decision you make might have on the environment and/or on the community? Ignoring the impact doesn't cancel it out.

How would it be if you included that mindfulness when making your next decision? How could you make it a creativity challenge, a time for innovation?

There were other lessons found with the 16 leaders. Some saw the invitation to creative thinking as a way to engage employees:

> You find people are more excited about what they're doing because of the opportunity to be creative, and I think that they are more motivated to do a better job. (Robert)

Another lesson connecting with innovative thinking was the confirmation of the truism that nothing is better than lack of money or resources to awaken our creativity. In some cases, the impulse to be creative sprang from the need to bring an idea to fruition within a very limited budget:

> Getting a company to be willing to incur initial costs – even though you can't absorb it, you have to be creative about how you fit it into your financial picture. No company can just afford to absorb it. So you have to be very creative about how you pull back somewhere else in order to do something. (Evan)

This suggests that if we succeed in expanding public awareness of the Earth's limited resources it may be possible to foster more creative ideas.

While many of us write ourselves off the list of creative individuals, saying "I am not a creative person," the capacity for imagination is nevertheless in everyone. As children, we interact with the world in a playful and creative way, without even noticing we are doing it. Later, the creative playfulness may get buried below the daily routines and self-constraining judgments. Harry, who was brought up on a farm, described it this way: "…That there is that seed in everybody of breakthroughs … of creativity."

Pam used simple questions to take employees into that creative mindset: "… when you hit a brick wall … figure out, "Okay. I can't go through it. Can I go around it? Can I go under it? Can I go over it? Can I find a different wall?"

Creativity and its product, innovation, are short-lived in a consumption-based market, and they demand organizations to permanently nurture imaginative thinking. Diego described it citing Hebrew ancestral teachings:

> In the Kabbalah, in Hebrew mysticism, when the spark of creation emanates, the minute it emanates it's captured and it's co-opted. Since it's an old agricultural religion, they have metaphors [from] agriculture. So what they say is [that] when the spark of creation is born, it's immediately surrounded by a husk. And it's the job of the Kabbalists to eliminate the spark from the husk. But as soon as it gets liberated, it gets the husk again, and that's what creation is all about. It's the same thing in Hinduism. And Buddhism can be defined as the same kind of philosophy. Anyway, applied to business … when you come up with a creative idea, it comes out there and things happen that husk it. The first is it starts to become institutionalized within your own organization. And rather than the organization serving the creative enterprise, the creative enterprise begins to serve the organization. That's what happened to Ben & Jerry's. That's what happened to all of the major good organizations that slowly become co-opted.

Daniel believed that to be visionary and to proactively be "in the creation of the new" is a key role of leaders, especially in times where planetary circumstances are "at the point of crumbling." In a similar vein, the Austrian ecologist and philosopher Fritjof Capra suggested that "in addition to holding a clear vision, leadership involves facilitating the emergence of novelty by building and nurturing networks of communications; creating a learning culture in which questioning is encouraged and innovation is rewarded; creating a climate of trust and mutual support; and recognizing viable novelty when it emerges, while allowing the freedom to make mistakes."[26]

Systems thinking

What is systems thinking and what role does it play when implementing sustainability initiatives? The last century has seen a paradigm change involving science, and, in the words of Capra, "with a tension between the parts and the whole. The emphasis on the parts has been called mechanistic, reductionist, or atomistic; the emphasis on the whole: holistic, organismic, or ecological. The holistic perspective has become known as "systemic." Systems thinking was launched by biologists during the 1920s, emphasizing the view of living organisms as integrated wholes"[27]. It brought up concepts like connectedness, relationships, and context. Systems thinking was enriched by the theorists of the Gestalt school and the new science of ecology, which found that Nature operated as a dynamic, large, and complex system.

According to Capra, "we do not need to invent sustainable human communities from scratch but can model them after Nature's ecosystems, which are sustainable communities of plants, animals, and microorganisms. ... A sustainable human community is one designed in such a manner that its ways of life, businesses, economy, physical structures, and technologies do not interfere with Nature's inherent ability to sustain life."[28] Capra indicates that we can learn about sustainability from the ecosystem, which has organized itself during the course of this planet's evolution. Biological sciences writer Janine Benyus notes that if the age of the planet were presented as a full calendar year, the human species would appear about 15 minutes before midnight on New Year's Eve. Our recorded history would be compacted into the last sixty seconds of the year, and all our plants, animals, and microbes, would have been slowly evolving since the month of March, some 3.8 billion years since the appearance of the first bacteria.[29]

The basic systems principles are interdependence, cyclical flow, long-term view, complexity, both/and thinking, and cooperation through partnership.

Interdependence refers to the interconnectedness of all members of the ecological community, in a complex network that Capra calls the "web of life." Interestingly, traditional biology has tended to concentrate attention on individual organisms rather than on the biological context[30]. But no individual can exist in isolation. In all of Nature we can see living systems that are included in, and are part of, other living systems. All these systems communicate with each other and share resources. No species can appropriate all the resources – there has to be some sharing, says Benyus. "Any species that ignores this law winds up destroying its community to support its own expansion," she says. And this expansion, as civilizations such as the Easter Islanders have shown, ends up destroying itself. The ecological disaster of Easter Island was deforestation, linked to human action, caused by over population and scarcity of resources. We and our community are one.

Who are the people you depend on?
Make a list.

Capra explains how in Nature the waste of one system is food for another, and that matter cycles constantly.[31] He traces the current clash between economics and ecology back to the fact that our industrial systems are linear, while Nature's ecosystems are cyclical. Our industrial business model takes resources from Nature, transforms them into products plus waste, and the con-sumers create more waste after they have used the products.[i]

The interconnectedness is clearly manifested in Nature. So why would we even consider that we humans are not equally inter-connected? Are we assuming that we are we not part of Nature, perhaps? Where did we get that idea?

But what may be true for traditional business is not always true for individuals. A study of 100 individuals committed to causes for the common good conducted by a team of researchers

---

[i] Sometimes, even very rapidly. Consider how much time of use we give to a plastic bag that helps us bring our groceries from the shop to our home. Thirty minutes, perhaps? While the decomposition of the bag, depending on its material, can take several hundred years.

led by Larry Daloz[32] found a recurrent mention of interconnected-ness. Some individuals referred to the universe as a web in which "each node is a living being, and each one is influenced by every-thing else in the universe."

In my study, six individuals talked about a holistic under-standing, about seeing the interrelationships and how all things are connected. Evan described it as "seeing the big picture," understanding "the whole" and how what one does fits within the larger system. Pam connected social work with environment and economy, and brought this idea into the organization by asking: "Do we really understand all the impacts of what it is we're going to take on?" For Connie it was a personal experience: "So I have to say it's something deep inside of me ... I feel I'm connected to the oneness of the cosmos."

Interestingly, six individuals in my study talked about the need to consider non-linear connections, and to be aware of the *cyclical flow*. Carl put it into these words:

> The biggest culprit in this decline is the industrial system that takes from the Earth, makes stuff that ends up as waste in the landfill or an incinerator very quick in a take- make-waste system.

This is similar to the reaction of an MBA student at Fordham University, who after watching "The Story of Stuff" reflected:

> We don't take into consideration the costs of extracting, transport-ing, making, and disposing stuff in our world. When we do, we are going to make drastically different choices individually and in our businesses.

Another was able to self-examine:

> ... our consumption is extremely high and I am guilty of adding to this consumption. I heed to fashion and shopping. The video made me think about how often I buy a new pair shoes because it is in trend. Also, I am part of the vicious cycle of shopping where I con-stantly need a new item. It also makes me happy after a stressing day. Again, the next time I buy a new shirt, I will rethink before I charge the card.

Some had an emotional reaction:

> I found this video quite disturbing, pointing out the "vicious" treadmill we all are on as consumerist Americans, working our-selves ragged, spending the little leisure time we have watching TV, and then shopping to somehow fill the void and attain some con-cept of happiness through the consumption of goods.

Nature operates in cyclical patterns. "After 3.8 billion years of evolution, Nature has learned: What works, what is appropriate, what lasts," observes biologist Janine Benyus. What can we learn from this? There is no cyclical pattern in our consumption habits, so perhaps CSR initiatives should review corporate practices from a cyclical flow perspective.

Understanding ecological interdependence means understanding relationships. It requires a shift of perception and thinking: from looking at a part to seeing the whole; from seeing an object to looking for relationships; from seeing contents to seeking the patterns that connect the parts. Western thinking has evolved through fragmentation, a way of thinking that creates divisions and separateness.[33] This fragmentation is reflected in how science is divided into distinct areas – chemistry, physics, economics, biology, psychology, astronomy, geology, zoology, physiology, sociology – which can distort, or even prevent an understanding of the connections between the components.[34] In a similar vein, we have, in the medical field, become used to consulting multiple specialists to treat the different parts of our body – frequently without any single doctor seeing the whole picture. In management, the fragmentation is expressed through decisions, plans, and measurements that focus on single aspects: business units, functions, projects, looking at performance of the individual. The assessment of the performance and the impact of the parts on the whole – which includes the internal and external stakeholders, the present and the future, the human and the natural resources – seems far too complex to be seized. This has interesting implications for management. It means that for leaders to get involved in sustainability initiatives, their way of thinking, measuring, and assessing results needs to shift.

The shift also reaches into how we set up *our time horizons* in business. Juliet Schor, Professor of Sociology at Boston College and author, observes that in the last three decades, the economy in the United States has become centered on finances, with the expansion of power and reach of Wall Street and other financial institutions. This in turn has intensified the pressure for economic growth. "When companies borrow money they need bigger profits, to pay off the bankers." Wall Street has applied more pressure on companies to deliver short-term results and higher profits. Today the consequences are widely recognized; companies think twice before investing in the long run – meaning a period longer than the quarterly shareholders' report – because they are pressured to maintain a continuous rate of growth, and this directly undermines the consideration of decisions that could preserve the social and natural environment.[35]

This is not a phenomenon unique to the United States, since the model has also been exported and, thanks to instant communications and globalization, spread like fumes throughout the world. Chandran Nair,[36] founder of the Global Institute for Tomorrow, analyzes in his book *Consumptionomics* the landscape of sustainability in Asia. He observes the attention that consumption-driven capitalism places on the present, ignoring in this "myopic focus" the effect of today's decisions on the future. "The discussion focuses on what to do with all the things we have available to us now. But what if markets encourage more consumption now to benefit people today but, in doing so, deplete resources or have an environmental impact that will make future generations worse off?" Nair challenges. His diagnosis is that economics focuses on short-term thinking, and therein lies the biggest problem.

Identify some recent decisions you have made that were beneficial to you, your workplace, or your community in the short term, but which could represent a problem in the long term.

Now identify some decisions that you have made with the long-term benefit/impact in view.
What made it possible for you to take the long-term perspective without creating potential problems in the short term?

In the study by Daloz et al.,[37] individuals acting for the common good reported a long-term perspective, not expecting to see the results of their actions immediately or in the same location they were taken. This shows an intuitive systemic perspective in these individuals who were committed to causes dealing with the common good. In similar terms, Rogers's study mentions the students who became sensitive to global environmental problems by paying attention to the long-term effects when planning their own actions.

CSR initiatives equally require long-term and non-linear thinking. Fortunately, some organizations are taking the lead and inspiring others, such as the cleaning products manufacturer Seventh Generation, which made a powerful statement of their values by incorporating into their brand itself the advice of the Iroquois natives, "to be mindful of the impact of our actions on the next seven generations." Five individuals in my study talked about how they integrated a long-term perspective into their decisions: "The consequences of my decisions affect generations to come, not just my lifetime" (Carl).

And we shouldn't forget the estimated more than one million grassroots and non-governmental organizations around the world who are actively working toward ecological sustainability, economic justice, human rights protection, political accountability and peace – issues that are systemically interconnected and intertwined. These organizations take initiatives and operate with the long-term in mind, and they are (unknowingly) shaping a new landscape for all.[38]

From a different angle, to see or find hidden connections that are not obvious is crucial to managing *complexity* and addressing complex challenges. To explain the hidden connections present in our every day, Harvard psychologist and adult development theorist Robert Kegan[39] gives the example of how we look at welfare recipients, who can be seen by some as people who have had bad luck and as lazy by others. But to look at the hidden connections would mean recognizing how the welfare system encourages and sustains poverty, or how the economic system creates an underclass that requires welfare. In my study, the background in natural sciences shaped Evan's thinking in terms of complexity: "My education is in botany and plant physiology ... What the education tended to provide me with was just an inability to look at anything and not understand how complex it was." Effective CSR initiatives may demand seeking patterns and connections beyond the obvious and the usual in the management of a business.

Another systems principle is *cooperation and partnership.* This refers to the tendency of all members of the ecosystem to associate with each other or link to each other or even live inside one another.[40] Each partner plays an important role. In human communities this translates into each partner understanding the needs of the other, and into both learning to change and co-evolve. This principle reaches beyond a mere behavior, and into the logic of a *"both/and"* framework. Interestingly, while ecology strives toward cooperation, conservation, and partnership, which are a visible manifestation of the "both/and" logic, economies as we know them (should I say, as we created and maintain them?), emphasize competition, domination, and expansion, a manifestation of the either/or logic. This represents another paradigm shift when considering planning and implementing meaningful CSR initiatives.

Are you an either/or thinker or a both/and thinker?
What have been some situations when you acted within an either/or framework, that might have been better addressed with a 'both/and" approach? Would the results have possibly been better?

Identify a situation you were involved in that solved a problem within a "both/and" framework.
What are the benefits and downsides of an either/or, and of a both/and framework? What could you do next time to consciously identify when which one is better for the occasion?

Systems thinking seems to be a key road that leads to developing a sustainability mindset. A few individuals in my study referred to MIT Professor and organizational learning author Peter Senge at some point during the interview, indicating they had been exposed to systems thinking through his writings or personal conversations. It is interesting to observe that Senge himself evolved from studying the learning organization from a systems perspective in the early 1990s, to sustainability and the role of corporations (2001). David Cooperrider, author and Professor of Social Entrepreneurship at the Weatherhead School of Management, had a similar evolution from organizational behavior and interventions using a process called Appreciative Inquiry, to seeing business as an agent for world benefit, highlighting the systemic interconnections.[41] Hillary Bradbury, Professor in the Management Division of Oregon Health & Science University, describes how she incorporated systems thinking into her teaching to develop the understanding of sustainability, helping her students see the larger picture, connecting the inner and the outer world. Another leadership author, Margaret Wheatley, indicated that our survival depends on our ability to become system thinkers, something equally recommended by marketing guru Michael Porter[42] who suggests that systemic models can be used first to inquire into, rather than to immediately strive to solve, sustainability challenges, thus allowing examination, learning, reframing, and action. Systems thinking is key for developing a sustainability mindset.

Yet my study pointed towards an additional dimension, to complement the systems and innovative thinking processes. I called it the dimension of *Being*.

Chapter 5

The Dimension of Being

We talk about ourselves as human beings. But taking a closer look at our extremely busy lives and endless to-do lists, we might perhaps be better described as human doings. In a recent study[43] of leadership mental models related to sustainability, author and Organizational Systems professor John Adams describes the "life orientation" on a continuum that stretches between the two poles of "Doing + Having" and "Being." The pole of "Doing and Having" is a good descriptor of an identity linked to what we do in life – to materialism, consumption, ambition, cost-effectiveness, quantitative growth, and financial performance. The pole of "Being" refers to a life oriented toward introspective practices, self-realization, valuing intangibles, the greater good, seeking qualitative growth and personal development, spirituality, detachment, and having enough.

Where would you put yourself?
Doing-Having--------------------------Being

And where would you like to see yourself?

Physicist and psychologist Peter Russell,[44] who explored the development of human consciousness by integrating Eastern and Western understandings of the mind, indicates that as our awareness of the global crisis deepened, "it became increasingly clear that, if we are to change our behavior toward the world, we need first to change our thinking ... developing a new sense of who we are and what it is we really want." This refers to valuing our inner development as much as, if not more than, our material development. He indicates that what we need is "a change of attitude, a change of heart."

In a famous address to the U.S. Senate in 1990, the former President of Czechoslovakia, Václav Havel warned boldly:

> The salvation of this human world lies nowhere else than in the human heart. ... Without a global revolution in the sphere of human consciousness, nothing will change for the better ... and the catastrophe toward which this world headed – the ecological, social demographic or general breakdown of civilization – will be unavoidable.

Russell indicates that a "truly holistic ecological ethic cannot be built into our attitudes, policies, and actions unless it is first built into ourselves." We tend to ask what we can do about the world rather than what we can do about ourselves, he observes, inviting us to focus on a deeper level of being. This was a concept that emerged in my study, and one that well described the discourse of ten participants. Whether they arrived at a shift in their worldview through traumatic experiences, trips, encounters, self-reflection, reading, journaling, or contemplative practices, the common thread was that different triggers had led them to self-examination. They made a determination to pause in their busy lives to review who they were, to scrutinize their values and their deeper selves, and to reflect on what identity meant to them. It permitted them to ponder what their purpose was: what was giving meaning to their lives and how fulfilling their lives actually were.

What gives meaning to your life today?

How fulfilling is your life today?

Eight participants in my study indicated that a quest for deeper answers related to the purpose of their own lives, their own roles in this world, preceded their sustainability-related initiatives: "And once you know who you are and where you've been ... [you know] where you want to go," Connie said. She reflected how everything started with pausing to look inside, describing how the "being" aspect took front stage in her life:

You cannot change anything until you change yourself. And that's one thing that's really become clear to me, that this deep work that I'm trying to do, this spiritual work, that's more important than what I do in the day, because that will drive and dictate any of the work I do … and it will give me the courage, wisdom, and insight, so it's got to be deep inside.

Pam talked about her transformation in terms of "being" versus "having" in these words: "There is more to life than the next gadget. I now see the world. I feel I lived in a cave."

Another leader in my study observed how he tended to look for someone who could serve as a wise guide to the outer world; he eventually learned a valuable lesson from a teacher at an Indian Reservation: to go out into the forest and cry for help:

So sometimes I used to go in my backyard or go in the woods and just cry out and say, "Hey, when am I going to get a mentor? When am I going to get someone to guide me in all this stuff?" And the answer would always come back, "No guides for you." You've got your own path. You've got to work it out."

An MBA student in my course on developing a sustainability mindset connected a reading with some self-examination:

When the author lays out the five or so points that detail how this system is lacking and what humanity is trying to find (wholeness, connection, etc.) I couldn't stop but think that this is exactly what I want to find and am searching for now. ... I am lucky and blessed to have a roof over my head, food to eat, friends to laugh with, and money to save and spend. With that being said, I am searching for this other component, the wholeness, the empowerment, the connection that currently lacks in my jobs, some of my relationships, etc. ... It's good to know that others are looking for this as well ...

It was interesting to observe that 13 of the 16 individuals in my study made comments that indicated an introspective attitude – not something I anticipated from a heterogeneous group of CEO's and corporate Directors! Nine talked about how they analyzed themselves. Willie talked about how he learned to listen to his conscience, thanks to an encounter with a spiritual master that led him to an immense awakening that changed his life. Michael learned to calm down and focus his mind thanks to a Zen Buddhist practice. Diego reflected on his long journey trying to understand himself and described it as a "constant series of deepenings and widenings."

In one way or the other, through different life experiences and in a variety of contexts, the quest for meaning was a profound (albeit uncomfortable) moment of self-examination. Connie described how she would get physically feelings of unhappiness, where she didn't care for the work she was doing anymore, she couldn't find any meaning in it, and felt what she described as a "hole in her heart." A traumatic event in her life was the turning point, and because of it, she began to think of the opportunity it presented for starting a new way of thinking, a new way of living her life.

She explained how important introspection was for her, since through it she realized the tension in her everyday existence:

> I live a fairly pretty strange life, I think. I have a strong interior life that kind of, I hope, is congruent to an exterior life, but it tends to ... the interior life is what tends to bring these things I think.

Introspection seems to be key, yet at the same time it is not a commonly accepted practice. Connie observed that more MBA programs and leadership programs are starting to deal with the deeper questions, "but people aren't comfortable going there. And then of course watch the language so it doesn't sound like you're at some Christian revival meeting, right?" was her self-warning.

Introspection also had its effect on colleagues. Carl recalled that people thought "he had lost it," and received feedback that employees thought he was a "freak," wondering if he "had gone 'round the bend." Others like Patrick and Daniel accepted it and took it as their identity, as being different, as being a rebel. Some found it difficult to communicate their awakening to others, including to me during our confidential interviews. Craig and Connie excused themselves, saying, "It'll sound soft, but I believe it to be true," (Craig), while Connie clarified that she was a corporate person, a lawyer:

> I know it sounds kind of woo-woo, I know that. And I mean, you might think that I'm like some hippie weirdo sitting here, but, you know, I'm (a lawyer) in corporate America ....

Willie took a more matter-of-fact approach, accepting his "craziness" knowing that others might be "laughing at him."

Is this surprising? The late Stanford professor, author, and global futurist, Willis Harman,[45] observed that Westerners, in particular, have neglected paying attention to the deeper, subjective experience of self, and this has had serious consequences in "our confusion about values." I recall a colleague who felt extremely uncomfortable with introspective questions, indicating they were "too much centered on self," something that she dismissed as tantamount to "inappropriate" behavior. However, "it is ultimately in this realm of the subjective, the transcendent, and the spiritual that all societies have found the basis for their deepest value commitments and sense of meaning," reflects Harman.

Being introspective, focusing on understanding one self, paying attention to feelings, or even asking profound questions like "Who am I?" is indeed unusual, and in many corporate contexts perceived as inappropriate. Yet it seems to be a cornerstone of the sustainability mindset.

Here is a question for you to stay with, during a full minute of silence:

Who am I?

Reflective corporate leaders

What are the implications of this "being orientation"? There is a close connection between developing consciousness of self and connecting with others. Gandhi centered his worldview in a model of individuals serving individuals, the family, the village, the district, the state, the nation, like concentric circles connected to each other through the services they provide to, and receive from, each other. In the center stands the individual and his values, anchoring the whole system. Patrick reflected that in his perspective, without achieving self-awareness, "it all falls apart":

> Particularly if you put it into a leadership context ... You can goad, you can punish, you can banish, you can harm and use that as a leadership tool to make things happen, but if you want to inspire and you want people to fulfill themselves in the most extraordinary ways, you have to know yourself well enough to be able to allow room for people to be who they are.

The focus on Being starts with introspection and questions about who am I, what is my purpose. And this leads to my relationship to others: What do I do for others? What is my role? My legacy? Eight individuals specifically referred to their frequent questioning of themselves: about their roles in life, in the world, and in their organization. For Mark, it was asking himself what he could do, what his purpose was, what his very life was about. For Connie, it was a journey of discovery that had her explore her talents and gifts, and connect them with who she was, who she had been, and where she wanted to go.

These questions led her to ask herself, "Who am I in the whole?" and sparked her first steps to relate to "something bigger." Daniel also reflected on his role, and replied that he was not afraid of changing the world and taking a leadership role toward that. Diego reported on his repeated reflections:

> I was sitting at my house years ago moaning to myself, "What's my role in all of this? ... Am I supposed to be a leader? Am I supposed to be a politician? Am I a helper? What is my role?"

If Patrick, a U.S. CEO of a hi-tech company mentoring employees to expand their self-awareness sounds eccentric, it becomes less unusual when we delve into the literature about spirituality and the workplace. Judi Neal, founding editor of the Journal of Management, Spirituality, and Religion, indicates that "know thyself" is the first guideline for leading from a spiritual perspective: all spiritual growth processes include self-awareness.[46] This is consistent with management professor Peter Vaill, who has written extensively about organizational behavior, and who suggests that organizations should pay attention to the "spiritual condition" of their leaders, which, he goes on to say is "the feeling individuals have about the fundamental meaning of who they are, what they are doing, the contributions they are making."[47]

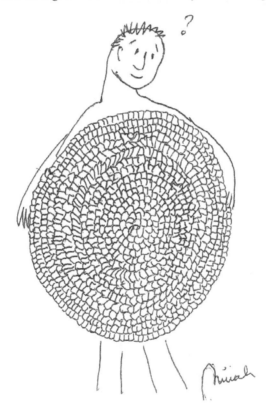

This is an interesting shift from the traditionally instrumental approach, where employee satisfaction is sought as a means to an end, which is to increase productivity, avoid turnover, or reduce absenteeism. Only one person in my study thought of introducing "more meaningful initiatives" initially as a means to an end, specifically to energize people in a time where morale was low because of restructuring and job instability. Later in the interview, however, she shared her surprise when seeing how employees "jumped on it," reflecting that there was a need for purpose that was not being fulfilled. What the findings of this study are pointing to is that the spiritual needs of purpose and meaning may constitute an end in themselves. Author Parker Palmer[48] referred to divided lives, which manifest when employees have "to check their soul at the door." This is an expectation, but how realistic is it, to do this? If we leave our soul at the door, who steps into the office? A soul-less body? What quality of interactions, of connections, of decision-making, not to say quality of life, does this imply?

Do you feel that you "check your soul at the door" when you enter your workplace? If so, what would it be like if you took your soul with you into your work?

Fortunately, a global movement to correct this issue has begun, and several business schools in the United States and around the world have, in the last decade, launched centers for spirituality in the workplace. Work is being discovered as a source of spiritual growth and connection to others.[49] Leadership programs include retreats, soul-searching, arts, and poetry. We can find a sign of change in the success of poets such as David Whyte, whose 1994 book *The Heart Aroused: Poetry and the Preservation of the Soul in Corporate America* is a bestseller, as are other books connecting work and soul: Moore's (1992) *Care of the Soul*, Bolman and Deal's (1995) *Leading with Soul*.

Still, there may be some challenges to solve. In a study on spirituality in corporate America, researchers Ian Mitroff and Elizabeth Denton[50] conducted ninety interviews with executives and analyzed 131 returned written questionnaires. They found that respondents generally differentiated strongly between religion and spirituality. Some viewed religion as a highly inappropriate topic and form of expression in the workplace, but they were hungry for models of practicing spirituality in the workplace that did not offend their coworkers or cause acrimony. Respondents indicated their desire to stop compartmentalizing or fragmenting their lives, and were curious if there existed examples of practicing spirituality in the workplace. Many interviewees – though not all – were afraid to use the words *spirituality* and *soul*. After recognizing a spiritual element in employees, the expression of spirituality at work requires accepting that employees want to be involved in work that gives meaning to their lives.[51]

The timing may be appropriate to bring the soul into one's work.

A different model of organization

While many employees do struggle to find meaning in their work, there is a growing number of members of senior management for whom spirituality at the corporate level refers to the higher purpose of the business. For Mark it was "purpose meeting profit," his dream of entrepreneurs who are like "Warren Buffet meets Mother Theresa," and corporations that are a place where employees love to work because they satisfy their higher values – and that satisfaction exists because the corporation itself contributes to the betterment of society or the restoration of the environment in a profitable way. Carl was able to convert his dream of becoming a restorative corporation into reality by disseminating his vision and engaging all employees. Diego describes himself as an activist who became a businessman to build the type of purposeful corporation he was dreaming of. He found business as a profound spiritual path, and was inspired by the founders of Golden Temple Tea, a company doing business in California and Oregon.

> They were being interviewed about how can yogis do a tea business, and they said that business is the hardest form of yoga because you're constantly coming up against your own values and your own limits. And then you have to make a decision. Am I doing this for the greater good, or am I doing this for myself?

Spirituality and workplace researcher Judi Neal[52] describes a new paradigm emerging among corporate leaders who define the purpose of business as a solution to world problems, using the creative energy of their employees. Creative work researchers Willis Harman and John Hormann had, as early as 1990, indicated that corporations were best placed to solve global social problems. They suggested that the role of corporations needed to change from that of economic production and consumption into a place for learning and human development. Leadership's role would be to apply spiritual principles to help bring about this societal transformation. That recommendation was tested in a study[53] of 90 businesswomen and businessmen from seventy organizations in 14 countries. The research found that the interest in spiritual and social values in the workplace was not limited to the United States alone. The common aspects of the organizations were that they: worked to enhance social equity and to protect the natural environment; fostered creativity; sought to serve higher purposes; had strong ethics manifested in business; and had the need for personal transformation in business leadership. Despite the controversy surrounding the topic of corporate behaviors, multinationals such as Chase Manhattan Bank, DuPont, AT&T, Apple Computer,[54] and others have tackled the subject of contribution by including a new question in their search for a corporate vision: "What is our higher purpose?" The question is a good first step.

Concerned with the issue of corporate footprint, Case Western Reserve's Weatherhead School of Management has created a center of excellence called the Center of Business as Agent of World Benefit (BAWB), which sponsors research into the ways business is making a positive difference in the world. And in 2006, the Academy of Management and United Nations sponsored the creation of PRME – The Principles for Responsible Management Education – which list the theme of corporate purpose and values as one of the six principles. We may be witnessing the rise of a conscious capitalism, says Patricia Aburdene,[55] mega-trends author and speaker, who listed spirituality in the workplace as one of the most important emerging trends of the 21st century.

As illustrated by the examples throughout this book, the findings of my study surfaced the steps some corporations are taking to combine profit with purpose. This is definitely something adult educators and coaches have to begin paying attention to in order to support students and executives as they focus on developing a new perspective of the purpose of business.

Promoting insight to connect with others

When Willie realized that it took engineers and business leaders "something different" to be able to design products and services that were respectful of Nature, he was not shy in trying to influence other leaders in his organization to become more introspective and to face the deeper questions. His intuition told him that these two things were connected. He commented on how he and some colleagues promoted this quest to explore their "role in the world" by taking hundreds of employees into the wilderness, and asking them on the first day: Why are you here? What are you to do in this job? How do we make your job and life seamless and meaningful so you don't go to a job that is unrelated to your own life, and your life and your job are not separate?

Several others adopted the role of bringing people along the path they had journeyed themselves, because of the value they found in this journey and how transformational it had been for them. Daniel saw this "guide" role as a key component of his current job, and was excited about it. He believed his role to be to "tap into the essence of the person, help find what purpose is at their core, what values. A huge role." Patrick, despite his position as CEO, made it a point to help people increase their self-awareness, taking time to hold one-on-one conversations. His rationale was:

> Why shouldn't business be holistic and open enough to allow people to emerge stronger, healthier from the work experience rather than depleted, annoyed, unhealthy, and dissatisfied?

What several of these leaders were doing was going from what was a personal experience to something that touched others. They wanted to share with others, to make a difference in other people's lives. This is the point where introspective practice and self-examination flowed into a stream connecting people with people in a significantly different way. Daniel explained the foundation of his work in these words: "Business has to deliver stuff, is a machine. It reduces the humanity in the person. We need to design a place differently, with love, sharing, wellbeing." Evan also thought about creating a working environment where people are able to grow, instead of becoming demotivated and their energy drained by what they often saw as an impersonal and soulless workplace. Diego reflected on how spirituality is present in every business decision: "You are constantly coming up against your own values and your own limits. And then you have to make a decision."

He realized that he had to constantly challenge himself by paying attention to the values he was demonstrating through the decisions he made, because they had an impact on others; he always tried to monitor if he was living up to his values, or if he was "falling off," and in that case what he needed to do to get back. This is not easy, he recognized:

> I'm a dad. Raising two kids in this environment, I'm a very dedicated father, so I'm at every ballet performance. I'm driving the kids around, dealing with play dates. It's very mundane in this world. In this business I've got to worry about the goddamn espresso machine broke. I've got to worry about someone calling up and they don't like the coffee this week. And I've got to try to keep my higher self during those times ... I know I could be doing more. I could be meditating more. I could be doing more yoga. There's so many things I could be doing I'm not. I've been very much captured by the husk, and I'm trying to break out. But it's okay. It's a good balance ...

Meister Eckhart, a medieval German mystic, connects the personal dimension with the outer world, arguing that it all starts at the center, and that all spiritual paths lead to the center, to an experience that could be called "enlightenment." The paths then lead from that center back into the world. Buddha, reflect spiritual intelligence researchers Zohar and Marshall,[56] went through many years of searching and suffering to achieve enlightenment, but when he had done so, he returned to the world, because he felt the obligation to pass something onto others. In the 1980s, corporate leader and management researcher Robert Greenleaf was the first to describe the connection of service and meaning through the concept of "servant leadership." This management concept, however, has roots in many spiritual traditions, say Zohar and Marshall. "Through the gifts endowed by their lives and personalities, these people have the opportunity to serve, heal, and enlighten those whom they lead, but the path calls ultimately for great integrity (wholeness)."

This spiral connection flowing from the personal to others is expressed in an anecdote Diego recalls, when he read an interview that Gandhi gave after the British left India. The reporter from the BBC asked Gandhi: "So what do you think of your role in liberating India?" And Gandhi said, "I wasn't liberating India. I was liberating myself. India was the vehicle I used to liberate myself." For Diego, there are parallels.

> And that's when I say this is a spiritual enterprise here. I'm working on myself here. And what makes it hard is I'm not in a monastery. I'm worrying about the price of coffee and whether or not the machine breaks down or the neighbors complain about the smoke. It makes it the hardest spirituality. So yeah, that was like a big awakening moment for me, realizing that it's not about changing the world. It's about changing myself, and that's the best I can do. And then using these vehicles of business, politics, whatever, as a place where that shows up.

Reflective leaders shape a different kind of organization, my data seemed to indicate. They exhibited a raised level of awareness of the problems of our planet, which caused a deeply felt need to do something about it. They had all the entrepreneurial characteristics of leaders innovating and trying to engage others through inspiring visions. Their sustainability-minded initiatives seemed at the same time to be anchored in a personal journey of self-inquiry and introspection, a path of personal growth.

Aware that today, the information about the problems of the planet is much more available and accessible for leaders across the globe than it was for the leaders in my study (albeit we were only talking of less than a decade in some cases), I began to wonder why change was not happening faster.

PART III
THE ELEPHANT IN THE ROOM

When organizational system's researcher John Adams collected frequency data related to how most people "did their thinking" most of the time, a high percentage of the responses clustered on the following options:

- Short-term thinking, rather than long-term;

- Reactive responses, rather than creative approaches;

- Focus on self or immediate group, rather than inclusive thinking;

- Either/or logic, rather than both/and thinking;

- Blaming others when facing a problem, rather than learning, centered on doing and having, rather than focus on being.

These behaviors manifested in the choice of values such as quantitative growth, cost effectiveness, financial performance, and consumption.

Adams concluded that "if these are the predominant styles of thinking (collective mental models) in contemporary organizations, then what sort of long-term sustainability can we expect to achieve?"[57] Adams is suggesting that the opposite of the way most people did their thinking (e.g., learning instead of blaming), or a combination of both (e.g., short-term and long-term thinking) would be needed for sustainability leadership. This is clearly an invitation to develop the new thinking.

I worked many years as a therapist, and helping patients to find solutions to their problems was important, but what seemed to be the shortest path – fixing the problem – was never effective for the patient. Certainly it was good to help them uncover a dream, a vision of how it would be to feel good, or better, or happy. But that was not enough. Instead, the road to real, lasting transformation always took longer and always involved certain detours to explore *why* something was the way it was, what wisdom and assumptions lay behind the visible pain. That pain was just a messenger, and we had to pause and listen if we really wanted to effect some change. If we didn't listen to the message, it would come back, soon, asking to be heard.

I spent much time reading and reflecting extensively on the findings of my research, reviewing the interviews, seeking key words, feelings, patterns, and wisdom. It was exciting to mine the rich vein of ore that these leaders taught us about how we should develop the next generation of sustainability-minded leaders. Yet one question kept coming back, insistent and persistent. Yes, these people changed and pioneered amazing initiatives in their organizations, efforts that evolved, grew, and transformed the culture of the business, making a positive footprint on the environment and the community, and even inspired competitors who began to develop sustainable practices themselves. But with all we knew, with all the news and scientific information being streamlined through the Internet daily about the planetary emergency ... *Why was change taking so long? Why was it so slow, so tedious?* Before thinking of solutions, *that* was the question that needed an answer, and in order to find the answer I began to explore what seemed like an elephant in the room.

 Why do you think change is hard for you?

Chapter 6

Why Is Sustainability Change So Slow?

Speed lies in the eyes of the beholder. What we consider slow or fast is a product of each individual's perception, sometimes validated by a collective perception. Changes may seem slow to environmentalists, and way too fast for industries that have to reconvert their processes, manufacturing plants, or even products they sell. The following is a short biography of our planet, which gives us a broader perspective of what is slow or fast.

Earth: A (Short) Biography

Four and a half billion years ago, the sun blasted off most of the clouds of elements and spun the rest into our solar system. Newly formed planets boiled as molten and gaseous materials, and each began its own geological evolution. One among them was the Earth.

Over the next half a billion years, as the Earth's surface quieted and cooled, an atmosphere began to form around it. The first rains fell upon the Earth, and the oceans emerged. Water was continually exchanged between atmosphere and ocean. Massive upheavals of the planet's crust formed great mountain ranges, and soil erosion carried rich minerals to the seas. These minerals, along with those arising from volcanic action in the depths of the sea, provided a creative, chemical womb.

Three billion nine hundred million years ago, this vibrant and fertile womb brought forth the first living cells. These primal beings had the power to organize themselves.

Over the next 200 million years, the cells developed a new order of creativity, as they learned to capture the packets of energy hurled by the sun at the speed of light, using these glowing quanta as food, thus inventing the process of photosynthesis. By gathering their hydrogen from the oceans, the sun-eating cells, in their vast multitudes, released oxygen into Earth's system. Over hundreds of millennia, the oxygen slowly saturated the land, the atmosphere, and the seas.

By two billion years ago, the sun-energized cells had unknowingly pushed Earth's system into a condition beyond their own capacity to endure. The vast majority of the earlier cellular communities perished as their interiors were set ablaze by oxygen. Yet out of this crisis, threatening the very viability of the living planet, arose a new and radically advanced being.

Two billion years ago, through the merger of separate and distinct living beings, the first cells with nuclei emerged. These new, more complex beings had the ability not only to endure oxygen, but to shape its dangerous energy for their own purposes. Thus, they seethed with creativity.

One billion years ago, life was drawn toward union as these cells learned to reproduce sexually, thus vastly increasing the creative potential for new life.

Six hundred million years ago, single-celled creatures took the daring step of submerging themselves into a larger mind, as trillions of them gathered together and evoked the first multicellular being. Early animal life flourished on Earth, as worms and spiders, snails, clams, and insects emerged.

Five hundred and ten million years ago, the first fish moved through the oceans with their fleshy fins, developing backbones to protect Earth's earliest nervous systems.

Four hundred and sixty million years ago, ocean waves left algae stranded on the shore. Unable to crawl home, they adapted to life on land, enlivening the long-barren continents in company with the insects that soon joined them.

Four hundred and twenty-five million years ago, plants developed wood cells and learned to stand upright, first living along the shores of oceans and rivers, and then transforming themselves into trees capable of covering entire continents with life.

Three hundred and ninety-five million years ago, insects, cooling themselves by fanning heat away from their bodies, unexpectedly took off and became the first creatures to inhabit the sky.

Three hundred and seventy million years ago, fish followed plants and insects onto the land, and soon the continents heaved with amphibians and reptiles.

Two hundred and thirty-five million years ago, the dinosaurs spread across Earth in all their wonderful diversity of form, size, and life ways. Some, reaching up into the sunlit canopies, reached heights unsurpassed by any other creature.

Two hundred and fifteen million years ago, mammals emerged from the reptile family, bringing emotional sensitivity into Earth's living community, a new capacity within their nervous systems for feeling the Universe. Their developed parental care for their offspring has eventuated today into our deep concern for future generations of all species.

One hundred and fifty million years ago, birds soared out of the dinosaur family and followed the insects into the vast vault of the sky.

One hundred and twenty million years ago, flowers appeared in an abundant array of colors and shapes, inviting the sky creatures, their partners in the ongoing creativity, into a new dance.

Sixty-five million years ago, an astronomical collision so changed Earth's atmosphere and climates that nearly all forms of animal life had to reinvent themselves or perish. In mass extinctions, many animals followed the dinosaurs into their graves. But such destruction also opened up new possibilities, which were seized upon by the birds, mammals, and others who proliferated in the wake of the disaster.

Four million years ago, our early ancestors stood up on two legs and emerged from their forest home to explore the African plains.

Fifty thousand years ago, modern Homo Sapiens emerged in the unfolding life process.

By 35,000 years ago, humans were migrating across the Bering land bridge, traveling down through North and South America. As if unable to restrain any longer their astonishment at existence, humans began a new level of celebration, with music-making and festivals that shaped ceremonials around the passing of friends and seasons. Deep within the Earth, cave paintings, with their artistic depiction of the animals, expressed some of the beauty that had seized the depths of human hearts and minds.

By ten thousand years ago, humans were consciously shaping the activities and patterns of nature through the domestication of plants and animals. A secure supply of food enabled populations to surge. Small villages arose around the planet, and pottery, weaving, and architecture were developed, as were calendars depicting the cosmic rhythms. Rituals and shrines to the Great Mother deity replaced devotion to totemic animals.

Five thousand years ago came urban civilizations, with soaring populations. Military systems arose to protect concentrations of power and wealth.

Three thousand five hundred years ago, the Classical Religions began to emerge with the teachings of Moses, followed, over the next millennium, by the teachings of Buddha, Lao Tzu, and Confucius. The Mayan civilization flourished. Still later, the lives and teachings of Jesus and then Mohammed led to the rise of Christianity and Islam.

Adapted from "The Cosmic Walk," originally created in the mid-1980s by Sister Miriam Therese MacGillis, of Genesis Farm in Blairstown, New Jersey, who was inspired by the "New Story" as told by Thomas Berry. A large portion of the text of the narrative is adapted from the "Prologue" to *The Universe Story: From the Primordial Flaring Forth to the Ecozoic Era*, by Brian Swimme and Thomas Berry (New York: HarperCollins, 1992).

Evolution has been accelerating. Using a one-year scale, if the Big Bang happened in the first second of January 1st, in the last thirty seconds humankind began the farming practice. The Industrial Revolution took place in the last half-second of the year.[58]

And if we think that the Industrial Revolution brought about changes, we should be aware that since then, human creativity increased exponentially, developing artifacts for transport, communication, food, shelter, and comfort beyond imagination. Less than 15 years ago, there was no Google in the world, and the avenues of Beijing and Shanghai were covered with bicycles. Since 2000, the number of cars in Shanghai has quadrupled, reaching close to a million by 2011, a number prone to continue growing since municipal governments encourage industrial growth by repressing bicycles in favor of cars.[59]

With all this comes our footprint on the planet. The following charts illustrate the recent spike in the impact that we are making on the Earth. Significant increases in rates of change occur around the 1950s in each case and illustrate how the past 50 years have been a period of dramatic and unprecedented change in human history.[60]

As the charts illustrate, our footprint is a significant footprint. In 2008, the Northwest and Northeast passages in the Arctic opened for the first time in human history, and commercial shipping sailed through them without using an icebreaker. It was not needed: *there was no ice.*[61] Some scientific inferences have been drawn from this and you may have heard them. As the ice vanishes, the reflectivity of Greenland and the Arctic changes, and the mirror of white ice is replaced by sun-absorbing soil or blue water. As the permafrost melts, tons of captured methane originally deposited there through decomposition of organic matter in ancient wetlands is liberated into the atmosphere. Methane is a greenhouse gas that is 30 times more effective in trapping heat in the atmosphere than carbon dioxide, which means that the permafrost melting is further increasing the already high CO_2 levels. Moreover, the feedback loop accelerates the process: more CO_2 leads to higher temperature, which leads to more melting, which leads to more CO_2. As the water temperature changes, so, too, do the currents. These in turn impact weather patterns, modify animal life, and have an effect not only on coastal communities that depend on fisheries, but also on employees in connected industries beyond the coastal villages. The oceans absorb more carbon, which in turn increases acidification, which damages the coral reefs, the base of our food chain. Warmer waters increase hurricane winds, which become more frequent, as does flooding. Mohamed Nasheed, the former president of the Maldives islands, announced that his low-lying nation started a plan to buy land and relocate its population to Sri Lanka or Australia before the ocean rises to threaten their survival. This is not the only island state starting such an initiative.

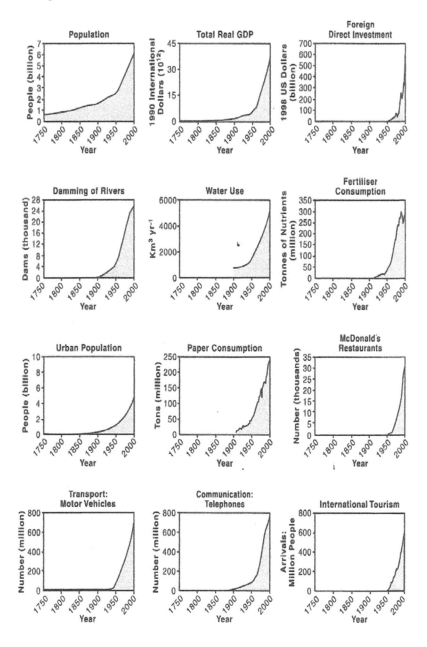

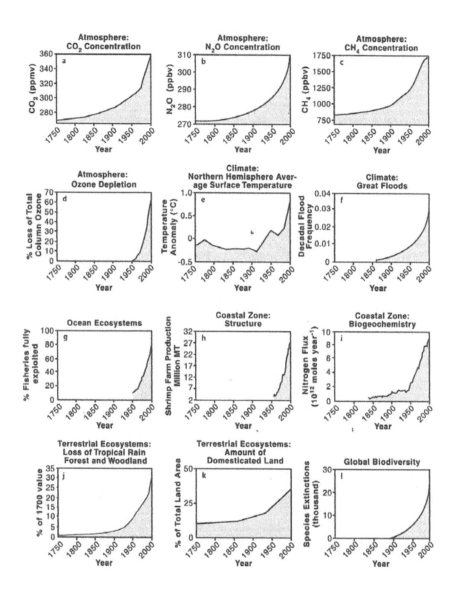

The impacts are difficult to foresee, since the systemic inter-connections create reinforcing loops where we least expect them. And while we all are experiencing some of the effects, we don't see the full picture. It's just a warmer winter in New York; suddenly there are frequent hailstorms or even tornadoes in Buenos Aires, something that hadn't been seen before; a beetle plague is dam-aging the Colorado forests; algae are floating in the Mediterranean and are hurting tourists; we read of smaller crops due to a damaged bee population that is unable to carry out necessary pollination[i]; there have been severe droughts in Somalia, Ethiopia, Kenya, and Djibouti, creating famine and a new humanitarian crisis. Twisters, floods, snow, drought, heat, and wildfire cost the U.S. alone over $1 billion in 2011. We may be able to see trees, but somehow the forest – that our planet's survival is in danger – is obscured.[ii]

Our planet is changing, and it is due to our accumulated behaviors. We may have an opportunity to mitigate or slow down the impact. So my question is: Can we afford a *slow* change in our habits?

---

[i] A recent study found that bees are suffering from the effects of neonicotinoids, a class of commonly used pesticides, introduced in the 1990s. Source: *The Economist*, March 31, 2012.

[ii] On May 5, 2012, a global event was organized by 350.org, a global grassroots movement to solve the climate crisis, to celebrate Climate Impacts Day. On that day, they invited people to issue a wake-up call, and connect the dots between climate change and extreme weather. The purpose was to educate, protest, create, document, and volunteer along with thousands of people around the world.

Something powerful is holding us back

Whenever you are in a situation where you are annoyed by some-one who is not acting as you expect, there is a golden rule: listen to the message behind his resistance. (This rule certainly also applies to the self, yet hard as it might be, it's always easier to try to figure out others before understanding ourselves).

Try this out: Think of something that you want/plan to do but are not doing, for some reason. It may be related to something that you're expected to do, and you agreed to do, but it is not happening.
What message might be hidden behind your reluctance to act?
Become a detective for a moment, and try to identify what message may be there for you to hear.
The purpose of this exercise is for you to practice seeing resistance not as something negative but perhaps as a source for understanding your motivations better—as a helpful hint for delving deeper.

Following that rule, and wondering why needed change was taking so long, I began to search for the powerful reasons that are holding us back, collectively, from altering our habits. The behavioral sciences indicate that resistance to change means that we hold dearly on to something we very much value, and that the simple idea of losing it severely threatens the individual. Following Maslow's hierarchy of human needs, it may be something that relates to our feelings of safety, to being loved, to our personal balance and realization, to food and shelter. But perhaps the most profound threat is the one to a person's identity, the loss of which would mean losing "who we are." This is a powerful threat, because we may not be aware of it, and because it is less obvious than doing without food or shelter. It has a real impact, but we are caught unawares because it seems to have grown, unobserved, in our unconscious. Peter Russell reflects that the need to sustain and reaffirm our sense of identity is apparent in the roles we play, the groups we join, the beliefs we adopt, and it can be so intense that we "become exploiters of our surroundings, of other people, or even of our own bodies."[62]

What are the aspects that may be core to who we are, that anchor our identity, and that would be challenged by the sustainability imperatives?

I began to identify several values that are central to our Western culture, which I will explore in detail next. They are: *Economic Growth*; *Achievement*; *Control*; *Wealth*; *Comfort*; *Independence*; *Competition*; *Knowledge*; *and Speed*.

These values are reinforced by other important enablers: *Science and Technology*; *Sophisticated Media that connects us*; *and Globalization*.

While this is not an exhaustive list, it shines a light on some of the aspects that are undeniably valued by society, and they therefore stand in direct conflict with, and are threatened by, sustainability imperatives. Let's take a closer look.

Economic growth

We, as a society, are collectively geared towards progress, growth, expansion, prosperity, and improvement in our standard of living. Corporations set annual growth targets, and develop strategies to achieve them. Shareholders (*financial markets?*) punish organizations that fail to attain those goals, and thus send a clear message of what is unacceptable. Responsible governments work to grow the economy and employment, and debate over how to achieve those goals. National economies are judged by how rapidly they grow, since growth helps countries improve their "approval ratings," leading to better access to credit. Money rules. Voters can sanction an administration whose policies have failed to achieve the promised prosperity. And at our individual level, we find motivation and inspiration in setting our own success criteria, such as making progress in our career, studies, income, or possessions.

Identify the different areas of your life where the values you describe as "growth" and "progress" manifest themselves, and indicate if and how the values become goals for you.

The impulse to grow is within Nature and within *our* nature (as if they were separate!). Nature's impulse to grow follows a cycle of growth, decline, death, and then mutating into nutrients that will support new life. In the Western culture, however, we are focused on growth, and in some ways want to capture and freeze the image there. We live with the illusion that youth as a symbol of growth potential can last indefinitely, and so we consume plastic surgeries, anti-aging creams and vitamins, fitness programs, magazines and entertainment that confirm the illusion of ever-lasting youth. We want to feel optimistic and positive, and that seems to entail the denial of decline as a natural step in the life cycle. We want to talk (and hear) about increasing prosperity and to be able to show it. What is now wrong with this?

Well, without giving much thought to is, we've been living with the assumption that we are not part of Nature and bound to natural laws, which happens to be a self-deceiving illusion. The fact that we collectively try to push that idea, doesn't make it more true. Growth is the Western mantra – which is being, unfortunately, increasingly adopted by the East. The world economy grew around 50 percent in total size between 1990 and 2008.[63] Markets are seen as the primary means by which societies realize their goals, because they deliver economic growth. In the U.S., 80 percent of the GNP is consumption spending, and it is promoted as essential for the country's economic efficiency.[64]

This has worked for ten generations, as environmental activist Bill McKibben notes. For two hundred years – ever since Adam Smith – we've assumed that more is better, and bigger is better, whether it's size of cars, homes, land productivity, or industrial output. And we actually could see an increase of comfort and security in the West due to a steady growth of our economies.[65] The capitalist system is very good at generating growth.[66] The problem is that growth, as we currently produce it, has become unsustainable.

Over the past twenty years, with our fossil fuel and coal plants and our consumption patterns, we have pumped carbon dioxide into the atmosphere at a rate that surpassed the optimal levels for life on Earth as we knew it, which is below 350 parts per million. As of June 2012, the rate is at 395.77 ppm and growing.[67] Economist and author Chandran Nair observes: "Unless we can shake off our obsession with growth, we can be sure that the dominant element shaping the direction of policy making will remain the economic one, not just in matters relating directly to the economy but in all others as well, including environmental and ecological ones. Given this, it should not be surprising that the debates surrounding such crucial issues as climate change are not fronted by environmental scientists or climatologists, but by economists."[68]

Economist Nicholas Stern, author of the *Stern Review on the Economics of Climate Change,* a report on climate change prepared for the UK government, called climate change the world's greatest market failure. There is a paradox in trying to solve the problem with economic instruments.

McKibben observes that of all the dramatic forces we're witnessing – stronger storms, melting ice, acid oceans – the most terrifying is to think of the end of growth, because "growth is what we do." But if our collective focus is on economic expansion, if we repudiate the idea of limits altogether, there is a main obstacle to our survival as humans. The obstacle is not in Nature, but in ourselves: in our mindset and in the consequences of our daily decisions.

Achievement

Think of a day when you felt proud of yourself. It is highly probable that it was a moment connected with some personal achievement. We are groomed from infancy into achieving goals and higher levels of performance. And we enjoy it! From potty training to our high-school report cards and college degree, from a weight loss to a sporting achievement or professional performance, we seek recognition, acknowledgement, respect, and appreciation. Consciously or unconsciously, we want to be worthy of love from others, whether they are alive or dead, whether they are current, past, or even imaginary relationships. We are willing to do our best to meet our internal expectations that we associate with those social recognition rewards.

Connected with the value of progress, prosperity, and growth, our drive to succeed leads to the pursuit of symbols: Where do we live? Do we own or rent? How many square feet? What car do we drive? What school do our children attend? Where do we go for vacation, where do we eat out, what objects do we collect, what brands do we wear? And since "achievement" and "success" relate to wishes or goals, to "fully" be ourselves depends perhaps not on where we are, but where we dream to be, or where we consider we ought to be.

What are the personal symbols of prosperity and achievement that you aspire to?

The language we use in this connection carries distinct messages. We can be a "winner" or a "loser." We can be seen as someone who has "made it," which secretly feeds our self-esteem and self-confidence, or we can torture ourselves with self-doubt and guilt because we are unable to "get it right." Perhaps we end up seeking alleviation in therapy, food, alcohol, prescription or illegal drugs, sex or gambling.

On the journey to achievement, we keep running on our personal treadmill, working harder and longer hours, and the cost can lead to feeling stressed, burned out, exhausted, lacking balance, and craving vacations and weekends. A 2007 study of the American Psychological Association found that three quarters of Americans experienced physical or psychological symptoms related to stress in a given month. About half of Americans (48 percent) felt that their stress has increased over the past five years, with money and work given as the leading causes of stress. Jobs that interfere with their family or personal time was cited as a significant source of stress by 35 percent, while 54 percent indicated that stress caused them to fight with people close to them. A study by the research firm Health IMS indicates that to combat sleeping disorders due to stress, Americans filled more than 50 million prescriptions in 2008 for sleeping pills and spent more than $600 million on over-the-counter sleep-inducing supplements such as melatonin and valerian root.[69]

Some of the business leaders in my study manifested feelings of emptiness and "a hole in the heart" that couldn't be alleviated by their professional performance or material acquisitions. But, ironically, even as they had that experience, they felt conflicted because it meant questioning the very positive social values of success and achievement.

Achievement is another ingrained value, difficult to let go of. It's not impossible, and I will address this later.

Control

Following closely on the values of growth and achievement, we have the value of *control*. I am referring here to the confidence we have in our intelligent capacity to analyze problems and creatively find solutions. We have imagination that helps us consider what is possible and what could be. We are told that "the sky is the limit," and this is an empowering inspiration to tackle any challenge. We create visions and take initiatives to change what is, especially what we don't like about the world. We are receptive to statements like "Yes we can," "Control your destiny" and "I have a dream." We create companies and organizations stating our vision as a first step. We learn how to craft plans that become the bridge we build between a dream and an action. We rely on our judgment, on our discernment and rational pondering, our "higher intellectual capabilities."

This aspect has roots that span millennia. Man, *Homo Sapiens* (literally "knowing man") has been defined by his superiority *vis-à-vis* animals, and has been fighting to control Nature in order to place its resources in service of his needs. Our confidence in human competency led our ancestors to undertake unthinkable journeys of exploration and conquest, expanding their mental borders by discovering new geographies. We have been able to exert power over the elements, soil, fire, water, and over other humans. We have developed the ability to influence, to expand our outreach, and to disseminate ideas beyond limits.

Religion has played a major role in defining the relationship of humans with Nature. The most ancient tradition, suggests Victor Ferkiss in his book *Nature, Technology and Society*,[70] considered the Earth a female entity, which female religions such as the cults of the Great Mother considered benign and actively fecund, while patriarchal religions considered the Earth both dangerous and passive. Nature was represented in Mesopotamian mythology as a "monstrous chaos" and it was the task of mankind to tame wild things.[71] This was manifested in destruction of forests to create irrigation systems and to underscore human power over natural resources; an example is described in the *Epic of Gilgamesh*, dating from over three thousand years before Christ, where a "heroic" king gave instructions to clear a forest to demonstrate his superiority over Nature. Ferkiss observes that the view of Nature serving as a resource for man has led to environmental disasters, such as salinization, flooding, and eventual destruction of the Tigris–Euphrates civilization.

The impact of this worldview can be seen in many activities, such as mining, logging, industrial fishing, oil exploitation, industrial farming, genetically modified crops, "chemicalization" of agriculture, nuclear waste depositories, canalization of wetlands, rainforest clearing, urban expansion, and dumping chemical waste into sources of fresh water. Our belief in the superiority of humans over Nature (as if we were not part of it) is evident in the destruction of ecological systems and the loss of biodiversity.

Mankind has been intent on altering the balance of Nature, and we now are experiencing the consequences of what ecologists call our "species arrogance" – specifically, our illusion of control. Others have called this the Sixth Mass Extinction,[i] and it's the only one resulting from human activity.

The alarm bell is ringing loud.

---

[i] The five mass extinctions were
    Ordovician – about 438 million years ago: Glaciers forming and melting
    Devonian   – about 360 million years ago: Another glaciation
    Permian   – about 245 million years ago: Asteroid or volcanic eruption
    Triassic   – about 208 million years ago: Massive floods of lava
    Cretaceous – about 65 million years ago: Asteroid or volcanic eruption

Wealth

The Merriam Webster dictionary defines wealth as abundance of valuable material possessions or resources. In a sense this is inadequate given the wide range of feelings that spring from the very contemplation of the word. They include:

- *Desire and motivation,* which connect with ambition, goal setting, planning, efforts, and perseverance to attain wealth;
- *Excitement* for initiatives and creativity to innovate how and what we do to get better results;
- *Envy* towards those who already "have it";
- *Resentment,* which connects with negative feelings, self-victimization, violence, crime, psychological abuse, or depression;
- *guilt, embarrassment, or shame* connected to experiencing How much we have compared to others, which may lead to intentional low profile attitudes, philanthropy, secrecy, paranoid behaviors;
- *Entitlement, sense of deserving what we have, pride* of what we obtained, which manifests in showing off, generosity, arrogance, sophistication, self-indulgence, elitism.

Explore the feelings that the word 'wealth'

generates in you.

With such a complex array of feelings, it is small wonder that discussion of wealth generates wide disagreement and can be a difficult topic. In addition, there are political rationales to support the more positive aspects of wealth. Wealth creation is a goal for a community, for a nation, for a planet. So what is wrong with wealth? Shouldn't we all have enough?

Ferkiss traces the reasons that made England a logical location for the emergence of the Industrial Revolution. England, he says, had embraced the basic premises of capitalism:

a. that the search for private economic gain is the major motivating factor for man;

b. that this is a good thing in itself; and

c. that economic freedom to seek private profit is the basis of all freedom.

The corollaries are that freedom includes use of natural resources, and that technology is a necessary help. Over the past century, we have developed a culture of consumption. Today over 2.2 billion people in Asia have access to mobile phones, including 80 percent of the Indian population – far more than have access to potable water or sanitary toilets.[72] We live in a world whose values are predicated on an economic system that rewards and provides incentives to those who can generate growth in consumption. For more than two hundred years, wealth has been created in large measure by exploiting natural resources. The planet was seen as a limitless resource, and resource depletion or environmental impact was not a concern of the exploiter. Problems that came up were "left for later," for economic reasons. Which corporation wants to act against its own profit interests? Which government wants to take unpopular decisions, such as limiting economic growth or disappointing dreams of "wealth"?

Yet we live in a world where around 80 percent of humanity lives on less than $10 a day, and half of the world's population makes do on less than $2.50/day.[73] In 2005, the wealthiest 20 percent of the world accounted for 76.6 percent of total private consumption.[74] Economists C. K. Prahalad and S. Hart, in their 2002 book *Fortune at the Base of the Pyramid,* mention that the 800 million at the top lived with an income of more than $15,000/year, while the remaining 6 billion people live with less than $15,000/year. This means *we* at the top are the minority that is trashing the planet and using up its resources, as if we were at a party where the bill is paid by everybody – yet mainly by those without savings, or the options to cash the insurance or move to another home. A mere 12 percent of the world's population uses 85 percent of its water, and these 12 percent do not live in the Third World.[75]

And things are not necessarily getting better. An analysis of long-term trends shows the distance of GNP between the richest and poorest countries was about:

- 3 to 1 in 1820
- 11 to 1 in 1913
- 35 to 1 in 1950
- 44 to 1 in 1973
- 72 to 1 in 1992[76]

Increased productivity has resulted in the production of more things – for fewer people. Economist Jeffrey Sachs reflects that a considerable amount of American spending "is not for the enjoyment of consumption per se, but to show off wealth, status, or sexual allure." He cited social critic Thorstein Veblen, who calls it "conspicuous consumption," referring to a form of consumption that has the main purpose of impressing others.[77] But now we have reached a point where the bills are coming due, reflects Nair. We are paying many of them, in weather-related or social crises. And affluent and "affluent wanna-bes" continue the pressure to get their "share" of wealth – whether it is to maintain what they have, or to get what others have and what they now "deserve" to have.

If wealth as we know it is no longer affordable in Earth-terms, may be should rethink the concept and find new definitions for it.

Comfort

Mankind has always sought to improve living conditions. The post-World War II years have seen an accelerating focus on boosting the technological innovations to make our lives more comfortable, particularly in the Northern-West hemisphere. Appliances made household chores easier; air-conditioners in homes and cars provided more agreeable temperatures; technology helped humans to feel safer, live healthier, and have more space in our homes. We now have more TV sets so we can avoid discussions, more cars per family to facilitate travel and to be able to do more in less time, more food options regardless of the season or our geographic location.

In the North-Western world it has become natural to "need" more things: we need heating; cell phones working throughout the country or outside it; fast Internet connections; different shoes for each sporting activity; elevators; freezers; email; nearby shopping facilities; insurances for home, life, long-term health, professional liability, flood and car; escalators; credit cards, bank accounts, ATMs; 24/7 filling stations; pet food; disposable silverware; gated communities; water filters; gyms; paper napkins, portable cups; spas; 24/7 convenience stores; 24/7 television programs; vitamins ...

What is wrong with this comfort level that we have gotten used to?

The problem is that the very resources that provide us with greater comfort are, because of how they are being exploited, causing a serious environmental impact. And corporations – and countries – have excluded environmental costs until now, accepting the damage or use of available natural resources as a necessary component of development.[78]

Let us consider minerals, for example – ubiquitous components of our every day life. The average automobile contains more than a ton of iron and steel, 240 lbs of aluminum, 50 lbs of carbon, 42 lbs of copper, 41 lbs of silicon, 22 lbs of zinc, and more than 30 other mineral commodities, including titanium, platinum, and gold. Every year, each person in the U.S requires more than 25,000 pounds of new non-fuel minerals to make the items we use every day. As large emerging economies, such as China and India, increase their participation in the global economy, demand for critical mineral resources is increasing at a rapid rate. That means that we are depleting our known mineral deposits at an increasing rate, requiring that new deposits be found and put into production.[79]

Moreover, we are witnessing the successful export of the American dream. The average American uses 250 kilowatt-hours of power per day, compared with 40 kilowatt-hours in China and 20 in India. If Asia used as much energy as Americans, the consumption would be 14 times as much. If they used as much as Europeans (150 kilowatt-hours per person per day) it would multiply nine times.[80]

While the World Bank, International Monetary Fund, and other forecasters see no problems in continuous growth, Lester Brown, environmental analyst and founder of the Worldwatch Institute, notes that in the 1950s, the world stopped living within its means and embarked on an eightfold growth of the economy. According to the United Nations World Water Assessment Program, the renewable water resources fell by more than half in the first five years of this century.[81]

Our market- and government-promoted consumption may bring affluence to many people – hundreds of millions. Yet sometime during the 1980s, we surpassed the planet's regenerative capacity, and now we are living as if we had a planet and a third. How is this possible? The domestic analogy would be that we're eating up our savings, the contents of our pantry, *and* the shelves, too. We're basing our comfort on resources that are non-renewable or, should I say, will take a long time to regenerate: another Ice Age to form the glaciers, some hundred million years to have extinct species create the fossil fuel, and, if we are lucky, about four billion years to perhaps have a new Earth crust formed with mineral deposits of coal, gold, titanium, or coltan – the minerals present in every electronic device we have in our home or industry.

Uncomfortable thoughts.

Independence

Now here we have a solid value, one that is deeply rooted in our human existence. Key aspects of the United States' Declaration of Independence have been adopted by many nations. We educate our children so they become independent thinkers and autonomous contributors to society. The search for independence is a motivation behind many who take off to explore new shores, new ways of living. The law protects the independence of the individual in many countries, and independence is seen as connected to freedom, free will, and sovereign decision-making. Democracies guarantee rights to the individual.

Yet what does independence actually mean ... and does it exist? One Fourth of July, to celebrate Independence Day, I invited friends over for a meal, which is a common tradition for this holiday. Except that this time I called it an *Interdependence Party*. I consider myself an independent person, and just out of curiosity I decided to review the list of the people I had depended on to prepare the *empanadas*[i] I served at the meal. I had bought the pastry at a store, so someone had packaged it; but before that someone had made the pastry; and before that, someone had planted and harvested the wheat to get the flour. As I filled the *empanadas* with meat, I thought of the farmer who raised the cattle, the truck driver who transported the animals to the slaughterhouse, the employees at that place, the person in charge of grinding the meat, the one packaging the meat, the person running the gas station from whom the truckers bought fuel, the person opening the doors of the supermarket, the person stacking the merchandise on the shelf (not to mention the person in the electric company ensuring there is power for the lights and refrigerators in the supermarket), the persons operating the water plant so people can wash their hands before handling my meat, the manufacturer of the Styrofoam trays, the manufacturer of the paper labels, the person who manufactured the scale to weigh the content ... and then also the managers at the different locations, the people taking care of the employees' children so all these people could come to work that day, the bankers, and let's not forget – the cow! This list didn't even include the oil I used, the eggs, onions, salt, spices, peppers ... I realized that I would not be able to do a complete list – ever.

---

[i] Argentine dish, consistent of a pastry turnover filled with either meat, corn, cheese, spinach, etc.

And we say we're celebrating independence. What is this myth all about?

Feminist author Susan Griffin observes that in Western cultures, independence and autonomy have been considered a traditional masculine value, with dependence being viewed as a feminine value. We find independence present in the archetypes of the adventurer, the pioneer alone in the wilderness, the sailor going into the sea, the cowboy, the crusading knight, the heroic marine, the courageous men who, depending on themselves alone, conquer and succeed. "Seeking liberation from traditional female roles, a woman is said to gain her independence," and dependence is an embarrassment to masculinity in the "idealized trajectory of male development," she notes.[82]

In what ways do you feel independent, and in what areas do you seek independence? What does independence mean for you?

Peter Russell traces the value of independence back to our psychological development. The newborn doesn't differentiate itself from the world, yet as we develop we learn to differentiate the "I" from the "not I." We learn to differentiate ourselves from others through our personal – and changing – characteristics, such as height, weight, age, etc. We also learn to base our identity on what we are not, i.e. shorter, heavier, older. The sense of individuality, Russell says, provides an inner "unity to all thought, feeling, perception, and action. That gives us the sense of "I-ness."[83] Yet, he observes, the paradox is that such an "I-ness" is extremely dependent on the outer world; our identity is based on our beliefs, possessions, status, and health. When those are taken away, we feel a crisis, become depressed, anxious, lost. "Some psychologists estimate that as much as 80 percent of our interactions with other people come from the need for reinforcement," indicates Russell. The road back to inner peace goes through connecting with others, the feeling of community, and interconnectedness.

Bill McKibben[84] noted the implications of what he calls our era of "hyperindividualism." We are less happy than we used to be, and there are not enough mobile devices on Earth to compensate for the lack of close bonds. We don't live on the Earth, we live *in* the Earth and are collectively part of the whole. Yet this doesn't match the thinking behind our decisions and daily actions that look after our individual interest disconnected from the context.

So the question I want to raise is: What is this myth of independence, this value we are pursuing that is only making our life difficult, since independence is a human abstraction, a concept, and an unrealistic expectation? And it is also making us profoundly unhappy!

Competition

We are early in life trained for competing with and beating others in a host of ways. These include children's' games, sports, beauty contests, school grades, business ideas, market share, innovation through R&D, and competitions from trivia contests to Grammy and Oscar awards. We try to match the size of our friends' homes or the make of our neighbor's car; we try to build a more impressive landscaping in the front yard. Thinking of real or imaginary competitors can inspire us to try harder, to persevere, to be creative, to set high goals to ourselves, to endure hardships. Competition can reduce prices of goods and improve their quality, and it may be the motivation behind many technological break-throughs that changed our world. Without competition, it is said that abuses in price setting or service occur more easily, and there is little drive to think of improvements.

Does competitiveness, as a deeply held value of our culture, have its downsides?

What role does competition play in your life?
What are the benefits to you of being competitive?
Can you identify any downsides? If so, what are they?

Evidence suggests that it has some subtle yet important con-sequences. We work longer to reach those higher goals and beat out the competitors; we train, sometimes beyond our physical capacity, to win first place, and frequently sustain injuries that last for life. Competition is a motivation that can inspire people to pur-chase things they don't need – and at times cannot afford – which is something marketing and advertising professionals know very well. We buy what "the other" has, only to realize that it didn't make us happier.

It was philosopher Herbert Spencer who in the late 19th cen-tury coined the term "survival of the fittest," creating a parallel between his economic theories and Darwin's concept of "natural selection." This has led to many misinterpretations, since people have understood it as a predator–prey relationship between species, as well as a struggle for dominance within a species. Yet Darwin's suggestion was simply that those who best adapt to the environment are better prepared to survive. Biologist Janine Benyus observes that silent collaboration is actually more the norm in Nature rather than explicit competition. In their book *Seven Life Lessons of Chaos,* John Briggs and David Peat indicate this is called "co-evolution," which describes for example how "100 million years ago Nature evolved flowering plants with seeds enclosed in fruits, at the same time animals enjoyed eating the fruits and evolved with them. The animals spread the plants' seed fostering new plant and animal species. Plant and animal evolu-tion were coupled together in one system," one interdependent system.[85] In linear thinking processes, differences can only be resolved via competition, which leads to conquest or compromise.

David Kinsley, in his book *Ecology and Religion,*[86] quotes Murray Bookchin, one of the strongest voices during the past 40 years on the relationship between ethics and ecological issues. Bookchin observes that "most features of contemporary capitalist society put a premium on a "free market economy," which is nothing less than a social license for vicious, selfish, harmful competition in which everyone is seen as a rival and success is measured in terms of how much economic and politic power one can accumulate over others in the scramble for one's share of the wealth that is being drained from the environment." This is echoed by Sachs, who observes that in societies where individuals are living within market values of bargaining, self-interest, and competition, they lose touch with compassion, trust, and honesty.[87]

Competing is a binary paradigm: one wins, the other loses. Someone is first, the other is second. It is founded in the either/or logic. And it generates isolation of the individual by definition. It's me versus you. That paradigm in which we are caught contradicts behavioral research that indicates the human need for connection. And it is not going to work in solving the big, complex planetary challenges we have to solve.

Knowledge

Here we have what seems like another "no-brainer" (what a para-dox!). What could be wrong with knowledge? Knowledge is power: Information helps us make decisions, judge situations and alternatives, solve existing problems, and perhaps prevent future ones. We increase our knowledge by reading, listening to others, learning from others, reflecting in order to extract lessons, observing and processing what we see. We invest time and money in educating ourselves and our children, and we permanently share and exchange information that becomes the foundation of knowledge. We communicate through our words and our actions, and we have little control in how far beyond ourselves our behaviors impact others – inspiring them, motivating them, creating some kind of reactions and contributing to their own knowledge database.

What, then, is wrong with knowledge? In the fast-paced world we inhabit, the rapid expansion of communication devices makes information accessible to us anytime, anywhere. In the early 1900s, Vladimir Ivanovich Vernadsky, Russian founder of geochemistry, postulated three phases of development of the Earth: the geosphere, (inanimate matter), the biosphere (biological life), and the noosphere, which is human knowledge transforming the biosphere. In what could be related to the current-day Internet, Teilhard de Chardin referred in 1922 to the noosphere emerging through, and constituted by, the interaction of human minds. Such availability of vast knowledge also brings with it the expectation that we "should know."

The Global Information Industry Center reports on a study that indicates the large increase in information flow: In 2009, the average American consumed "information" for about 11.4 hours a day, up from 7.4 hours in 1980. Information reaches us through cable and TV, mobile devices, DVDs, books, newspapers, magazines, radio, telephones, movies, plays, music, and computers, including games, the Internet, email, and social media.[88] Indeed, so omnipresent are the sources of information that failing to hear about a technological innovation, a scientific discovery, some weather-related catastrophe on another continent, or the latest argument of local politicians can make us feel awkward, as if we were living outside the world.

Brain researcher Iain McGilchrist makes detailed distinctions between how we process information, and differentiates the contributions of the left and right brain hemispheres. While the left brain provides us with the analytical, linear, organized, and decontextualized way of knowing, the right brain provides us with the holistic experience, the multidimensional immersion into the world. While the left hemisphere fragments reality in order to "manage" it, it's only through the right hemisphere that the full picture is understood. Think of a broken egg and trying to put it back together. As the children song goes: "All the king's horses and all the king's men couldn't put Humpty together again."

So the problem with knowledge is that we tend to become avid collectors of fragments. The more we collect, the more we realize that we don't have the "full picture," creating a self-reinforcing loop of dissatisfaction and a race to collect even more data. The reality is that what is actually missing is closer than we think: It's inside us, not outside. It's called wisdom and if we just stopped running and are silent, we can hear it.

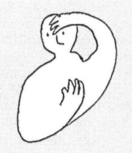

How do you feel about knowledge and information? As a treasure hunter seeking gems? Or perhaps as someone trying to drink from a hydrant? Or inside a bunker hearing the storm outside? What image fits best how you deal with the available information?

Speed

Knowledge and speed are connected. We not only want to know, but we want the information *now*. While many talk about the ever-accelerating pace of our lives, Ferkiss traces the drive for speed in America back to the early 1800s. Prompted by the Industrial Revolution, mechanical innovations were occurring at an ever faster pace. Farmers quickly saw the benefits of new instruments in agricultural technology; progress was achieved in faster modes of transportation, and emphasis, as Ferkiss observes, was placed above all on speed – "getting there first so as to be able to settle the land and get its products to market. America developed a passion for steamboats, built more for speed than safety."[89] The steamboat was followed by the railroad, and later planes and rockets. The Model T car evolved in a relatively short time into a Bugatti Veyron car, which achieves speeds of up to 267 mph, and can go from 0–60 mph in 2.4 seconds.

The value of speed accompanied us in an increasingly visible way over the past two centuries. Griffin observes how the "most intense efforts were made to save time"[90]: faster and faster computers, with the seductive idea of a data highway where information can reach the opposite corners of the planet within milliseconds. Yet the faster our technology, the more we seem forced to undertake in order to keep up. Willy nilly, we find ourselves responding to what comes our way.

Take emails for instance. You send out a message to your team members, who receive it a few seconds later. Every one processes what you've written, and replies. So now you get six replies within a few minutes. You process what they have written and now have to respond to them. As on a squash court, the faster you hit the ball, the faster it comes back, and the more times you will hit it within an hour. The result of this speed is to-do lists that nobody can realistically accomplish, and the items are dragged on from one day to the next, with a few of them fortunately expiring by themselves. Not surprisingly, we are spending more time working than ever, observes McKibben. Our leisure hours today are at their lowest since 1950 – roughly a third less – and we keep thinking that if we could just do things a little faster, we could save some time. Organizations provide employees with Blackberries so they can be contacted 24/7.

But time cannot be saved, Griffin reflects, nor increased. Only lived. With speed there comes stress, and that deprives us of the profound experience of conscious living. We float on the surface, racing through the day, our feet barely touching the ground, having superficial encounters where we cannot really tell what mood the other person was in, remember the face of the waiter, or if the bus driver was male or female. Velocity! While we long for the intense experience of being, we seek to get it through quantity and volume. So we multitask, we change subjects rapidly, our interactions are fundamentally to say what we have to say, not for listening to the other. We seek to fill a hole with the adrenaline of velocity. If people are not fast enough, then machines may help us: drive fast, surf the Internet fast, download at higher speed.[91]

In an interview with a candidate who wanted to attend my MBA course, I warned that the course was slow-paced, and that I had deliberately included opportunities to pause and reflect. "That is great," the woman replied excitedly. "I think it's wonderful if we take one minute to reflect!"

What is this value of speed? What is velocity all about? To go faster – to get where? To do more – to get what?

How do you feel about the speed of your life?

What could you do to change it ?

Chapter 7

Enablers

While the values described in the previous chapter are core to the Northern and Western hemispheres (and have been exported throughout the world), they are enabled by some other elements that are equally rarely discussed. I will address these in this section.

Science and technology

It is difficult to imagine our life without the benefits that science and technology bring to us. We conduct video conferences that save us the hassle of traveling; we distribute information in a milli-second over five continents; we chat with family far away and don't feel the distance between us; we watch movies at home, or on our mobile devices anywhere, anytime; we transport and eat fresh food from countries we may never visit; we design smarter homes, safer buildings, cleaner cities; we help people access water where there is none available; we develop devices that help expand education and give broader access to culture; we produce cheaper, better products more efficiently. Our dedication to scientific research has helped us to understand our bodies better and to cure or treat dis-eases with greater effectiveness; in parts of the "developed world" we live longer; oceanographic or Earth sciences allow forecasters to anticipate weather related threats; our understanding of geology helps us to find the resources provided by the Earth's crust; and social sciences help us understand each other a bit better.

Science and math education have become key areas to focus on in order to remain competitive in the global market. For instance, China is planning to invest 2.5 percent of its GDP in research and development by 2020, so as to become a leader in innovation and intellectual property, according to Denis Simon, professor at Penn State University – who is also the science and technology adviser to the mayor of the Chinese city of Dalian.

Techno-optimists consider that human ingenuity and creativity can handle any challenge, and that in this lies the solution for the problems we currently face. Technology can definitely bring us much-needed hope. So why should something be wrong with valuing and betting on science and technological progress?

The problem seems to be not in science and technology itself, but in the thought process that underlies scientific thinking – and the roots of the problem reach far back into the past.

The Reformation could be considered the first great example of the search for certainty in modern times. As German theologian and philosopher Friedrich Schleiermacher puts it in the mid-1800s, the Reformation and the Enlightenment have in common that "everything mysterious and marvelous is proscribed" and in the search for the one truth, myths and metaphors are replaced by the pursuit of unambiguous certainty.[92] The Enlightenment was the age of reason, ignoring the fact that reason is based on conceptual frameworks, which are always embodied and contextual. We measure with the instruments we have available, then make assumptions based on these measurements that result in our interpretations. When the assumptions are socially shared, they might seem more real, yet they are still assumptions. The Enlightenment is based on the belief that man can control his destiny, and we can see how its legacy is reflected in the thinking of today's techno-optimists.

The Enlightenment also first conceived Nature as a "vast collection of objects that could be subject to scientific investigation and experiment."[93] Power came from knowledge gleaned by extracting Nature's secrets, and Isaac Newton thought of the natural world as mechanical building blocks interacting with one another. To understand the natural world, things had to be broken down into their components in order to explain the causal links between them. Nature became a great clock that could be disassembled and reassembled. The new driving forces were human prediction and control.

The reliance on mathematics as an abstracting tool meant that science could only deal with what is measurable, quantifiable, and numerical – which created an oversimplified and fragmented approach to reality.[94] Scientific research became objectivist, meaning that there is an objective universe that can be explored by methods of scientific inquiry; it became reductionistic, meaning that phenomena have to be explained in terms of more elementary components (i.e., color explained in terms of wavelength) and positivistic: What is real is what can be measured. Nevertheless, a suspicion remained that something was being left out, and it was something important. Some phenomena just could not be explained, much as they were analyzed. These include predictions by clairvoyants, telepathic communications, levitation, spiritual healings, placebo effects, and psychosomatic syndromes. As global futurist and visionary Willis Harman notes in his study of what he calls the "scientific heresy," something as simple as deciding to raise an arm – and there it goes up! is a sign that the reductionist approach just is not enough – something as immaterial as a thought seems to have effects in the physical world.[95]

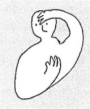

What do you think about telepathy?
Did you ever experience a telepathic connection?
Do you pay attention to your "gut feelings" or intuition?

If so, how have they served you?

Psychiatrist and researcher Iain McGilchrist makes an interesting analysis of the thinking involved in traditional scientific reasoning. Every thing we apprehend, he posits, is the way it is because we see it in that way rather than another way. When science adopts a view of its object from which everything human is removed as much as possible, it is merely exercising another human faculty – that of standing back and seeing something in a very de-contextualized, unnatural way. There is no reason to consider this the privileged way of approaching reality – other than to do certain things more easily, use things or have power over some things. Ultimately, objectivity requires interpretation of what one finds, and it depends on imagination, McGilchrist observes.[96]

But the objectivist paradigm continued throughout the Industrial Revolution, with the myth of science as a unity with one logical path to knowledge, irrespective of context (whereas science is, quoting British philosopher and historian Stephen Gaukroger, more like "a loose grouping of disciplines with different subject matters and different methods, tied in various ways each of which work for some purposes but not for others"[97]). In addition, the scientific method was considered sovereign, though the greatest advances of science are often the result of chance observations and personal intuitions. With the Industrial Revolution, the capacity to produce objects using mechanical processes reassured the supremacy of man over natural world.

This over-reliance on, and prioritization of, our scientific and rational approach to the world has kept us in a bubble where, for us, reality becomes what we can measure and see. This view excludes rich and profound aspects of our world and of our experience, as Rabbi Joshua Heschel would observe. Citing McGilchrist: "An increasingly mechanistic, fragmented, decontextualised world, marked by unwarranted optimism mixed with paranoia and a feeling of emptiness has come about, reflecting the unopposed action of a dysfunctional left brain hemisphere."[98]

The good news is that we have another half brain hemisphere that could serve to help us out of this social and environmental planetary mess.

Media that connects us

Media has become the circulatory system of planetary knowledge. We are more connected than ever due to all the innovative kinds of mobile devices that keep us hooked into the "noosphere" wherever we are. Eighty percent of India's population have a mobile phone, many more than have sanitary installations or running water in their homes, and Taiwan heads the world ranking, with 106.45 phones per 100 people.[99] China has 1.17 billion phone subscribers between landlines and mobile phones, which is close to its total population (1.34 billion), suggesting a cross-generational phenomenon. By the end of February 2012, Facebook reported 794,565,000 active users worldwide, with 50 percent of them logging on any single day. After the U.S.A., Indonesia has the second largest number of Facebook users, almost 42 million.

Media connect us, transforming the meaning of distance and location. Swifter communications methodologies accelerate decisions, and also allow us to expand, in an unanticipated way, the horizons of our learning. We get insight into far distant cultures, and startling views from space and under the oceans. As the Arab Spring demonstrated, any individual can start a movement with the ability to put an end to an entrenched power, and can even inspire others to launch similar actions. Media is changing the power dynamics of the world.

Media also shapes perceptions, introduces or reinforces values, influences what we do and how we do it. Sachs observes that for over a century now, we have been receiving loads of commercial advertising, campaigns, and official propaganda, which have molded our opinions and desires. We have been groomed into wanting more and more, enticed by stimuli that aim directly at sensitive places in our psyche: belonging, forestalling aging and death, sex, fame, happiness and fulfillment, and attractiveness, to name a few identity boosters. Advertising professionals know how to connect our desired feelings with the purchase of an item, selling the illusion of fulfillment via consumption. A 2004 survey of eight- to eighteen-year-olds estimated the total media exposure of this group (by computer, handheld devices, TV, movies or DVDs, video games, audio consoles) was, on average, 8 hours, 33 minutes per day.[100] We get non-stop messages about what we need to buy, where we need to spend, borrow or play. The promise is happiness, and when the promise goes unfulfilled, we just pass over in our mind to the next item that will get us that satisfaction. In the meantime, we deplete the resources of our planet, create more waste, increase our carbon footprint, and increase, also, the social divide. Of course, we do make money on the way. So we can buy … another planet?

Identify some recent purchase decisions you made, decisions that were strongly influenced by the promise of happiness you received from the media.
Can you identify other moments when your values, preferences, and purchases were shaped by advertising messages?

Furthermore, media also has a powerful role in shaping our culture. The new array of devices is designed for the individual, rather than for collective usage, which exacerbates the isolation of the individual. An international study conducted to explore the relationship between television viewing and social trust indicated a statistically significant inverse relationship: the higher the amount of daily TV viewing, the lower the feelings of social trust.[101] In other words, when we finally get out of our personal bubble to interact with others, we feel suspicion, anxiety, and distance from one another. Not the ideal situation.

Finally, media creates a perception of reality, simply by repetition in one medium, or by portraying the same perspective in a variety of media. If we hear about depressed people, stories of violence, or stories of corruption on several TV channels, or on the radio, or reading print media, we then get a "picture" of how the world is. And this impacts our feelings, our reactions, our thinking, and our attitude as we go out into "that" world. I am not suggesting denying, or not reporting, negative stories; what I'm observing is how a lack of balanced news gives us a biased image of the society we live in. And, as economist Jeffrey Sachs notes, our brains are malleable. "Scientists use the term 'neuroplasticity' to describe the fact that our brains are continually being rewired depending on the kinds of stimuli that we receive and the ways that we choose to behave."[102] We are not just what we eat; we are also what we see and hear, Sachs reminds us.

How does the way you think impact
what happens to you? Do you notice
the connection between how you
think about something and how you
act as a consequence?
And how might this be influencing the
responses you get from others to your
actions?

Globalization

Globalization began over five hundred years ago, reflects Paul Hawken in his book *Blessed Unrest,* when, realizing that the Earth was indeed round, Western Europeans started circling the globe to bring commercial ventures to wide-flung nations. In the 19th century, the concept was presented by economist David Ricardo, who developed the theory of comparative advantage: If Britain could make cloth more cheaply, and Portugal wine, each country should specialize in that commodity. McKibben observes that in Ricardo's framework, the capital was expected to stay at home "due to the natural disinclination which every man has to quit the country of his birth."[103] That of course didn't happen. Capital flowed between countries, and international financial markets and multinational corporations succeeded in easily breaching country borders. Globalization in our time results in interconnectedness of our economies and the weakening of political borders. It has expanded employment opportunities, and with it income and education. And access to goods. Take a look around the room and identify how many of your objects are locally manufactured, or peer inside your fridge and list which foods have originated within a radius of 50 miles of your home.

But globalization, playing as it does a big role in enabling the values we discussed in the first section, also has complex side effects, as many protest movements have highlighted over the years. Hawken mentions some of the liabilities: worker exploitation; unregulated manufacturing practices with a high CO_2 footprint; destruction of communities through urban settlements; and loss of the economic resiliency of regional communities to endure bust and boom cycles. Freelance writer Eric Randolph, based in Delhi and London, observes that many Indians, especially the poor and tribal people, view globalization largely as a source of intrusion, dispossession, and pollution.[104] Sachs reflects that the winners of globalization include: the owners of physical capital, who can shift their operations around the world; the owners of financial capital who can invest abroad; and the owners of human capital, who can export skill-intensive services to the emerging economies. In the U.S.A., this has meant that capital owners have been the big winners, and workers with low educational levels are the big losers, as they are not able to compete with the cheaper wages paid to workers in the emerging economies.[105]

In addition, globalization has also brought about the export of the Western model. On a recent visit to Romania, I had the opportunity to drive around on secondary roads. A Romanian manager at a multinational company I worked for asked me, "Why would you, coming from the U.S., be interested in traveling around the small villages of Romania? We are fifty years behind ..." I replied that they may in fact be 50 years ahead. As we were driving through the small villages we came across more horse-driven carts than cars, and the former are impervious to fuel shortages. I noticed the front yards of houses were not ornamental, but consisted of vegetable gardens, with rows of different produce carefully laid out. This resulted, too, in organic farming, not because the owners had a sophisticated sustainability education, but because they continued tending their food gardens as they have been doing for generations. It also made the food local, and thus affordable. Each house had a well in the front, which meant that they had their own water source. In the small villages they had several stores that sold used clothes. Finally, I noticed so many people were outside their houses, sitting in front of their homes and talking – kids playing, teenagers hanging out together, women standing in small groups chatting. Coming from suburban Miami, where I rarely see a person walking, and hardly any children in the yards or on the street, it caught my attention. They have community bonds, I reflected. In many parts of the North-Western world, developers are creating "new communities," where only so many families can live; they share an organic vegetable lot, a community center to meet and gather, and the internal streets of the community encourage walking and biking. "We are beginning to re-create

artificially something that you already have, something very valuable," I said to the Romanian manager.

What have been the personal benefits you have
derived from globalization?
What have been the negative consequences to you
of globalization?

PART IV
THINKING OF ALTERNATIVES

In the previous section I shared a few values that are central especially in our Western culture, and explored why they were so important to our identity, and in what ways they played an important role in the problems we are facing. In other words, I began to think of how our adherence to some of these values can lead to self-inflicted, if unintentional, damage.

It doesn't have to be this way. While our planet is rapidly changing, we also have the opportunity to change ourselves, and to begin making a different imprint on our Earth. Taking a closer look, I believe that the values that are part of our problem can be grouped into different categories: those that need to be redefined and reshaped; those that invite us to develop our whole brain; and those that present an opportunity to evolve as human beings towards a higher level of development.

Part IV addresses the alternatives available to us for converting what are unsustainable values into new opportunities for our world to thrive in a sustainable way.

Chapter 8

Redefine and Reshape

Several dearly held values of our culture conflict with sustainability, as we have seen. But the problem may not be growth, wealth, comfort, the media, or globalization, but the way we understand them, the way we practice and organize our lives around them.

Let's take economic growth. "Questioning growth is deemed to be the act of lunatics, idealists, and revolutionaries," observes Tim Jackson, British environmental economist and professor of Sustainable Development at the University of Surrey.[106] Chandran Nair, founder of the Global Institute for Tomorrow, is one of those "revolutionaries." Nair realizes that across the Asian region, hundreds of millions of people live in poverty and don't have enough money to consume. "They cannot even consume the basic necessities, such as food, housing, sanitation, education, and health care."[107] They are not rich, and are looking to improve their living conditions. Nair argues that in emerging economies, growth is necessary. Restricting the growth of consumption is not an option, and I agree: To me it would even be immoral. The key question centers on whether or not there is a way for emerging economies to grow without depleting and trashing our planet.

Nair offers several solutions. For some resources, such as rainforests, fisheries, and various metals and minerals, sustainability requires a total or near total bans on exploitation. In the developed world, which is responsible for the bulk of the consumption and resource utilization, Nair goes further. Nair suggests in his book *Consumptionomics* (one of the most daring books to challenge the values we take for granted) that, for the developed world, the twin strategies of restricting the growth of consumption and making production more efficient in the use of resources, are key opportunities for change.

Making production more efficient sounds good – but restricting consumption and economic growth as Nair and others advocate is a difficult idea to swallow in a world that is built on the promise that economic expansion will ensure happiness for all. It is unacceptable in the world we're living in. But, as Sociology Professor at Boston College Juliet Schor warns, there is a little caveat: We shouldn't be thinking of business as usual any more. The ecological devastation "will not only lower the average returns available, but the market will also become more volatile. The instability of climate and the running down of ecosystems are not smooth processes," she notes: "Expect a rockier road."

It's a scenario that makes it suddenly more interesting to consider our alternatives. There are two types of growth – "extensive" and "intensive" growth. *Extensive growth* moves along "a horizontal plane on the surface of the planet," suggests Ervin Laszlo, founder and president of the Club of Budapest, an international think tank. Extensive growth is characterized by the conquest of territories, colonizing people, and larger markets, and it generates unsustainability. *Intensive growth* centers on the "development of individuals, and of the communities and ecologies in which they live.[108] What if we would focus on "intensive growth," meaning green innovation to produce more sustainability – specifically, shifting to organic and local agriculture, wind power, and passive solar energy generated in our homes? And as you may have learned at the HSBC airport ads, 0.3 percent of Saharan solar energy could power Europe.

This is the perspective suggested by author Frances Moore Lappé in her 2011 book *Ecomind: Changing the Way We Think to Create the World We Want*. She argues that talking about no growth is scary, especially for the jobless: it's unappealing, and provides little motivation. Instead, we should pay attention to the "deadly economic models" that we are supporting, and to which consciously or not, we are giving strength.[109] Some of these "models," Lappé continues, are: government representing big corporations' interests through their lobbyists; advertising and media creating a biased picture that we ultimately buy; and taxpayers paying for the "externalities" – the cost of damaged ecosystems that are not included in the balance sheets. She suggests focusing on qualitative growth, on growing community-operated businesses; Lappé cites inspiring examples of how this is already happening in places such as India, Central America, Europe and even in some cities in the U.S.A.

In a similar vein, Schor reflects that the mantra of "grow or die" needs to be revised. If we consider the way a small mom-and-pop operation functions, we notice that the owners can use the positive difference between costs and revenues (their profits) to upgrade their equipment, but they are not required to *grow*. A business that generates a decent profit can operate as it does for years, or it can keep up by innovating to improve quality or to lower costs through greater efficiency. Improving productivity becomes then the key for success, rather than growing size or output. This applies also to many larger companies, observes political economist Gar Alperovitz, who studied employee-owned companies, cooperatives, and credit unions. These organizations don't depend on Wall Street and the big financial system, which demands growth. Schor reminds us that it has not always been like this, anyway: It is only since the 1980s that the economy became "finance dominated."[110]

As a reaction to something that is not working well, venture capitalist and entrepreneur Woody Tasch founded the Slow Money movement, where people invest where they live, for the long term, and in ways that enrich the soil, communities, and human welfare. Slow Money's long-term objective is for one million investors to commit 1 percent of their assets to local food systems.

Michael Shuman, Fellow at the Post Carbon Institute and author of the 2012 book *Local Dollars, Local Sense: How to Shift your Money from Wall Street to Main Street and Achieve Real Prosperity*[111] reflects that the traditional financial institutions don't even offer as great a return as smaller, local business does, and their profits don't even really go back to the community. Instead, he suggests, investing in our neighborhood not only helps where we live, but also develops trust-based relationships.

James G. Speth, author of *The Bridge at the End of the World*, explored the concept of a post-growth society as described by Australian author and Professor of Public Ethics Clive Hamilton: a society that consciously promotes social structures and activities that improve individual and community wellbeing.[112] In the U.S.A., he points, we still need growth, but of a different kind. We need growth in good jobs and in income for the poor; availability and efficiency of health services; education and security against the risks of job displacement, old age, and disability; investment for urban and interurban transport, water, waste management; and the replacement of the energy system and in restoration of ecosystems.

Is it thinkable to slow down our growth in such a way that it doesn't have a painful impact on employment and incomes? Schor asks. She is not the only one asking that question. It's true, preserving high employment levels is one of the most cited justifications for maintaining the mantra of economic growth and consumption. And at the first International De-Growth Conference, which took place in Paris in 2008, the ecological economist Peter Victor observed that to simply stop growth would be a disaster. But, according to Victor, if we reduced the working hours for an individual worker, we could hire another worker to share that job. Not only would more people be employed, but they would also have more free time. Besides, organic agriculture and local small businesses are more labor-intensive, therefore they make a clear contribution to employment.

This is a curious perspective, since for decades the objective of less labor-intensive jobs has been a cherished goal of innovators. It is called efficiency and productivity, doing more with less. It sounds as if now that we've made some headway in that direction, we are trapped in a vicious circle of consume more so we can produce more so we can maintain the margins and the employment – yet we are also generating more waste and depleting the planet resources, which means facing limits to our growth and consumption. And, interestingly, unemployment has not necessarily decreased.

Given the increasing visibility of the crises, it may be the right time to review the purpose of growth other than the strictly economic or financial reasons. We have come to accept the economic perspective as the only "right" one. But, is this rationale valid?

If today we think that to live happier lives we need to grow, we need to revise that paradigm. Growth has been linked to prosperity, but as author Tim Jackson points out, things other than economic expansion are needed to attain happiness: stronger family and community bonds, good health, trusting community relationships, satisfaction at work, the ability to find meaning and purpose in our life. These speak more to the quality of our lives than the material concerns of economic growth.

What are some alternatives to economic growth and prosperity that you can think of incorporating into your life?

What would it take, and what could be a first step in that direction?

Certainly we live within economic systems, and it is not my intention to deny that. Fortunately, there is an increasing number of thinkers exploring and suggesting alternative ways to consider how to adjust, correct, transform, and innovate our financial and economic systems. Global futurist and visionary Willis Harman observed that "the world macroproblem will be satisfactorily resolved only through a fundamental change of our mindset." This is precisely what I want to focus on – the one area that is in our full control, which is our mindset, the inner constellation of our personal values. They are the forces that shape our daily decisions, and it is through their use that we are at our most powerful.

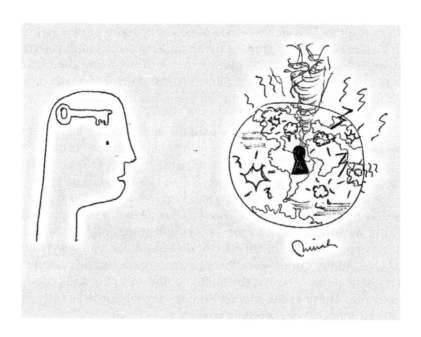

I am what I have

Redefining growth connects closely to our concept of *wealth.* How we live is the visible manifestation of our wealth and prosperity, at whatever level we may be. As we have seen in the previous chapter, wealth is a cherished goal for many, yet it has become an impossible dream to sustain unless we redefine it. Tim Jackson refers to the "age of irresponsibility," where we are willfully blind to the limitations of the material world. He describes the blindness as "the inability to regulate financial markets ... and our inability to protect natural resources and curtail ecological damage."[113] To maintain our dream of wealth we have created "financial and ecological liabilities." I found this a fascinating description of our current circumstances, and realized how critical it is for us to *acknowledge* it, as a first step. Then, I suggest we look one step further, and ask ourselves *Why is this happening?*

The words "ignorance," "short-sightedness," and "denial" come to my mind. Ignorance and myopia can easily be addressed with information and education, as the business leaders in my study have shown, and as the students of my classes repeatedly confirm. But when we explore denial, we have to listen to the wisdom of resistance again. What attitudes, mindsets, and values are at the foundation of our choices and decisions? What fears and (fragile) supports of our personal identity?

In a group dialogue at an MBA class, as we were discussing the values behind the goal of wealth, one student reacted in a perturbed tone, saying, "But if you take away all my goals, of having a better home, a better car, affording better vacations, or even better education for my kids, what is left?" I could feel the pain in his words that reflected no less than the beginning of a higher awareness. We're all seeking fulfillment; we're just looking in the wrong places.

Part 1
Take a moment and write down the key factors that make up your identity. Which of your possessions do so? What about your profession and career? Your interests? Places you visit?

We have anchored our identity in the symbols that our culture has handed down to us. The messages are that we are what we have, what we do, where we go on vacations, and how we educate our children.

Consumer researcher Russ Belk labeled as *cathexis* the process of attachment that leads us to think of (and even feel) material possessions as part of "the extended self."[114] This message is reinforced permanently through the promise that by consuming this or that, we will "be" or "become" what we dreamt of, and therefore we will feel happy and fulfilled. And since the promise is vain, as soon as we re-encounter "the hole in the heart," we find the new answer in the next product to shop. Jackson observes that the "restless desire of the 'empty self' is the perfect complement for the restless innovation."[115] Our economy fosters and builds upon an inner emptiness, which holds consumption (consumerism?) dear, but which never fulfills the promise of profound satisfaction. Is that the only concept of wealth we can relate to?

Part 2
Taking a new look at the list you generated:
What alternatives can you think of that may
give you a feeling of satisfaction and
happiness that are not related with your race
to acquire or maintain material possessions?

What if we looked at wealth in terms of setting our goal to reduce the depletion, so we allow the restoration of natural resources, fresh water and air, healthy soils, restoring the planet's capacity for absorbing our waste, and providing a life supporting ecosystem? Is there something that we could personally do (or stop doing), to restore that wealth? What if we looked at wealth as the rich outcomes of satisfactory relationships – of spiritual wellness and quality time with oneself, with loved ones and with members of our community? Tim Jackson thinks of a society with low carbon economic activities that employ "people in ways that contribute meaningfully to human flourishing."[116] Jeffrey Sachs cites America's greatest late 19th-century capitalist Andrew Carnegie, who suggested that the "duty of the man of wealth" is "... to set an example of modest, unostentatious living, shunning display or extravagance; to provide moderately for the legitimate wants of those dependent on him; and, after doing so, to consider all surplus revenues which come to him simply as trust funds, which he is called upon to administer, and strictly bound as a matter of duty to administer in the manner which, in his judgment, is best calculated to produce the most beneficial results for the community."[117]

If we look at our current examples of capital management, we are a long way from Carnegie's ethical position.

Author Cheryl Pallant stresses the importance of focusing not only on what we want to dismantle, but also on what we want to cultivate. She envisions a scenario where we shift from large houses to small, collect good will rather than material goods, and invest time in art and introspection over ceaseless industry.[118]

Ervin Laszlo reflects that we forget that it is not "the world but we human beings who are the cause of our problems."[119] First president of the Czech Republic Václav Havel, in wondering what could change the direction of today's civilization, observed that "the only option is a change in the sphere of the spirit, in the sphere of human conscience. ... We must develop a new understanding of the true purpose of our existence on this Earth. Only by making such a fundamental shift will we be able to create new models of behaviors and a new set of values for the planet."[120] That may be an alternative definition of wealth.

A young MBA student described her experience with these words.

> I am also consuming FAR less than when this course started ... the desire to shop has honestly left me. This makes me a bit sad, almost as if I broke up with a boyfriend ... since it was an activity that I considered fun, and it used to make me feel happy ... but I've moved on ... and shopping no longer has that "happy" effect on me, not even a fleeting happiness. ... There are so many other activities that are far more fulfilling ... for my soul. I want to focus on feeding my soul rather than satiating my materialistic cravings. I am still as ambitious as ever, I just no longer feel like living my life aspiring to materialistic goals that ultimately won't give me happiness or any lasting sense of contentment and satisfaction. I'd rather aspire to living and working in a sustainable way, creating value for society, consuming as little as possible, and giving as much back as I can ... and if I can inspire even one other person to join me, living in a simpler way, I feel that is the best way to spread sustainable practices – it will mushroom.

Luxury redefined

On a recent trip from Mumbai to Pune, India, we stood stranded under a bridge for a couple of hours, waiting for our taxi to be repaired. I noticed the traffic on the highway, and the long-distance buses that kept streaming by caught my attention. They were rather old vehicles, their paint was beginning to peel, they had small windows, and piled baggage on the roof. The temperature was high, and I noticed people with their elbows sticking out of the open windows. No air-conditioning, I thought to myself. The buses were not miserable, but they weren't modern either. My eye captured one sign on one of them: "Luxury redefined."

I reflected on the standards of comfort I had gotten used to. Having spent most of my life in a developing country, Argentina, I was certainly surprised when I moved to the U.S.A. by the many manifestations of comfort that North Americans had and took for granted. Naturally, after a while they became my new standard. I spent ten years living in an upscale condo that was easy to keep clean, since we didn't open the windows very often. When people asked me how I endured the hot Florida weather, I always replied that it was actually not a problem at all. All homes, cars, and shops were air-conditioned, and the only moment when I felt the heat was taking the short steps between a shop and the parking lot. In fact, I had always to carry a sweater because malls and offices tended to keep the temperature rather low all year round.

It took a personal change of mind for me to notice what had become my "new normal." As I became more involved in sustainability, I began to observe my own habits and behaviors. I was driving a car of 3,616 lbs to move my 135 pounds around. I never considered the option of (a scarcely adequate) public transportation. I enjoyed the air-conditioned gym with its extra fans to create a breeze for the sweaty aerobics class; I noticed the brightly lit but empty meeting rooms in my building; I didn't think twice when shopping, in Atlantic Miami, for shrimps shipped from Thailand, or golfing on manicured courses that were watered carefully, regardless of rain or the dry season. I liked the seasonal replacement of all the flowers around the building and on the streets of my neighborhood. One day, as I drove down the street, I watched workmen clearing a block, their heavy machinery lifting trees and bushes to make space for the new community recreational park. On the curbside, there was a man, supervising the bulldozer, and next to him, there was a white egret, also watching. At that moment something felt extremely wrong to me. The bird, whose ancestors had lived here for generations before the community was developed, was watching how his remaining small environment was being ripped away. If I had to attribute any feelings to the bird, I would say it had no feelings of sadness – just amazement at what we humans were up to. The white bird was so much wiser than us, I thought. He had lived there without polluting, damaging, or depleting the ecosystem he was a part of.

When we moved to a house built in the 1950s, the first night I noticed something strange yet familiar: the breeze that was coming through the many open windows. It brought back memories of spring evenings in Buenos Aires, and all of a sudden I remembered there were other ways to keep cool.

Frugality is becoming a competitive advantage, says Bruce Piasecki, author of *Doing More with Less: The New Way to Wealth*. And it may not be so difficult to redefine comfort, after all. "Waste not, want not" was the mantra of the Depression years, and a friend of mine wondered if we aren't perhaps revisiting that theme, when she read about reusing zipper bags, and recalled how her mother used to wash and store every plastic bag.[i] I saw it a couple of years ago on the hills of Athens, plastic bags drying on a clothing line, next to shirts and underwear. I remember stopping to take a picture, not sure what was more picturesque to me, a clothing line in a capital city, in the 21st century, or the plastic bags put to dry in the sun.

Today I'm connecting this image with my experience of the Romanian villages, and with the more post-modern GEN, Global Ecovillage Network, the growing network of sustainable communities and initiatives like ecovillages and transition town initiatives. These are different names falling under the new concept of intentional communities, where people strive together with a common vision, small developments where a limited number of families with a common vision and values live and create a community , cultivating local organic farming, using renewable energy, and practicing mutual support. That sounds like luxury redefined to me.

---

[i] No one wants "to go back"! warns author Frances Moore Lappé, suggesting we frame things as "innovations." This should make us aware of how we came to worship "the new" ascribing to it a higher value than "the old." Food for thought.

What unstainable comfort have you become used
to?
What could "luxury redefined" be for you?

A new responsibility for media

To review our personal definitions about wealth is important, but the media will also have a major role to play. Have you ever considered the power of media in shaping our reality? In indicating what is valuable? In what we ought to have and do in order to "fit"? And if this is already happening, is this the reality we want? What is the responsibility of media in contributing to the betterment of the world?

A few years ago I was invited to a conference about media as an agent for world benefit, an event organized by Images and Voices of Hope, a non-profit organization started in New York in 1999 by Judy Rodgers, "to expand awareness of the choices those in media make that raise public trust, generate constructive meaning, and amplify human hope, enhancing humanity's capacity for life-promoting action."[121] Persuaded that change starts with awareness, the organization promotes community dialogues and summits in different parts of the world, and features inspiring cases of individuals taking their responsibility in the media to a higher ground.

In 2008, CNN launched a yearly contest titled *CNN Heroes*, where people nominate individuals for their selfless contributions to the greater good. The campaign featuring the many candidates shows a "different reality," and provides inspiration to the broad audience. The world seems to be suddenly a better place when we watch stories that speak to us about humanitarian causes – stories about ordinary people doing little things that make a big difference. I recall the story of one woman who used to jog in the mornings and one day, jogging by a shelter, invited one homeless man to join her. He did, and after a while there was a whole group of residents of the shelter that joined her every morning. They collectively figured out how to get the appropriate sporting gear for their runs, they laughed together and had fun; that simple activity boosted their self-confidence, so that many took on a determination to get out of the shelter, and worked out a plan for it. Or another person who, at her acceptance speech, looked puzzled by receiving a special award for something she considered unimpressive and just simple acts of kindness. What times are we living in? she wondered. Stories like this one are like a mirror suggesting what we, too, could do personally, just using our little gifts.

Other media contribute to stories of inspiration, such as: *Positive News* (positivenewsus.org); the *Good News Network* (www.goodnewsnetwork.org), an electronic media that finds amazing or small things that make this planet a better place; *Good*, (www.good.is), a collaboration of individuals, businesses, and non-profits started in 2006 that features amazing acts of kindness in a magazine, videos, and events; and Odewire.com, a website with "news for intelligent optimists." More recently, a Romanian and an Argentine woman founded in Canada an organization called *The Good Collector* (www.thegoodcollector.ca), and post on their website innovative projects to improve the quality of our life and environment, and to inspire others. Magazines like *YES!* (yesmagazine.org), and the *Kosmos Journal*, "The Journal for Global Citizens Creating the New Civilization," founded in 2000 by Nancy Roof, are other valuable publications shaping the new world.

The news creates particular feelings in us. Imagine this: You wake up and turn on the news, just to listen to the latest speech of one politician blaming the opposition for all evils. You switch the channel, and listen to news of violence, domestic or foreign, of explosions, or of a new corruption scandal. You decide to switch off the news, and glance over the headlines in the newspaper. Not much more enticing. You fold it and jump into your car, and the radio tells you about the accidents on the highway. Maybe you don't need to imagine this scenario, since it probably constitutes your daily experience.

Now think of a morning where you start listening to a story of a coffee shop where everyone pays for someone else's coffee. Or the young entrepreneur who found a way to convert leftover fruit and vegetables from large food retailer Costco into a rich 100 percent organic soil that doubles the nutrients of chemical-based soils. Do you think you might head out into the street feeling a bit differently in this alternative scenario? We take in news like we take in food, and it becomes part of us. What will you have? Ice cream or poison?

 Take a moment to reflect on the type of news you discuss with friends, family, or coworkers. Do you ever comment on positive, uplifting news? What kind of positive news could you comment on?

Media has become more than TV, billboards, radio, or print. We take in information from other channels, too, and the most interesting to me is social media. Social media definitely "democratized" the access to information and opened new venues for speaking up, and so it is shaping reality in new ways. In times when anyone can upload a YouTube movie, launch an awareness campaign, raise funds for a cause, or collect signatures to create change, the dynamics of power have shifted.

One.org is an example of this power shift. Co-founded by Bono and other campaigners, ONE is a grassroots advocacy organization that fights extreme poverty and preventable disease, "by raising public awareness and pressuring political leaders to support smart and effective policies and programs that are saving lives, helping to put kids in school and improving futures." Through their web, anyone can add their voices to advocate for campaigns for clean water and sanitation, health, trade and investment, climate, and development, among many other causes.

Change.org is another such initiative. Launched in 2006 by two former classmates from Stanford University, Ben Rattray and Mark Dimas, *Change* is a social action platform that gives anyone, anywhere in the world, the chance to start or support campaigns for social change. Every month, millions of people launch or sign petitions on issues that range from human trafficking or women's causes to immigrants' and animal rights, environment, and food. Some months ago, the *New York Times* featured the story of a group of fourth grade school children who started a petition and won their cause with Universal Studios. They had read the Dr. Seuss story "The Lorax" and valued the message about protecting the natural environment. But as they visited the website of the movie that Universal Studios was making, they were disappointed to see that there was no mention of the book's environmental aspects! They thus created a petition at *Change.org* that went viral and soon collected over 57,000 signatures – so many that the studio updated the movie site with the environmental message that the kids had dictated.[122]

The Arab Spring and its cascading consequences is another demonstration of the power shift, and how media can be redefined for new purposes. And the good news is that it's not up to "them," whoever that is, to make the shift. Now anyone of us is able to shape the media – and reality.

 How are you using the social media? Whether you intend it or not, you're shaping the world with what you post, forward or ignore. Anything you would like to do differently?

Inside or outside the globe

Much has been said and written both about the benefits and of the negative impact of globalization. In the previous chapter, I explored globalization as an enabler of our values, particularly since in a world where geographical borders vanish, values that don't support a sustainable planet also spread and expand rapidly.

Globalization may look like bringing distant cultures closer to our lives, but it is actually the expansion of a Western monoculture. Globalization is having ten different brands of jeans in remote villages of the planet, genetically modified seeds replacing indigenous varieties, and Coca-Cola dispensers in native communities. And, unfortunately, the model that is being exported is far from providing a more healthy, happy, or safe life.

The question, then, is how could we put the mechanics of globalization to serve a better purpose, one that helps us restore resources, develop new patterns of thinking, or introduces new perspectives before making decisions?

On a pragmatic level, today more than ever, we need global awareness and international collaboration to solve our problems, as linguist and writer Helena Norberg-Hodge observes.[123] She has extensively studied the impact of globalization and the spreading of Western values into the traditional culture of Ladakh, in the northern region of India, which led her to found the Counter-Development movement. We need policies that promote small scale on a large scale, allowing community-based economies to flourish and spread as a concept. We need international treaties to protect the local and the global commons, which are the natural resources of our planet. Globalization is not an inevitable, evolutionary force, Norberg-Hodge indicates, "and the active proponents are less than one percent of the world population."

On a deeper level, we have the opportunity to see globalization as the phenomenon that has been building connections and bridges among people that were unthinkable before. Maybe the best contribution of globalization is teaching us how we are all interconnected. When an unethical, unregulated behavior in the U.S. mortgage system creates a global financial ripple effect that touches the lives of individuals, rich and poor, in far-away countries, we are being taught a lesson about interconnectedness. And we learn that collectively faster than attending a Globalization conference.

This may be the way to get outside our bubble, and notice that we have been connected all the time. Developmental psychologists research how to advance human consciousness to go from an ego-centered perspective of the world to a holistic integration of the self into all that is. If every problem is something life is teaching us, then the shadows of globalization certainly are an opportunity to take one step in our personal development (provided we pause to

notice and reflect on the message that seems to be shouted at us).
As Laszlo pointedly observes, when we become conscious of these
connections, human thinking is lifted from the outdated ego-centered level to the urgently needed community-, ecology-, and
planet-centered dimension. Actions emerging from this new
mindset will automatically take us into different places.

Chapter 9

Develop Your Whole Brain

In a culture that places such a high value on our intellectual capability, how would we feel if someone told us we are underutilizing *one half of our brain?* British researcher Iain McGilchrist suggests that there are two fundamentally opposed realities for us as human beings, two different modes of experience. Each one is of extreme importance in connecting and understanding the human world, and their difference is rooted in the bi-hemispheric structure of the brain. The hemispheres seem to be specialized for different functions, observes neuroscientist V. S. Ramachandran. The right hemisphere provides us with a more full experience that comes to us initially as an intuitive understanding, which researcher Robert Ornstein[124] describes as being shortsighted and taking off the glasses. Our left hemisphere then applies linear and sequential analysis of this message, forcing "the implicit into explicitness,"[125] and bringing clarity. The left hemisphere plays a key role in "decoding" what we first perceive through our right hemisphere in a holistic way. At the same time, in doing so we connect with the world through fragmentation, and the "whole" is lost to us. The hemispheres need to cooperate, but as McGilchrist reflects, they are "involved in a sort of power struggle," and this explains in his view many aspects of contemporary Western culture.[126]

The way we look at the world shapes our reality, making us partners in a creative process. If we see ourselves living in a fragmented, mechanistic, and "rational" world, if we experience at the same time extreme optimism and feelings of emptiness and paranoia, we may be subject to too much of a left hemisphere and too little of the balancing act contributed by the right hemisphere.[127]

McGilchrist cites a story related by Nietzsche. Once upon a time, there was a wise spiritual master who ruled over a small and prosperous domain. He was respected as a selfless man who knew how to take care of his people. As the population grew in number, his domain expanded and he needed to delegate to emissaries, whom he entrusted to look after the distant regions. He trained his emissaries so they could be trusted, but eventually the most ambitious and clever vizier, the one he trusted the most, began to see himself as the master and used his authority to gain more wealth and power. This upstart vizier saw the forbearance of his master as a weakness, not as wisdom, and before long, he took on the position of master, and the domain became a tyranny, and finally collapsed. This story is for McGilchrist an analogy of what happened to us: while our hemispheres are meant to cooperate for us to achieve a more complete connection with reality, the history of philosophy is a story that describes the battle that has characterized Western culture over several millennia. These days our civilization is in the hands of the abusive vizier, who is very gifted, ambitious, and driven by his personal interests. The right hemisphere, which is the Master in the story, the part that can bring peace, wisdom, care, and security, is chained and largely ineffectual.[i]

Among the forces that currently hold us hostage to unsustainable behaviors, *Control, Knowledge,* and the enabler *Science and Technology* reside in the domain of our left brain hemisphere. I suggest that we can "develop a whole brain mindset" if we learn how to more effectively engage (listen to?) our right hemisphere.

The illusion of control

It is clear that we do not know on any day what that day will bring. Depending on our tolerance of uncertainty, we may feel more or less comfortable with that fact. Yet our work or even the simple management of our daily chores demands planning to make things happen, to anticipate obstacles, and to resolve challenges. To do that, we use our capacity of language and linear, sequential analysis to help us pin things down, and make them "clear and precise." This gives us a sense of rationality and objectivity, and helps us feel

---

[i] Ornstein observes that while positive emotions have a seat in the right hemisphere, emotions of anger, disgust and fear also have their origin in the frontal section of that hemisphere (p. 73).

we are staying "real" and true to "what is." We are immersed in a culture that is strongly reliant on our intellect to master and control the world with logic and imagination. We use abstract, decontextualized, and "disembodied" thinking, to guarantee ourselves that we manage reality in a step by step, brick-by-brick approach. We use either/or logic to make decisions; we avoid ambiguities and try to come to fixed conclusions, statements, and concepts. We set clear boundaries, and we seek to explain in order to be fully understood by others.[128] Two hundred years of philosophy have dealt with reality in these terms: real versus ideal, subject versus object.

The left hemisphere gives us a sense of self-sufficiency, as we fragment the complexity of the lived experience into small pieces that we then place in some type of order. We try to detach the experience from complex ingredients, such as emotions or relationships, which escape our capacity for rational analysis. "The left hemisphere is competitive," indicates McGilchrist, and its prime motivation is power. If that is how we see the world, it becomes clear why we have competitive relationships, are driven by winning and conquering, have a win/lose mindset, stay in a myopic vision seeing only what we have in front of us.

Using our left hemisphere, we feel in control. Problems arise because reality is like water that keeps leaking through the cracks of the walls we try to build around us. Reality is complex, presents us with multi-causal events, exceeds the instruments we have available to measure it, and explodes with emotions, feelings, and other "irrational" aspects. The reaction is to try to combat these leaks with more analysis and rational thinking. As in Nietzsche's story, the vizier has to use more and more tyrannical power to control the population, and even so, or because of it, the domain eventually collapses.

Can we see the signs of how our way of handling our reality is collapsing? Some are evident in the financial markets, where we become blinded by competitive and myopic short-term gains that end up costing citizens their savings and jobs; some are seen in numerous armed conflicts, where we seek to solve our differences by using force to overpower opponents, costing lives, time, and money to rebuild what we destroy (while developing more animosity and enemies); others manifest themselves in our attempts at maximizing profits at the expense of planetary resources as we deplete or pollute, impacting the climate balance, our health, or even the livelihood of our and future generations; and others appear in the social gap and disparity of access to food, water, health, and shelter.[i]

The evidence is all around us. We have been relying too much on our intellect, and we need to balance and bring in our intuitive voice and the deep-seated wisdom that we have inherited from our ancestors. The predominance of conquest as a way to solve problems and to progress, has resulted from a "masculine" drive that shaped our patriarchal civilization. For some (bizarre?) reasons, the contributions of our right brain hemisphere have been seen as "feminine," with an accompanying connotation of "second class." These right-brain perspectives are the ones that connect us with others through compassion, especially when we don't fully understand others; or they are expressed in the desire to include and

---

[i] The worst drought in the U.S. in the last 50 years is affecting 88 percent of the corn crop, a staple of processed foods and animal feed as well as the nation's leading farm export. According to a *New York Times* article of July 26, 2012, this will have an impact on ethanol production, pig farms that use the corn as feed, and global food prices. This is an interesting example of systemic implications. If we have less corn, whom should we feed: people, pigs, or cars?

seek integration via collaboration with people who are different; or they use empathy to explore how others may be feeling. These right-brain perspectives can give us a very different approach to problems.

How important is being logical, reasonable, and objective to you?
How do you get in touch with your "gut feelings," intuition, or emotions?

Certainly relinquishing our need for control entails opening the doors to uncertainty, which can make us anxious, especially if we are caught in the belief (illusion) that we can be "in control" of reality. But there is much to gain when we integrate our right brain into our thought process. To begin with, our understanding of reality will be more integral, holistic. If we are able to incorporate a broader picture, our chances of developing more accurate interactions with the world increase significantly. Secondly, the sole fact of listening to our emotions and connecting with others in a non-defensive way gives us a feeling of relaxation. We need to remember that in order to maintain control, plan, and think in an analytic and linear way, we have to keep a short grip on the reins of our feelings, and not to "deviate" from logical reasoning. That means that when we can momentarily relax that tension, a sense of élan pervades. We have all experienced this feeling in a variety of situations: when dissolving in tears at a joke, when playing with children, when taking a ride in an amusement park that makes us scream, when arriving home and kicking off our shoes, when crying in emotion or getting into a trance listening or dancing to music.

In what circumstances do you find yourself enjoying the "right brain" dominated activities? Do you have enough of them or would you like to have more of them?
What can you do to help this happen?

These may be brief moments, but they are intense and leave us feeling somehow "better persons," who are positively open to others, and feel trusting without any particular reason. Now if what we think shapes reality, how would our interactions with the world be if we integrated our right brain contributions in our day-to-day existence? The need to control could be mitigated by the enjoyment of trusting the process. And when we trust others, research suggests, we address what is best in the other, triggering a response that seeks to deserve the trust granted. This already sounds like a better and less stressed world.

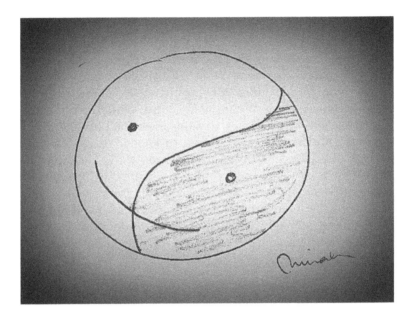

Unleashing ancestral wisdom

Thinking about **knowledge**, a story comes to mind. In May 2012, I was invited to attend a four-day retreat organized by the international spiritual university Brahma Kumaris, just outside Oxford, England. The retreat, facilitated by Dr. Peter Senge, is part of a yearly gathering under the title "The Call of Our Time," where leaders from different continents acting on causes for social service are invited to meet, network, dialogue, share, and reflect in silence. The initiative is the brainchild (or should I say soulchild?) of Dadi Janki, the Administrative Head of the Brahma Kumaris World Spiritual University, who 15 years ago saw the need for such a meeting place.

In a particularly peaceful setting, we pondered the theme of "awareness and right action," exploring what awareness means, and how to put consciousness at the service of the world through focused action. But the interesting aspect was that the four days were not about sharing data, crafting plans, or making decisions. Through different guided meditation exercises or shared reflections, Dadi Janki and several others conveyed an invitation to make silence in our minds, to notice our thoughts and empty our minds by gently pushing them aside. Only then, the conveners insisted, will we be able to listen to the wisdom that we carry, a wisdom that connects us with the universe, with the Source, God, Energy, or whatever name we choose to give to It.

Now you may wonder why would these bright executives, judges, psychiatrists, entertainment, consultants, deans, educators, and top sporting coaches, to name a few, be brought together with their multifaceted contribution to knowledge and asked to experience ... silence? The answer is simple: We all thrive in a culture that rewards left-brain thinking. Business, education, politics, science, technology ... we know how to think to get our points across. But nevertheless this keeps us thinking with half our brain. We are able to get a full half picture of the world, and act upon it. Maybe this is not enough?

Take the next minute to close your eyes and just do nothing. No need to reflect, to ponder, to plan what you will do later or review what you've done. No need to answer a question or imagine anything. No need to even pay attention to the flow of your mind. If thoughts come up, notice them but remember you don't have to do anything. No need to push them away, or fight them. Enjoy the opportunity of experiencing a moment of nothingness.... with no guilt.

McGilchrist points that we are used to the utilitarian perspective of our left hemisphere, which pushes us to find the "what for" of everything. It always has an end in view, and "downgrades whatever has no instrumental purpose in sight." The right hemisphere, on the other hand, is simply alert to connect with whatever is; it is concerned and cares for what is happening. Our left hemisphere provides us the clarity and power "to manipulate things that are known, fixed, isolated, decontextualised, disembodied, general ... but ultimately lifeless." The right hemisphere yields "a world of individual, changing, evolving, interconnected, implicit, incarnate, living beings within the context of the lived world, but in the nature of things never fully graspable, always imperfectly known."[129] It is not perfect as the left hemisphere aspires to be, but it sees *more* than the fragmented focus presented by our left brain.

Paying attention to our right brain takes practice. Pretend you are your cat. Or your dog. Think of a person you know, and try to imagine how you would "feel" when you see that person. Don't engage your thinking, just your gut.

When we shut down our left brain's analytical processing of the world, which is the equivalent of pushing our thoughts aside during meditation, we stay in a receptive state to connect with whatever is, and this means both with the outside and the inside. Outside and inside may even seem to merge, as our borders vanish, yet we are neither asleep nor unconscious. We are in an augmented state of alertness, which at the same time is profoundly quiet and relaxed. As a result of that experience, ideas may emerge that suddenly provide us solutions, insights, and a clarity we perhaps didn't anticipate. This is because by enabling the right brain's holistic view of the world, we connect with a broader wisdom that is integrative as opposed to the fragmentation of knowledge gleaned from data. We may not be able to put the wisdom into words easily – that is the task of our left brain – but we will have the intuitive certainty that "something is still missing" to reach the better solution or the more accurate decision. The wisdom remains as our intuition's voice.

With our head filled with judgments, preconceptions, assumptions, rationales, and expectations, how could we possibly listen to such a voice, which has been culturally dismissed and devalued, which we are not even trained to pay attention to? Because the right brain is soft spoken, it's a "gut feel," an "impression," a vague feeling, an inner voice that we ourselves are prone to disqualify in disbelief. The Inquisition burned the witches who listened to those strange voices. If every lesson learned alters our biology by leaving a genetic imprint, we may still carry those hard lessons inside us. Interestingly, in contrast to Western culture, intuitive wisdom has been profoundly respected and perpetuated in aboriginal cultures across the globe, and cared for as a key part of the cultural heritage.

We don't need to attend a four-day retreat to open the doors to our right brain. Innovation and creativity trainers know other ways that can help. Developing playfulness, expressing ourselves through the arts, walking in Nature, practicing paradoxical thinking, writing or reading poetry, listening to music, and creating metaphors are all other techniques available to gradually learn to listen to our intuition and integrate the ancestral wisdom our right brain hemisphere has for us.

Let's try taking a walk in Nature. Find a place and go for a walk. Switch off your phone, or better yet, don't take it with you. Don't take music with you, nor anything to write on. Go alone. You don't have to walk far, just be present wherever you are. Just connect with the natural surroundings. Take the experience in.

Bringing back the scientist

The aspiration of the traditional scientific paradigm (still the paradigm most generally adopted by the scientific community) is to provide a rational, observable phenomenon that is described in an objective way, free from any influence by the observer. Well, that assumption has been proven faulty throughout history. It didn't take more than inventing a better instrument to realize that the conclusions drawn previously were particularly biased and influenced by the type of man-developed instruments. Scientific arrogance (sponsored happily by our left brain) assumes the non-existence of what we don't know. Up to the 1950s, we believed our galaxy was the entire universe. Today we know that there is a metagalaxy that contains billions of other galaxies. And that metagalaxy is just our universe: There may be millions, perhaps billions of other universes in the "meta-verse."

The focus our left brain provides is definitely important because it allows us to study something in depth. What is missing is the "betweenness," which is not absent, just denied. And, as McGilchrist notes, there is "no reason to see that particular way as privileged, except that it enables us to do certain things more easily, to use things, to have power over things, the preoccupation of the left hemisphere."[130]

American poet Henry David Thoreau wrote in 1852, "I must walk with more free sense. It is as bad to study stars and clouds as flowers and stones. I must let my senses wander as my thoughts, my eyes see without looking. ... The more you look the less you will observe. ... What I need is not to look at all, but a true sauntering of the eye." He referred to a different way of seeing, where instead of analyzing what the eye perceives, he was opening himself to the experience of the whole of existence with "the whole of himself." And that way of grasping the world "does not yield less insight, rather the scope of vision is larger."[131]

Nobel Prize winning geneticist Barbara McClintock was said to work on her research with a non-traditional approach. She developed a particular way of observing, similar to meditation, staying during hours in proximity to the corn she wanted to study. She began in this manner to understand genetics in a dramatically new way, reporting on chromosomatic behavior that was "much more marvelous than the scientific method allows us to conceive."[132] It is clear that the separation of the material world from the world of mind and spirit did not prevent great scientists from exploring the relationship between object/subject that had been denied. The fathers of modern science were in a way "integral thinkers": Giordano Bruno, Galileo Galilei, Copernicus, Kepler, Newton himself, also Einstein, Niels Bohr and Carl Jung, to name a few, all had intuitive and even mystical insights.[133]

If these were individual, personal moments in the life and work of these great scientists, it was quantum physics that launched a whole different paradigm. The classic interpretation of the natural world had already begun to erode at the end of the 19th century, when the atom was found to be not the ultimate indivisible unit but actually host of a number of components. And the particles dissolved ultimately in a stream of energy. It was Max Planck who discovered that light was not a continuous stream but packets of energy called quanta. After this, the theories of electromagnetic fields were developed, and Einstein's theories of relativity. The quantum world appeared weird to traditional thinking. Physicists investigating the behavior of particles carrying light, matter, and force found that, until registered by an instrument or another act of observation, these particles have no specific position, nor do they occupy a unique state, observes Laszlo.[134] Furthermore, the new physics has found that all energy packets in the universe that share or have ever shared the same quantum state remain intrinsically connected with each other. Einstein proposed an experiment to divide twin particles, and when they are separated and subject to altering conditions, the changes in one are automatically manifested in the other, no matter the distance in between. It is as if one particle "knows" what is happening to the other. The speed of the transmission was estimated about 20 times the speed of light in one experiment, and up to 20,000 times faster in subsequent experiments.[i] This phenomenon appears both in the smallest as well as in the largest known structures of the universe. There are no straight lines in the Universe, as we would like to conceive it with our linear left-brain reasoning. There are parallel realities, and experiments have demonstrated that not only quanta but entire atoms can travel, as shown in the studies of teleportation carried out in the U.S.A. and Austria.

What are the implications of these discoveries? The understanding of the natural world is not a mere matter of interest to physicists, biologists, or philosophers. It is at the foundation of our cosmovision, it shapes our world in that we (most of us unknowingly) buy into one interpretation as the larger frame of reference that provides meaning and makes sense of all that is; this again is not an abstract philosophical issue, but something at the foundation of our day-to-day actions and interaction. Take one simple statement: if all is energy and every particle remains connected with other particles altering them, this means that all things in the world are interconnected, us included. What are the implications of our decisions, our interactions? If we approach the world from our rational perspective, we see mechanical relationships, linear and simple. But if we view our environment from an energy perspective, of interconnectedness, of consciousness beyond the five senses, of belonging to a larger stream of energy, how would we act differently, use resources differently, consider the impact of our behaviors differently? And if what we think shapes reality, as the physicists' experiments have shown, what type of reality do we choose to create? wonder authors Briggs and Peat.[135]

Here again we have the opportunity to engage our whole brain in the scientific approach to understanding our environment. Laszlo reflects that civilization has been characterized by particular paradigms, which are useful and instrumental for their time. However, as reality changes, at some point these interpretations lose their capacity to maintain order and provide a framework to address human challenges. They cannot be held, and thus

---

[i]   Laszlo, E. (2010). op. cit., p. 85, cites the experiments of Aspect and Nicolas Gisin, as well as the studies of the National Institute of Standards in Colorado and the University of Innsbruck in Austria. In Austria, particles are routinely teleported from one side of the Danube to another, a distance of about 700 meters.

collapse, giving origin to a new cosmovision that is better fit to deal with the world. He cites the age of Mythos, guided by mythical consciousness; the age of Theos, with a theistic mindset; the European Middle Ages with a theistically colored Logos; and the Modern Age, with a mechanistic and manipulative Logos.[136] I wonder if the present seems to be *TM-TM*: Trade Mark, Technology and Money?[i] Whatever the label, as we are experiencing all around us, the financial, social, ecological, and spiritual crises indicate that something in the current cosmovision is not working anymore.

In the previous chapter, I mentioned science and technology as powerful enablers of our cultural paradigm. The suggestion is to approach them with our whole brain, in order to deepen their potential. Technology is already a key enabler for transparency, and by being aware that our actions can be public, it promotes a more ethical behavior. [ii]

Technology has launched a connected humanity, with widespread access to others and to information: This makes us feel closer to each other, understand the sameness in our differences, which in turn allows us to connect in a more compassionate way with others. We actually have the foundation for a more peaceful society, if we learn to harvest the new possibilities these enablers are offering us.

---

[i]   Erich Fromm observed that we live in a society "that rests on private property, profit, and power as the pillars of its existence. To acquire, to own, and to make a profit are the sacred and unalienable rights of the individual in the industrial society." While private ownership is seen as a natural and universal category, it is in fact "an exception rather than a rule," Fromm notes, "if we consider the whole of human history (including prehistory) and particularly the cultures outside Europe in which economy was not life's main concern." Source: Fromm, E. (2011). *To have or to be?* New York: Continuum International Publishing Group, p. 57

[ii] In a session of the European Community in 1989, environmentalists presented a report about the dangers of industrial agriculture to an audience of policy makers and industry leaders. As they described the environmental problems in Western Europe, an executive from a leading French corporation threw up his hands exclaiming: "Yes, yes, OK! But just leave us the Third World!" Can you imagine this happening today, in our Facebook and Twitter world?

Chapter 10

An Opportunity to Evolve

What if all these problems we're facing were in fact opportunities to get away from what is haunting us? There is a Buddhist saying that difficulties and pain are our teachers. So what is here for us to learn, so that we can evolve, transform, grow, do a leap of consciousness?

I found that four of the aspects and values that are part of the problematic mindset – *Achievement, Independence, Competition,* and *Speed* – are actually opportunities to evolve in a profound way. Let's see how.

I am the 'It' if I make it

In Chapter 6, we extensively explored the presence and effects of achievement as an important value in our society and, we could say, in the history of human civilization. The drive for achieving a goal is an important fuel that has led generations to overcome unthinkable obstacles; allocate enormous physical effort; and develop virtues such as patience, persistence, and resilience – not to mention the breakthroughs of disciplined intellectuals. The drive to achieve has shaped civilizations and progress.

Yet there are strings attached. **Achievement** has slightly "moved off center," and become a value manifested through symbols of consumption and status; this has taken a high toll on our planet, and thereby on our collective civilization's home. Our sense of identity is bound to what we "do," to what we achieve and obtain. This not only pushes us into longer working hours, and reduced family time, but it stretches our physical limits and stresses our psychological health. We have become what we do, and depend on how we do it not to mention *if* we do it; otherwise, we sense that for some reasons we are not able to meet our self-set expectations. We are *human doings.*

Our market-driven civilization is both a product and a cause of this pervasive value, creating a circular loop that self-replicates. Receiving the messages of corporations, we are invited through advertising and sophisticated marketing campaigns to measure our imagined achievement through the objects we can purchase. From the consumer side, we buy into a tacit language of symbols, to communicate to our environment "who we are." From the workers' side, we just need this to continue because it contributes to our employment security. The loop, however, moves in a spiral, and we have to work harder, do more to get more, and follow a moving target. Behavioral researchers of the 19th and 20th century from Sigmund Freud to Jacques Lacan (representatives of the achievement civilization) conclude that the desire just never stops, it must be the way we are built: We will always be missing something, and are doomed to an eternal chase.

Try this: Take a blank piece of paper and draw a vertical line down the middle, creating two columns. On the left hand column, list "what makes you *you.*"
Once you've finished, review the list and remove some items, which you would prefer not to lose, but would not deeply impact who you are.
Once you've done this second step, do one more round, removing some further items.
What did you discover about yourself?

But what if we uncovered the connections between achievement and our ego needs? What if we realized that it is *we ourselves* who tie our identity to externalities, only to find the fragility of those ties, and then live in fear they might fray? What if we each realized that our deeper self is actually untouched by what we own or what we lose? This was something that several of the leaders in my study mentioned. For at some point in their careers, Pam,

Connie, Ronald, Daniel, Paul, and Suzanne stopped, perturbed by why they were in that "race" and what they were really after, and questioned the values that were manifested in the achievement and consumption rally.

Some time ago, I had come up with an exercise to explore the ties of identity and to provide an experience of the deeper self. The exercise consisted of preparing a list of "What makes you *you*." The next step was to review that list and remove a few aspects that were "not nice to lose" but that, thinking twice, would not really make you stop being you.

A friend did the exercise over a playful moment during a lunch we shared. She didn't like to take out things, but followed the instructions. Once she had completed the second step, I asked her to go back to the list and take out even more aspects. It was certainly not that she would *like* to lose things such as her job, her intellectual skills, or her partner, but the point was what she could take off the list while still feeling she was who she was. At that point she didn't like the game any more and had a hard time remembering we were playing. She became anxious, and in an irritated tone she handed over the paper and the pen, saying "You can have it all!" in something that sounded like a full resignation of life, not simply of the external anchors of her identity. This is a phenomenon that mirrors what is happening at a societal scale. As we are confronted with the potential loss of the symbolic anchors of our identity (in the form of threats to our security, fears of losing savings, job, possessions or our standard of living) we more easily react from an emotional state, either with violent reactions, excessive defensiveness that manifests as aggression, or denial and depression.

As we talked about her emotional response and what feelings had caused it, she realized that the ties were intense, yet surprisingly there was something of herself that remained after giving away the piece of paper. This may be the question to test: What remains when we let go of the identity anchors? Nothing? What about *being*? In an early morning conversation, spiritual guide Dadi Janki invited the audience to get in touch with what possessions mean. "I don't even own a suitcase," she shared. Now this is a long way from where we are, but the message is not in what we own or strive to achieve, but how much of our identity we anchor on these achievement goals.

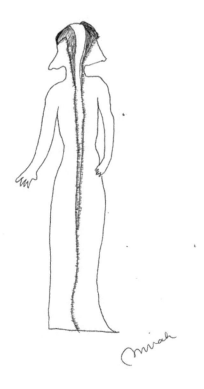

An MBA student reflected about her personal journey confronting her achievement needs in these words:

> I am still as ambitious as ever, I just no longer feel like living my life aspiring to materialistic goals that ultimately won't give me happiness or any lasting sense of contentment and satisfaction. I'd rather aspire to living and working in a sustainable way, creating value for society, consuming as little as possible, and giving as much back as I can ... and if I can inspire even one other person to join me, living in a simpler way, I feel that is the best way to spread sustainable practices. ... People will soon realize how much happier life can be if they quit their jobs and pursue their passions ... if they let go of their fears of not being able to get a new car next year, or having the biggest house ... if they can let go of the fear of abandoning the materialistic value-system ... we can live happier, more sustainable lives where we don't exploit people or the Earth. I want to just stop ...

What happened to this student was a shift in her values, with a direct manifestation in her behaviors, lifestyle, and impact on her social circle. But this shift in her values was more than switching preferences, like from being a fan of one sports team to becoming a fan of another. She found a way to detach her identity from some material symbols of achievement, and still be "herself," or perhaps a more profound and gratifying sense of self. As she expanded her consciousness, she took a step in her personal awareness and this is an irreversible evolution of her self towards a higher level of development. This is what we all collectively need now, and while it sounds intimidating, it is actually just a few steps away from each of us.

I am, you are

Let's face it, the dream of **independence** is not only unrealistic, but also something that only brings trouble when we try to make it happen. As Laszlo points out, all nations of the planet claim sovereignty and independence, but their autonomy is an illusion in a world with "transborder economic and financial flows,"[137] information, goods, weapons, people, and multinational corporations crossing borders permanently in physical and virtual ways. The most intangible travelers are ideas, and we all know that ideas are the seeds of the largest changes humanity has launched.

If ideas are the seeds of changes, what ideas are you harboring that will bring about the changes you want for yourself, your family, community, and environment?

Autonomy and independence are a masculine myth that seeks to enshrine the need for personal power and self-sufficiency in a vain attempt to deny the very order of Nature, which is *absolute interconnectedness* of all that is. In a recent class at the MBA program a student mentioned his surprise and delight when reading a chapter in Paul Hawken's book *Blessed Unrest*. "He provided some background on living organisms and demonstrates how humans are similar to them; in fact, there are very few distinctions," the student wrote. Yes, centuries of civilization may have developed a different perspective, but still we are not only *not different* from Nature, we are actually *part of it*!

In his book *Ecology and Religion*, David Kinsley[138] indicates that the Earth and humanity are part of a cosmic evolution, and to think of ourselves as "different from, separated from, or in control of the natural universe is to define ourselves as rootless, homeless, and estranged." This is precisely how many people feel these days, and in a perpetuating cycle we try to overcome the emptiness and anxiety brought by those feelings of disconnect, seeking more focus on self and self-satisfaction. In justification, we all have heard the analogy of the passengers in a plane – in case of an emergency, oxygen masks will fall, and you first fix yours before helping someone else. What needs to be added is – fix yours *and* help someone else! And even so, I still ask myself when do we know that "our mask" is sufficiently fixed so that we can turn to do something for the others? This analogy of "me first" may be another trick of our ego to keep us focused on self, with an ever-moving target of unmet minimal satisfaction. As Laszlo suggests, in the past, coexistence worked as long as we believed we were capable of meeting our own needs independently of each other.[139] But we have enough proof by now this is no longer reality, if it ever was. Individual salvation, self-determination, autonomy and freedom to pursue our personal interests and needs are manifestations of an atomistic worldview that no longer holds us to account for the world we live in. We may want to continue defending and pushing that interpretation through, but from environment to economy and society, our newspapers are filled with reports of the push back. Protestant theologian Sallie McFague observes that Christian theology has focused primarily "on the relationship between individual human beings and the divine, minimizing the importance of social and ecological fabric in which human beings live." The importance of the Earth has been downplayed, and in many traditional theologies "became merely the temporary stage upon which the drama of individual salvation is played out."[140] We may dream separately but we must act together and *inter-existence* may be the new word.[141]

Author Peter Block reflects that the "absence of belonging is so widespread that we might say we are living in an age of isolation." The world has become smaller because of globalization, yet this has not necessarily developed a wider sense of belonging. Media, education, institutions, and professions, particularly in the Western culture, promote the inward attention to ourselves, and we live as fragmented units, each one working on its own purpose and needs. The work, Block says, is to overcome this fragmentation in order to create a more positive and healthy future.[142]

Small changes in the way we do things can help foster the connections. To give an example, in my classes we push all the tables against the walls, and leave only chairs in a circle. A student described the impact of that experience in the following words:

> I felt the large open circle was a great way to facilitate discussion and dialogue amongst classmates. Instead of the traditional class-room set-up where everyone faces one direction, the circle allowed every participant to see everyone else. This induced more of a back and forth due to the eye contact and "volleying" of comments.

How do you feel about your level of
connectedness with others?
Very happy? Somewhat happy? Not very
happy?
Is it the number or the quality of connections
that could be improved?

Can you identify in what ways you're
contributing to this situation?

What is one thing you could consider doing
differently to get the outcomes you want?

And another added:

> ... for the first time in my MBA, I could interact and get to know my fellow classmates. The times we spent sharing our beliefs and sometimes very personal details helped create a bond that I hope to keep for a long time.

True, biologically speaking, our bodies self-regulate, our DNA is unique, and our personal history makes us distinct from everyone else. We develop our sense of "I" in the unity of our thoughts, feelings, perceptions, experiences, which give us our "I-ness." Yet, as Russell observes, "when the skin-encapsulated self is taken as the *only* sense of self, we end up seeing the world solely in terms of "I" and "not I."[143] And that is a misleading perspective that takes us into problematic behaviors. *Because no organism lives on its own.*

We need to begin understanding that very basic principle as a first step to bringing it into our awareness in our daily decisions and interactions. Imagine how we would make decisions if we were conscious of the impact they have on a wide, universal scale? This was a question one of the business leaders of my study asked, which triggered a whole revamping of the design and manufacturing processes of the multinational corporation she was working in.

How would we interact with others if we kept in mind that we depend on others, even when we don't even imagine we do? I learned this lesson many years ago, and my teacher was the doorman at the Argentine Consulate in Paris. As I was leaving the building he greeted me and asked me if I had found what I came looking for. I was tempted to give a mechanical nod with my head and continue walking, but I thought it was impolite from my side, and stopped for a moment to reply to his question with a full sentence. Actually no, I said. But I guess I came to the wrong place, because I was looking for a working permit. And what do you want to work as? he asked. Reluctantly I replied that any work would be fine since I just wanted to stay in Paris. Can you tutor children in Spanish? he asked. And so I ended up having a never-dreamt-of experience of living a month in a 16th-century castle in the heart of Normandy, giving Spanish lessons to the children of a family to which he had recommended me.

Do you have an anecdote about someone who, without their knowing it, unexpectedly helped you and meant something very important in your life?

What would the concept of interconnectedness imply for how we deal with those who think differently, those who act in violent ways or in ways we don't approve of? Here, too, developing the awareness of how we are all interconnected has a major consequence in our interactions and can build more peaceful environments. Numerous religious teachings and modern self-help texts suggest that when we hold resentment towards other people, the main suffering and pain remains with us, impacting our health of body and mind, and with it our quality of life. These teachings invite us to let go of our feelings of resentment, vengeance, and anger. This concept opened the path of reconciliation in South Africa after the end of apartheid, where offenders were invited to voluntarily attend community meetings, face the family of the victims, and ask for forgiveness. Interestingly, those who had been offended were able to accept a candid expression of repentance; as Psychology Professor Michael McCullough[144] observes, we are wired to switch rapidly into compassion when we sense pain and honest repentance, becoming the consolers of those who actually had harmed us.

When considering the possibility of interconnectedness, the (masculine) fears of dependency as a synonym for powerlessness need to be confronted. But are we really more powerful on our own or, instead, when we act collectively? Small fish gather to be safer when cruising the waters. Birds fly across the hemispheres in flocks rotating their positions. Tsunami survivors in Japan joined to help each other. The financial or housing collapse, the fumes from a volcano in Iceland that paralyzed travel worldwide a few years ago, the climate change related impact on our day-to-day life are unwelcome – yet timely lessons on interdependence. Being confronted with the limits of our "independence and autonomy myth is an opportunity for us to evolve, dropping a value that has not helped us much, and embracing instead a more ancestral one: I am because you are.

The more I base my identity on interdependence, the less I fear losing it. And that awareness brings at the same time a new sense of responsibility: What is the contribution I'm making to the whole? Mike Eldon, Director of the Symphony Group of Companies in Nairobi, Kenya, put his insight into a poem:

The pool of life

Standing over the pool
Close to noon.
The high sun
Casts my puny shadow
Onto an insignificant corner.

I am but a flimsy swaying observer
On the vast surface of the water.

Can I make the slightest impact?
Do I dare try?

Confident, bold,
I plunge in
Swiftly reaching the far end.

Everywhere my motion is felt.
All around the water comes alive,
Is energized.

I turn and swim more slowly, calmly.
And now my calmness
Also spreads.

Lose, so I can win

Is life possible without competition? I asked this question one morning over breakfast with my family. Interestingly, the male responses were uniform. "Absolutely not! You take away the fun! Competing is the challenge, the excitement." The female responses were the opposite. "Definitely! Collaboration is good for all." In her book about ecology, gender, and society, Susan Griffin observes that while women tend to fear competition because it may harm the other or lead to retaliation, men fear closeness and intimacy, which they see as a threat to their power and autonomy. Yet the need for connectedness doesn't disappear, Griffin notes, and historically men were able to find the profound satisfaction of collaboration by bonding for a common cause – which could be fighting for the same purpose, against the same enemy, or cheering for the same team. Through those means, men are able to escape the fragmentation, the "separation from the other" felt when competing.[145] The desire to serve and feel an active part of a larger whole, bringing to our life meaning and purpose, remains, and there are just different ways to achieve those deep-seated human drives.

Author and filmmaker Helena Norberg-Hodge studied the population of the Tibetan region of Ladakh, and was made aware of the assumptions she carried from her own culture: that human beings were "essentially selfish, struggling to compete and survive." Instead, she found in this village another reality – "the Earth nor other human beings are separate, there is no strict boundary between self-interest and the needs and concerns of others. One person's gain is not another person's loss. Mutual aid, rather than competition, shapes the economy."[146]

This finding is not an isolated phenomenon, contrary to what we may have come to believe based on the "Darwinian" interpretations of survival of the fittest, and the kill-or-die binary paradigm. European archaeologist Marija Gimbutas, who studied extensively ancient civilizations, found in her excavations in Southeastern Europe and the Mediterranean artifacts that pointed to a different interpretation of the Neolithic cultures. She discovered an extremely peaceful Goddess-oriented culture, with seemingly no weapons or war artifacts and no traces of hierarchy in the society, but a practice of complete equal rights between the sexes, socially, politically, and spiritually. The artifacts found denoted widespread artistic crafts, sculptures, musical instruments, and woven products. The most interesting aspect of these discoveries that challenge the traditional archeological theories of a "male-dominated, warrior characteristic of human nature," is that this civilization lasted for at least 25,000 years!

Gimbutas's findings (which were very controversial and attacked by traditional archeologists) became the foundation for social scientist Riane Eisler's influential book *The Chalice and the Blade.* Motivated by her early childhood experiences of the Nazi regime, Eisler explored in her book (now translated into 23 languages) whether domination was indeed a part of human nature. Going beyond the traditional dichotomies of right versus left, religious versus secular, Eastern versus Western, Northern versus Southern, and capitalist versus socialist, she looked for patterns and found the dichotomy of *Domination versus Partnership system.* Researching throughout history, myths, and prehistory, she was able to identify an early Partnership system in civilizations such as the European Minoan Crete, which, "while not ideal, was more peaceful, had a more equitable distribution of wealth, and was more gender balanced." Before that, Neolithic societies, such as Catal Huyuk in Anatolia, were equally peaceful, and more egalitarian, and they honored and venerated Mother Earth, "as we still see in some indigenous traditions today."[147] Eisler found the Partnership model in the early Western traditions, followed later by a Domination system. The Domination system has been evident throughout history in different versions: men dominating men, men dominating women, religions dominating other religions, men dominating Nature. Interestingly, it was followed by yet another evolutionary shift, manifested in numerous movements challenging the Domination model. She finds the signs of this shift in the abolitionist, anti-colonial, civil rights, and women's rights movements, fighting the domination of one race, one civilization, or one gender over another. The challenge to the Domination model is also manifested through other causes against different types of violence, and even in the environmental movement, which is challenging the superiority of men over Nature and proposing a partnership. The findings about a cycle of *partnership–domination–challenge* may be not exclusive to Western civilization: A recent study performed in China found a similar evolution cycle in the Asian civilization.[148]

Cooperation has also been found among the hunter-gatherers, where with the exception of times of extreme deprivation, the rule seemed to be that when some ate, all ate, according to anthropologist Michael Gurven.[149] University of California anthropologist Sarah Blaffer Hrdy equally found that humans survived mostly because of cooperative skills, rather than fighting over territories.[150] This is also found in primates' behaviors, where aggression and combativeness would mean the destruction of the more subtle cooperative behaviors that hold the monkey colonies together, ensuring the survival of the group, according to primate biologist Kim Wallace.[151]

Think of a situation where you acted with another person very much in mind.
Then think of another situation where you realize you did not act with the other in mind.

How were your actions (and the consequences) different?

What new insights does this bring you?

Eisler warns that cooperation does not necessarily mean entering a partnership paradigm, since within the domination model there are numerous examples of individuals teaming up and cooperating for subduing others and exerting violence or abuse. We need to think of cooperation as it is manifested in Nature.

Fritjof Capra describes partnership as the essential characteristic of sustainable ecosystems, where there are cyclical exchanges of energy and resources. "The tendency to associate, establish links, live inside one another, and cooperate, is one of the hallmarks of life."[152] In human society, partnership is democracy and personal accountability, with each single member of the community playing an important role and acknowledged as such. As members act with the other in mind, they can co-evolve, learn, and change.

In addition, while pursuing our self-interest we may not necessarily mean to act in socially unacceptable ways, yet the hidden consequences of our daily decisions, habits, and behaviors may be the ones that are unethical, suggests Willis Harman, as he describes the global mind change we need to adopt.[153] I reflect that as he wrote this, in the mid-1990s, he was thinking of the impact on future generations. But today, we know that it's no longer a concern for the livelihood of those not yet born, but our own, very current life as we've known it.

Considering the perspective of the other is not only a way to expand our understanding, and to avoid polarizing conflicts, but also helps in transcending the limiting framework of the "either/or" logic.[i] Developmental psychologists affirm that in human development there is a progression from a self-centered, egotistic, either/or thinking, to an inclusive, cooperative, both/and thinking. I recall a conversation back in 2005, when I was starting my doctoral research. Over lunch with a colleague we were discussing environmental illiteracy, and he brought to my attention a recent article in which a journalist was "declaring war on Nature," claiming that since it looked like Nature was raging over humanity, it was about time to fight back, instead of becoming naturalists taking care of the Earth. Nature is not with us, it's against us, this journalist wrote, in a clear either/or paradigm that was threatening his existence. If we consider the collapse of our economic, social, and ecological systems that were anchored in the either/or paradigm, in self-interest with a short-term focus, and in promoting conquest over collaboration, we realize that our paradigm is vastly expired and no longer useful.

---

[i] In a previous chapter, I referred to our binary either/or thinking pattern. This, I observed, was an aspect that the business leaders of my study had abandoned when addressing sustainability-related challenges. They knew – or discovered – that they had to often think both short- and long-term, and that the paradox was part of their complex reality.

Transcending the either/or framework is our real task. Hiro Saionji, President of the Goi Peace Foundation in Japan, observes that we are raised to believe in the existence of enemies. "We harbored conflict and disharmony in our mind." We declare war on terrorism, on poverty, we fight sickness, evil, crime, climate change, and the list goes on. We fill our minds with enemies and focus on defeating them. This struggle will continue for as long as we stay caught in the paradigm of opposing forces. "We must first and foremost rid our own heart of conflict and divisiveness. Only when we are able to achieve wholeness and healing in our own self will we be able to achieve peace and harmony in the world."[154]

So, how is life without competition? Briggs and Peat refer to chaos theory, and suggest we need to think of both/ands here, too- or, as David Bohm would say it, separation without separatedness.[155] This entails competing within the framework of cooperation, agreeing on the broader rules that will allow us to collectively thrive. In sports, the rules of the game permit the game to exist; in our daily relationships, what are the tacit rules that we should be considering, rules that will allow us *collectively* to grow?

What are the activities that you engage in that are very pleasurable for you?

Now picture them as endorphins releasing opportunities that can improve your immune system, reduce stress and charge your batteries—and take them "more seriously"!

Don't leave their occurrence to chance, make time for them to appear.

And this may not be that big of a challenge, after all. According to a 2002 study at Emory University of Atlanta, we are wired to cooperate. In this experiment, a group of women could choose to cooperate or to compete. They not only primarily selected cooperation, but MRI studies conducted during the experiment indicated a release of dopamine in the brains of cooperating participants, showing brain images similar to the those of a person eating chocolate, connecting with sensations of pleasure and satisfaction.[156] Since the experiment was conducted only with female participants, it may not be generalized to both genders. However,

McGilchrist cites scientist Robin Dubar, who connects our "indulging in 'futile' activities" to the release of endorphins observed for example when grooming, listening to music, dancing, smiling, laughing, practicing religion, or experiencing love and togetherness.[157] Feeling good is a good enough reason to evolve.

No time to waste

We have all heard it or talked about it with friends; days are going by faster and faster. "Is it a matter of us aging?" some would ask, recalling that our grandparents used to say time went faster. But nowadays, it's also the youngest generation who notices it. A cosmic acceleration perhaps? And how are we playing in that rhythm, or rather, how are we contributing to it?

In Chapter 6 we explored how doing and getting things faster has become an important value of our civilization, so much so that failure to keep up with the speed expectation can mean a problem. It could mean losing a client if we don't have a "quick" training program; risking our job if we don't keep up 24/7 with emails; losing the attention of others if we don't quickly make a point; or losing market share if we don't keep rapidly developing new products or services. I also named some of the downsides and unwanted consequences. We're running frantically, collectively – we're just not clear where to. The fact that we're collectively doing it, in a sort of tacit agreement to abide by the rules of high speed, does not necessarily make it right. Shared assumptions may appear to be true, but they are not borne out in reality.

A few days ago I was reading the Facebook entries of a friend, who went on a trip that covered Madrid, Marrakesh, Zagora, Girona, Dubrovnik, Split, Hvar, Korkula, Zagreb, Athens, Santorini, Mykonos and I may be missing a few other cities in the list, all in 14 days. His posts were exhilarating, fun, filled with multisensory descriptions of the very diverse experiences, and they left me with the feeling that in reading about them I had been on a rollercoaster ride that lasted two weeks. This vacation didn't seem any different from the rhythm many have in our daily life. Paraphrasing the saying that "whoever dies with the most toys, wins," I would say "Whoever ends up with the most lived experiences, wins." That's a maximization principle. Quantitative maximization.

There is something however that cannot be accelerated or zipped into a compressed time fragment: making meaning. To make meaning of events or encounters, we need to pause, process, quiet down, make an inner silence. Several leaders in my study mentioned that they had to stop at some point and reflect about what they were doing, about the larger picture, about their contribution to society and environmental problems, and about the purpose of their work, their role, their life. Some did it by going on a trip that provided an opportunity to stay away from obligations, while others achieved it in a retreat, or through introspective practices and meditation. During one program, I invited the Masters students to spend one hour in Nature, with no phones, iPods, books or journals. Just staying for one hour on their own, in Nature, with no particular task. One of the students went to a park, and watched children at play. That suddenly brought back memories of her sister, who remained in another country. She cried as she went back in her mind to happy times when they played together, and realized that she hadn't been thinking of, or connecting with, her sister for very long time. She realized that in the vertigo of her busy life in the U.S., she had missed something important. She wrote in her posting how thankful she was for having been triggered to have this strange experience of being in silence, with nothing to do, for one hour.

So what if we slowed down? What would we gain, and what would we miss? In his study on communities, author Peter Block observes that one of the obstacles to overcome is the expectation of speed and scale; when we can overcome this obstacle, we are able to gain depth of connection with self and with others.[158] Speed is a narcotic, that anesthetizes our senses, and we lose the capacity to notice and perceive the more subtle aspects of life. To make it through our shortened attention spans, we need louder volume in order to hear, and brighter signs, such as the advertising competition displayed in Time Square, Manhattan, where brighter and bigger signs are designed to capture the attention of passers-by.

A few years ago, I was visiting the International Fair that took place in Germany. Many countries had their booths, and I was particularly impacted by the Dutch stand. As I stepped inside, I followed a ramp that turned a few times, the equivalent of climbing up to the third floor of a building. Arriving at the end of the ramp, there was a long wall with a picture of a forest landscape, in 1:1 scale. In front of the picture, on the floor, there were some stones and water, and a wooden balcony, along which people were standing. I couldn't understand what this was about. I had climbed the ramp, and there were all these people just watching a picture on a wall? Suddenly, one mother whispers to her son, "There, look there!" What seemed to be a static picture was actually a movie, with the caveat that it was a movie of a forest landscape, and nothing was happening in it. Almost nothing. Every now and then a soft breeze would move some leaves, a cracking noise would indicate there might be some animal (but not visible to the camera). People just stood in silence and watched. Now remember the context: an International Fair displays the best and newest the different nations want to exhibit. Competition for the attention of visitors was paramount. This booth, however, was in sharp contrast with the style of all the others. It was not loud, nor colorful; it didn't have rapid motion, or changing stimuli. Yet, it was more profound for me than any other in the Fair. It made me suddenly stop and reflect. It provoked me to take in the life of Nature, despite the fact that my sensory thresholds were set up for high stimulation.

 What is one area where you would like to try slowing down?

In many parts of the planet, the need to slow down has begun to develop into something that could be called "*the Slow Move-*

ment," emerging as a reaction to the speed trap in which we live. In Australia, a family of three generations took on the initiative to promote and provide information on their website[i] about programs and people taking on "slow" actions. Initiatives of the slow movement make us realize that we are not only rushed at work to complete impossible to-do lists (which, don't get eliminated even if we attend to them in our weekends or evenings), but we also rush our meals, our commute, our meetings, our reading, our family time, our vacations, and our recreational activities. The slow movement is a call to become aware of our self-inflicted speed trap, and suggests ways to take control of our life by slowing down.

We can find the *Slow Food* movement, initiated in Italy in 1989, by Carlo Petrini, to counter the propagation of fast food, threatening the local traditions of growing food, preparing it with family and friends, and paying attention to the tastes while eating. Today, the grassroots organization has over 100,000 members in 150 countries, 1,300 chapters and a network of 2,000 communities committed to the sustainable production of food.[ii]

Città Slow[iii] is the *Slow City* movement, started in 1999 in a small village of Tuscany, Italy and is now in 25 countries. The organization has set out several criteria and cities may apply to become part of the Città Slow network. The cities have to have less than 50,000 habitants, and some of the criteria refer to the city's environmental policy, infrastructure, encouragement of local produce and products, and community and Città Slow awareness. To qualify to be called a Slow City and to use the snail logo, a city must be vetted and regularly checked by inspectors to make sure it is living up to the Slow City standard of conduct.

Following similar values, *Slow Living*[iv] is the name of a summit meeting in the state of Vermont, U.S., that promotes "a more reflective approach to living and work; an approach that is mindful of impacts on the environment, on Earth, and on communities; and that incorporates resilience – our ability to 'bounce back' from the consequences of climate change, resource depletion, and other changes and stresses." The summit is an invitation to realize how we can lead a life that is not guided by the conventional "faster and cheaper" but by slower and better, "where quality, community, and the future matter."

---

[i]   www.slowmovement.com
[ii] www.slowfood.com
[iii] www.cittaslow.org
[iv] www.slowlivingsummit.org

Slow Schools is another manifestation of the slow movement. As University of Colorado Professor emeritus in Education Michael Holt reflects, "the process of education is not about supplying students with lumps of information to be regurgitated on demand. It is about enabling students to learn how to learn. It is also about giving them opportunities to hear what others have learnt (knowledge) and to then discuss, argue, and reflect on this knowledge to gain a greater understanding of its truth for them and of how this knowledge will be of use to them." This approach is not new, and has been used by the Montessori and Waldorf systems for a long time, as well as by home schooling.[159] This perspective led to a major change in the educational system in Japan, where in 2002 the public schools changed the curriculum offering the students much more free time. As Ken Terawaki, a senior official of the Japanese Ministry of Education explained, "our current system, just telling kids to study, study, study, has been a failure. Endless study worked in the past, when Japan was rebuilding. ... But that is no longer the case ... telling them to study more will no longer work. ... We want to give them some time to think."[160]

Slowing down connects with mindfulness, explains Jon Kabat-Zinn, Professor of Medicine Emeritus and founding director of the Stress Reduction Clinic and the Center for Mindfulness in Medicine, Health Care, and Society at the University of Massachusetts Medical School. And mindfulness, a concept used in Buddhism, refers to expanding our consciousness, becoming more profoundly aware, refining the perception of our senses, of learning to listen to our intuition, to our body, and to our mind. When we make silence and slow down, we are better able to develop that awareness, which is a door to wellbeing, compassion, and wisdom.

So when thinking about whether slowing down is at all possible, we can reflect on the fact that hunter-gatherers "worked" about two hours a day, and even at peak harvest times Amish farmers average just eight hours a day. Juliet Schor invites us to try out small changes that can give us more leisure time.[161] Making time and taking time, we may not only discover that we live happier, but also evolve as human beings.

So close

When all the sounds are gone
The chatter silenced
The open eyes don't see
That's when the experience of the Big Self
Takes place.
Not me, but the Universe in me
And me in it.

IR

PART V
BEYOND THE TIPPING POINT: BIG BANG BEING

My interest in sustainability was initially piqued when I wondered why some leaders would decide to champion sustainability initiatives with all the resistance and problems that stance involved as they attempted doing business in such an unusual way. My attention had been drawn in the past few years to a growing number of stories about environmentally friendly initiatives, about examples of corporate citizenship, and about innovative business ideas for products and services that could "do good" while bringing in "good money." Then, I became intent on delving beyond the newspaper stories; I wanted to explore *the persons* behind these initiatives. I was curious to uncover their motivations, what inspired them, what informed them, or what pulled them towards an uncertain goal, and I assumed that I might find something that we could replicate as we developed the next generation of leaders.

Who would have guessed where my initial questions would take me! Listening to their stories I learned a lot about what inspired them, the numerous triggers and moments of deep insight that pushed them to act; and I was fascinated by their interesting personal transformations, and by the way they were now looking at themselves, their roles, and also at the world itself. Insights about their values, their spirituality, and their mindset began to emerge through the accounts of their journeys. Aware as I was that this small number of cases was not enough to permit me to draw any generalizations, I still reflected on the findings from an exploratory perspective. I felt like an ethnographer studying an uncharted territory.

The findings triggered my next question. These leaders went through a particular personal journey that led them to new insights. The information they gleaned about the impact of human behaviors on the environment played an important role, since their expanding awareness motivated them to take action. But with the increasing attention detailed in the media towards climate, financial, and social crises, why was change not happening faster? I decided to take a closer look searching for the aspects of the mindset that we collectively share in the Western culture that were contributing to our "unsustainability." There must, I reasoned, be powerful reasons.

Chapter 11

It's Personal, It's People

And so we have arrived at this point where, after exploring the forces holding us trapped in a model that is collapsing, it becomes personal. "Personal," because it was the idiosyncratic way of thinking of each individual I studied that transported them into a different evolutionary level. In fact, it was also beyond thinking; it was some kind of *inner experience*. Robert Walsh, professor of Psychiatry and Anthropology at the University of California at Irvine, has studied the common wisdom at the heart of hundreds of different cultures and traditions. Among the commonalities, he found that there are two realms of reality. One is the dimension of the everyday, where we feel in familiar territory among objects, animals, and people. But beyond this dimension, there is another one, more subtle and profound: "the realm of consciousness, spirit, Mind or Tao."[162] This dimension, Walsh argues, is not where we conduct our business or have our daily interactions. It is a dimension to which we are not trained to pay attention, yet when we tune in to it, it gives us a feeling of deep familiarity. In a recent workshop, a participant – an engineer in a car manufacturing company – described it in these words: "I don't know what happened ... I am not the same person as two days ago ... I connected with something inside, like a place that is profoundly familiar to me, yet where I notice I haven't been for years, for many years ..."

 Do you know what I'm taking about? Have you had a similar experience? If so, how would you describe it? Have you ever talked about this to anyone?

Some people access that dimension through meditation, reflective practices, closeness to Nature, and through observing or expressing oneself through art. Independently of how we access this other dimension, it is an inner experience, and it is not about the "doing" and handling of our daily chores and businesses. It's not found in the technical thinking that aims to solve our problems, and yet it is at the foundation of finding deeper solutions.

The experience of two realities is not a new phenomenon, although it may become more obvious as more and more individuals seek a deeper meaning for their lives. British religious thinker and author Karen Armstrong studied what German philosopher Karl Jaspers called the *Axial* a period between 900 and 200 BCE that was key to the spiritual development of humanity. In a period of seven hundred years, the world received the wisdom of Socrates, Plato, Euripides, Jeremiah, Confucius, Lao-tzu, Mencius, Buddha, Rabbi Hillel, and many others. What is particularly interesting, Armstrong observes, is that prophets, mystics, philosophers, and poets emerged in a time of extremely war-torn and violent societies. Thus, within the context of that one reality, they pushed the frontiers of human consciousness and addressed the transcendent dimension in the core of human being: the other reality.

During that time, the foundation was laid for what would become the greatest spiritual traditions: Confucianism and Taoism in China; Hinduism and Buddhism in India; monotheism in Israel; and philosophical rationalism with the roots of democracy in Greece. The Axial Age was together with the Western scientific and technological transformation in the 16th century, one of the richest periods of "intellectual, psychological, philosophical, and religious change in recorded history."[163]

But wait a moment! *War-torn and violent societies?* Add climate-related catastrophes and it sounds like our evening news. Helena Norberg-Hodge observes that the introduction of the Western model of progress via consumption and "technological modernization" has been – and is – playing a major role in the breakdown of traditional families and communities. Having lived and studied the culture in the ancient population of Ladakh since the mid-1970s, she could witness how the balanced, self-sufficient farming economy was disrupted by the introduction of imported seeds, fertilizers, and a variety of other imported products against which the traditional agricultural practices could not compete. Men migrated to the larger cities, multi-generational families became more like the Western "nuclear family," and the rich web of community relations was torn apart, creating religious intolerance and a sense of poverty as they compared themselves with Western lifestyles. She quotes words of a resident, Tsewang Paljor, in 1975, saying "We don't have any poverty here," and later in

1983, "If you could only help us Ladakhis, we're so poor." This story is not unlike others in different parts of the world. I recall a presentation by coach Elena Espinal at the International Coaching Conference in Lima, Peru, a few years ago. She was hired by a Mexican government agency to coach and support members of an indigenous community in the southern Mexican state of Chiapas to become self-sufficient by using government-provided loans at very favorable conditions. After a few months into the program, they asked her to travel to the region and explore why people were not applying for the loans. She interviewed them to understand what they were currently doing and how they were managing their subsistence. Are you poor? She asked one man. No, I am not, he responded to her puzzled. "Poor is when you don't have children! Because children help to work and then get married and keep the community going …" A woman who had taken the loan used it to buy a truck, which she kept parked with pride (since no one was driving it). The community leader had accepted a deal with Coca-Cola to allow a soda dispenser in his village in exchange for a new house. He never moved into the house, where he instead kept his cattle. It's very good for cattle! he exclaimed. We didn't move in because our homes are better, our homes don't have tiles on the floor because the earth is cooler in summer and keeps the heat in winter; besides we have the entrance facing east. What Elena Espinal learned and came to share with the audience was that poverty is a descriptor created from within our Westernized-capitalistic perspective; when we apply it to indigenous communities, we disrupt their self-sufficiency, and we *create poverty* by introducing new standards of having that are impossible to achieve, leading to a downward spiral of community breakdown, loss of indigenous traditions and ancestral wisdom, cultural impoverishment, and new urban dwellers.

But we don't need to travel to remote locations to experience this situation. We know this model from up close. Even having grown up in Argentina, part of the "developing world," it became natural for me to hold up models of living that came from the Northern hemisphere: city trumps countryside; intellectual work trumps hand-work; driving a car trumps taking a bus; bigger trumps smaller; faster trumps slower; new trumps old; getting your own apartment trumps staying with your folks. These values were so "natural," unconsciously taken for granted as they shaped my life, that a different perspective felt weird to the point of eccentricity. I recall when my nephew decided to stay in a small village in the mountains, explaining that he didn't like to live in a city. What is wrong with him? I wondered. It took me almost a decade to understand his perspective.

Go back in your mind to when you were growing up.

Were there different values and priorities? What was different?

Living or working in densely populated urban centers, we seek contact with Nature in a flower pot on the balcony, driving to get to a park, or flying to experience a mountain. We have become used to live fragmented lives, isolated from our neighbors under the banner of "independent living." The atomistic worldview that we adopted from science and shaped our mental models has left us prisoners of our own "separatedness," and the lack of connection with the other creates a more fragile sense of identity. So we do more so as to have more, with the hope to "be" more happy. Wanting always more is even declared an essential part of being human, and behavioral scientists that shaped the thinking of several generations warned that our essence is selfish and narcissistic – and only societal culture tries to tame it. But is it so, really? It may be so … in the Western civilization, but not universally, reflects Norberg-Hodge, describing the ancient culture she experienced and studied. We just happen to live in an anthropocentric, materialistic, reductionist, rationalistic and nationalistic culture, ego-centered and left-brain dominated, which makes us fall into the collective assumption that this is all that is. Mistake. This is just *one* reality, and one described from within a particular bubble.

The unmet need

The search for connection does not go away. We seek it in Facebook, LinkedIn, Twitter, and other outlets in the ever-multiplying social media. The search for meaning and deeper values sometimes comes back in the shape of a fundamentalism that clings to a worldview while, in a desperate attempt to make it valid, its defenders declare war on what is different. The search for fulfillment is channeled in the religion of Success and its god, Money. As Danah Zohar and Dr. Ian Marshall observe in their book *Spiritual Intelligence: The Ultimate Intelligence*, we are "spiritually dumb,"[164] searching for deeper purpose in the wrong places.

The Axial philosophers and prophets turned their eyes away from the world, and penetrated the interior world of the individual. It was something that had its origin in the personal realm, and then became manifest in interactions with others.

Turning one's eyes away from the world and tuning into the innermost self opens an interesting window. Since the time I first learned the word "sustainability" in its modern meaning, back in 2005, we have all become more informed and have developed some kind of awareness about how things are not going well on a planetary scale. We have all been looking extensively to the outside. How bad things are going is difficult to establish. We can select from those that claim that irrevocable changes are already happening and we are, as a humanity, moving towards a collapse – the "doomsday" perspective, where we cannot really influence what will happen – to the other extreme, the "we will handle it" with new inventions, ingenuity, human superiority over natural forces, everyone relax and just trust that someone will come up with the right solutions at the right moment. In this connection, an interesting story happened as I was writing this book. An unprecedented heat wave covered the U.S., creating extended drought. One town in Illinois experienced the adverse impact as the water level of their lake sank so much that it made impossible the traditional summer boat race. The lake was barely three feet deep, compared to the minimum five feet needed. Human ingenuity can solve this! A system was set in place to fill the lake, pumping water from the river. This solution was not without its own problems, from the cost of gasoline to overworked pumps burning. But nothing seemed to stop the desire to maintain the entertainment, provide the touristic attraction, and ensure the expected income to the town. Seven days into the pumping, "a few more days will do it," a truck owner explained. Approved by local authorities and a division of the EPA (Environmental Protection Agency), an environmentalist interviewed expressed concerns that the ecosystem of both the lake and the river would be altered. As I listened to the story, I thought it would make for a great joke for stand-up comedians. What next, maybe we can use bottled water imported from … France?

Between these two extremes, from doomsday scenario to "we can solve this" bravado, there are those who are going on with "life as usual," perhaps recycling and sometimes buying organic food, but overall not spending much time pondering the impact of what they consume, drive, produce, or do in their daily life; and there is a growing number of individuals concerned with what they can do to contribute to the change.

Yet there is a very interesting phenomenon: If we pay real attention to the outside, we may feel pain, concern, fear, uncertainty, some urge to act for the greater good. If we are living oblivious to the larger picture and are not paying attention to the critical times of which we're in the midst, this, too, seems to leave us with a "hole in the heart," something that we try to quiet with our next purchase, maybe a vacation, a better job, a better partner, parting, or partying. Victor Frankl said that our search for meaning is the primary motivation in our lives, and when this need is not satisfied, we feel we're living a shallow and empty life. Certainly this deeper need is well understood by marketing and advertising professionals, who tap into this unfulfilled need with the next magic offer that will take care of it; and we are all to some degree happily buying into that illusion, which (we unconsciously assume) would make things so much easier.

But the emptiness comes back, like an unmet need. Several of the individuals in my study mentioned they pondered questions such as "Why am I? Who am I? What does my job mean? What is my life all about?." Authors Zohar and Marshall observe that two of the top ten causes of death in the Western world are suicide and alcoholism, frequently related to a crisis of meaning.[165] And we have many other less dramatic symptoms, such as workaholism, addictions, or stress, that are either socially accepted or dealt with by means of cruise-packages, Red Bull, or Prozac.

Helena Norberg-Hodge didn't find any signs of lack of meaning in the Ladakh community. There is definitely something connecting these symptoms with the way we have organized our lives.[i]

Shift the focus and the paradigm will follow

Now thinking of organizing our life differently is not necessarily the right ,approach, because it may take our attention away from the real focus, which is our deeper self. It doesn't seem to be something to just fix "on the outside," but, rather, to first address in the inside. Going back to the findings of my study, the cornerstone of the wonderful initiatives those leaders championed was not found in the motivation to do better business or to develop more sustainable products: *the cornerstone was in the shift of their mindset*, in the deeper questions they pondered, in the systemic understanding of their context, in the awareness of the interconnectedness, in the personal quest for meaningful action.

It seems as if their breakthroughs came because of a shift from

doing (activity, busy-ness)

having (material possessions)

being (someone)

to a focus on

being

knowing-what-to-do (purposeful action)

having (inner balance and peace).

And these leaders were not alone in their unplanned journeys of mindset shift. They may have not noticed it, but the shift has been happening in different places on our planet, in a rather disconnected way. Willis Harman observed over a decade ago the signals indicating that we were into a mind change. He saw it in healthcare, education, business, and finances, and in a rethinking

---

i And at the same time, we may be entering into a new phase of evolution, expanding our consciousness. If you look back into your own life, do you find that your consciousness has expanded? If you watch movies from 15, 20, or 50 years ago, do you find them naïve? Are the themes and the dialogues impossible to imagine in our day, as if people then were looking through a narrower cylinder?

of national security and delegitimizing war.[166] This wave has only been expanding since, and at a faster rate.[i] Professor and author Peter Senge commented recently about a project to fully transform our educational contents and methods, which are still based on the Industrial Revolution concept and are definitely no longer relevant to the challenge of our times. Paul Hawken started a global inventory of grassroots organizations working for the betterment of the world, and estimated that there are over a million such organizations worldwide. The Institute of Noetic Sciences, California, found a subculture in the U.S. based on a shift from competition to reconciliation and partnership; from greed and scarcity to sufficiency and caring; from outer to inner authority (inner wisdom); from mechanistic worldview to systemic perspective; from separation to connectedness and wholeness.[167] Peter Russell, author of *The Global Brain Awakens*, indicates that the number of persons actively involved in consciousness work is rapidly increasing, doubling every four to five years.

The "hole in the heart" became also manifest in the famous "course on happiness," which was the name students gave to a Harvard college course on "Positive Psychology." Already in 2006, this class had the highest enrollment in the university – 855 students, surpassing the traditional Introductory Economics, and motivating Professor Tal Ben-Shahar to create an online version a couple of years later. The class focuses on the psychological aspects of a fulfilling life, exploring happiness, empathy, self-esteem, friendship, love, success, creativity, spirituality, and even music and humor, all from a "serious, respectable scientific perspective," of course. Let's not forget that our left brain is still in charge.

---

i   The global edition of the *New York Times* posted a blog on July 4, 2012 connected to the UN's meeting to discuss the International Arms Trade Treaty, pointing out that there are around 639 million small arms and light weapons in the world today, and 8 million more are produced every year. This means one small weapon for every one person out of 11 in the world. As a commentator on National Public Radio reflected, weapons sales are big business, particularly for the five permanent members of the UN Security Council – the United States, Russia, China, Britain, and France – which, along with Germany, are the largest suppliers. Someone must be planning how to arm the other 10 people. The transparency that uncontrollable social media and the Internet are bringing to our world is what prompts and accelerates change. It was easier to be inconsistent – to advocate for some values and behave in contradiction to them and get away with it – when it was all kept in the dark, hidden from the public eye.

It's a nice start, though. New York University Professor Carol Gilligan[168] extensively explored the masculine perspectives shaping Western civilization, and the impact of our civilization's neglect of the feminine contribution. In previous chapters, I have already suggested the connection of the undervalued right brain perspective and the aspects that are characterized as "yin" or feminine: compassion, intuition, empathy, connection to Nature, sensitivity, feelings orientation. It's easy to think in terms of opposites:

- Law and rules versus relationships and exceptions
- Autonomy and competition versus connection and collaboration
- Confrontation versus conciliation
- Power versus service
- Logic and analysis versus perception and intuition

Now the invitation is precisely to step away from our *either/or* logic, and to think of these as *both/and* polarities, not as mutually exclusive choices. Some of these opposites need to be redefined to allow space for the other polarity – as we discussed when addressing competition, independence, rational thinking, or power – because the way we are used to thinking of them doesn't consider any other option: Power is "power over" not "power with"; confrontation implies right/wrong, and does not allow the coexistence of different perspectives; competition is either me or you, not "let's both perform at our best"; autonomy is "I will do what is best for me," not "let's do individually do what is best for the whole."

Polarity Management author Barry Johnson indicates[169] there are situations where we are confronted with a false choice, and we struggle because we cannot just select one option. Collaboration and connection are important, but we also need privacy and time for self. Intuition is important, and so are words to break down the holistic perception and share our thinking with others. We know that we are in front of a polarity when we cannot take just one option. As my colleague Beena Sharma said it eloquently, we cannot choose breathing in; we also need breathing out.

Besides, studies have demonstrated that creativity is augmented when the two brain hemispheres function in an electro-magnetically integrated, whole-brain manner. In addition, meditative states reveal a balanced, whole-brain functioning. When both hemispheres work as one, awareness is heightened, perception and recall are clearer, and flexibility increases, getting us into a state of "superlearning."[170] We may be ready to pay more attention to these aspects, whether it is to live a more holistic life integrating yin and yang or, if we prefer to stay in the pragmatic perspective, to use our brain capacity more fully.

The one personal task

What doesn't change is the fact that the mindset shift is definitely a personal task. Christopher M. Bache, Professor of Religious Studies at Youngstown State University, observes that the experiences of the great mystics in humanity's history were a journey from ego-attachment and separateness from others, through a period of transition described with the metaphor of a "dark night of the soul," to a spiritual rebirth, entering a new stage of consciousness. Anyone visiting this planet from outer space and observing how we live and interact, and the problems we're facing, could easily report that we're living that dark night – and this would be good news, since dawn must be close. As American author and philosopher Henry David Thoreau noted, "Only that day dawns to which we are awake." (Are you awake?)

But I want to make an important distinction. The personal task is not reserved for the enlightened, the philosophers, the gurus, the sages. The mind-shift is a personal task for everyone, and we all are fit, prepared, and equipped to accomplish it – or should I say, to *flow* into it. It is not so much connected with what we learned, but with what we know deep inside, and I'm referring to a wisdom that is equally distributed among all people. This is the reason that great spiritual traditions invite us to espouse silence, to go inside, to connect with self, going to the center from the center. No age, gender, ethnic or economic discrimination here.

The questions are personal, since they are about our own lives, and so are the answers we have to find. We all have our own particular history and characteristics, which make us different the same way the cells of our body are differentiated for particular functions. Russell[171] presents an excellent example: On a micro level, each particle is different and pursues its role. We have several trillion cells, each acting in its own interest. As we look at them from a broader perspective, we can observe how each cell is playing its role for the whole body to function. Cells are part of a high degree of synergy, and we know that when one part doesn't play its role, the impact can rapidly be felt in several other parts of the body.

Russell considers that human society today appears to be in a state of low synergy, and this is a reflection of the way the members of society perceive themselves in relation to the world around them. A recent story comes to my mind. Given the extreme heat wave and drought in several regions of the country in the summer of 2012, several communities banned fourth-of-July fireworks and barbeques to prevent further wild fires. I heard on the radio a man in the Midwest indicating that he was not stopping a tradition that was nice for him and his kids. They can come after me later, he said, quietly and defiantly. Democracy is messy, I thought, especially when we act on our "autonomous rights" as if we were a separate cell outside of any body. But then I also think of the many community actions, where individuals come together for a common cause but with very disparate ideas of how to proceed. Conversations become challenging yet agreements are reached and proposals are implemented. They are the uncountable, small initiatives that are making this world a better place.

Democracy is messy, yes, when everyone is acting as a separate cell, unaware of the body to which we all belong. Once we understand this basic principle of interconnectedness, we realize how our actions are impacting others, and vice versa. This is the turning point, when we can feel from the other's perspective; we empathize, just as the leader in my study empathized with a farmer not letting go of a single coffee plant, even though it meant losing the house Habitat for Humanity came to build for him. And when we feel the connection to the other, something in our thinking shifts, too. We have a harder time going back to how we saw things before.

There is a joke where two men talk in a bar. Do you like Jews? one asks. No, the other replies. What about Protestants? Nope. And Muslims? No. What about Hispanics? No... But you like blacks? Nope... Hey, you really don't like anyone!! Well, *I do like my friends!* the other replies.

When we get to know someone better, their skin color, ethnicity or beliefs vanish in the background. That person becomes a person, not a demographic data.

Think of sometime in your life when this happened to you, that as you met someone personally, you changed your perspective and dropped some of your prejudices and assumptions.

What insights do you get from this?

Feeling–thinking–acting is a reinforcing cycle. We shape our reality with the way we think, with the assumptions we hold and share, with the thoughts that manifest in our actions and interactions. A famous quote of Lao Tzu advises *"Watch your thoughts; they become words. Watch your words; they become actions. Watch your actions; they become habit. Watch your habits; they become character. Watch your character; it becomes your destiny."* Helena Norberg-Hodge, who marveled at the sight of the peaceful and joyful community of Ladakh, observed that community members showed a healthy self-esteem and inner security, and little signs of self-doubt. As a result of such positive energy, they interacted with high degrees of tolerance and patience towards other community members, accepting their differences. And as a result, the community was safe, void of aggression, and relatively conflict-free.

In a different context, just consider your feelings when you talk to a stranger who looks at you with a stern, serious face, and how they change when the person suddenly offers you a bright smile. Unconscious fears about the "stranger" vanish, and we naturally feel safer. Our conversation will be tinted by those feelings. I recall many years ago I was traveling for the first time with the man who later became my husband and life partner. We arrived at a secondary airport in the northern region of Brazil, and half a dozen poorly dressed local men approached us to sell us services – taxi rides, hotels. I immediately associated the situation with the warnings I had heard in other places, even in Buenos Aires – don't talk to strangers, don't accept offers from strangers. I began to rapidly open a path for myself, avoiding eye contact, when I noticed that my traveling companion remained behind, engaging in a conversation with one of the men. Neither one spoke much of one another's language, so I stepped back trying to help him "get rid" of the dangerous stranger. To my surprise, they were smiling and laughing, using signs and manifestly having a good time. When I suggested we walk away, he replied, "Wait a moment, he has a hotel for us, an excursion, he has some tourist information we need"! Long story short, we received wonderful attention, advice, and help for what we wanted to do. And the whole interaction was so joyful for everyone who was involved – except for me, who was still learning and processing in disbelief... It took me some time to learn that lesson: we live what we think, our thoughts create reality.

What power we have, if we realize we can decide what to think.

At a recent retreat in Oxford, UK, Dadi Janki was asked what to do when we "go back into the world," with all its negativity, fears, and violence. "Watch your thoughts," she replied. "Pay attention to the thoughts you let into your mind. If they are toxic, it will not help you or the others. Think of your mind as a boat, floating among some toxic waters. If you let the water in, you won't be able to bring others into your boat, it will sink. Use the mind-boat to bring positive thoughts of hope and compassion – and so you will create hope and compassion in the world."

When we evolve inwardly, we generate outward evolution.

This is what makes the change of mind, the change of heart so powerful. As we become aware of our pace, our values, how we're self-inflicting our problems, we can pause to ponder, and simply be in silence. We have the opportunity at hand any time during the day. Nothing in the outside is powerful enough to stop us from going inside and listening to ourselves, to take a minute for a quick trip into our deeper self. The spiritual organization Brahma Kumaris has a habit of playing soft music every hour, for one minute. Whenever the music sounds, people stop what they are doing – eating, writing, chatting, giving a speech, moving. They stay where they are and simply do nothing to experience the silence of the nothing.[i] Many participants consider this habit one of the most valued take-aways.

It's people

A few years ago I was taking my morning walk on the beach, picking up garbage, when I picked up a pair of sunglasses. They looked pretty new, so I kept them in my hand. A few yards later, I saw a pair of goggles. I picked them up, and since they seemed in good shape, I kept them. Not too many steps later, I saw a snorkel mask lying on the sand! I picked it up, and thinking of my husband, who likes to snorkel, decided to keep it, too. So here I was, walking with these three objects, when I suddenly became aware that they were all "looking" devices! Is there a message here for me? Should I be seeing something? *Is this something personal?* I had barely finished

---

[i] We have adopted this powerful habit, and in our Minervas (Minervas.org) sessions we call it "The minute of the Butterfly." In some Hispanic countries, they say that when there is a sudden minute of silence in a group, an angel passes by.

thinking that question when I noticed a little red shimmer in the sand, something that looked like a rubber bracelet. I bent over to explore it, and saw a bracelet like the ones for certain campaigns. I looked at it closely to find out what campaign it was about, and saw the engraving: IT'S PERSONAL. I froze. I looked at it again: Had I read it clearly? Yes. *IT'S PERSONAL.* I turned it to see what campaign it was, and found another engraving: IT'S PEOPLE. Unable to understand what this meant, yet profoundly touched, I put the bracelet on. I knew it was a message, but I couldn't understand it, and I decided to wear it until I figured out what I had to learn. Coming from an individual-focused worldview as I was, I could understand that something was personal: self-awareness through personal therapy, personal development through coaching, personal learning through reading and training ... but what was this connection with *it's people*?

Research has shown that people meditating together tend to move into collective patterns of synchronized brainwaves. This connects with what is called "phase lock" in chaos theory. Phase lock occurs in Nature when individual systems shift into an integrated resonance. Bache gives the example of individual cells, taken from a chicken embryo heart, that are separated from each other and continue beating, erratically. When they are recombined, once a certain number of cells is reached, it becomes a tipping point and they all synchronize to beat in unison again.[172]

We all have experienced some kind of "phase lock" when attending a live concert and connecting with the multitude, or when watching a live football game and tuning in with the crowd, or when participating in a public demonstration supporting a cause.

Aimee Bernstein, who is an energy coach[i] and used to be a rock singer in the 1970s, shared how she misses the "magnetic energy" she experienced when the band was performing; there was something larger than the sum of the musicians. Something similar was mentioned by pianist and composer Lynne Arriale, who described that when playing music with others, suddenly something magic happens, and "it's like the air fills with bubbles." Physicist David Bohm discovered that the same phase lock can be produced when people sit together in a dialogue. After a period of individuals just sharing what is on their mind, suddenly meaning

---

[i] Aimee Bernstein works with people to unleash their energy through Aikido-type exercises and movement that help bring consciousness of our inner strength. openmindadventures.com

begins to be created collectively, as in a dance. Everyone dances alone, yet the group moves in tune with a rhythm.[i]

Physicists have long been researching the behavior of matter and particles, and as early as the end of 1800, it was discovered that the supposedly indivisible atom had a variety of components, and these elementary particles were dissolving in energy. In addition, packets of energy, called "quanta," appear to have a space- and time- transcending interconnection, a phenomenon physicist Erwin Schrödinger called "entanglement." Since the 1930s, several experiments have confirmed this discovery. Entire atoms, not only packets of energy, can be entangled, and when one is measured, the others show the same unanticipated measurements although far apart from one another. Matter is not composed of parts but of sets of connected relationships.[173]

What implication does this have on our life? One consequence of interconnectedness relates to what we *do*. If we are all connected, it's as if we are all under a blanket, and when someone pulls on one side, it will impact others. What we do, at a personal level, does matter, and so what others do also impacts us. We may not be aware of where the blanket was pulled or by whom, we just experience a change. This thought alone has vast implications in our day-to-day lives: What can be the impact of the decisions we're making? Of the quality of our interactions with others? Is thinking exclusively of personal benefit a realistic option? Or are we just a bit myopic?

A second consequence relates to *thoughts*. As we have been examining earlier, thoughts generate feelings and actions, and thoughts create realities. And thoughts are ultimately energy. We are shaping our reality, and since we act within our context, we are also shaping the reality for those around us. We don't even need to enter the domain of quantum physics for this. I recently realized how different spiritual practices have in common the importance given to intentional thoughts. Whether it's through prayer, meditation, blessings, or chanting, the widespread wisdom seems to give a particular value to intentional thoughts. If I look back at the lesson I began to learn in the Brazilian airport, thinking the best of the other person created a self-fulfilling prophecy, it brought the best out of the other. When we launch this loop, it bounces back to us, with a good feeling of care and respect. And then this elicits our

---

[i] A similar "phase lock" may be the reason that during fascist regimes, so many otherwise ethical individuals bought into actions that later in time seemed totally unacceptable for them.

next positive response again, and it begins to expand beyond the initial scene. We are left with a warm, fuzzy feeling that the world today is a good place – and with that in our mind, we enter smiling the next shop, and after a moment of puzzlement, the person possibly begins to relax and smile back. That on which you focus grows. Maybe we forget that we decide what to think?

> We are all expanding circles
> Circles of intention
> Circles of attention.
> With each interaction
> We send out waves
> To shores we will never see,
> And not even imagine.
> But there is one thing
> We must remember:
> With each word
> With each look
> And each thought
> We are all expanding circles.
> *IR*

Another implication of the connectedness is more subtle than acting or even thinking. This one is about simply *being.* Jon Kabat-Zinn , founding director of the Stress Reduction Clinic and the Center for Mindfulness in Medicine, Health Care, and Society at the University of Massachusetts Medical School,[174] indicates that we can impact others just by our pure presence. We can calm someone down just by being calmly present, or we can switch the mood of someone who is worried without doing anything other than showing up. A presence filled with lightness, a floating presence, shines something that is perceived by others at an intuitive level, not at a rational one. "There is something different about you today … Did you change your hair style? That color suits you well … I like your socks." We are simply not trained to acknowledge when we connect to the energy of the other in a non-conscious, intuitive dimension. So it's more common to seek something tangible to attribute the imprecise perception. Yet our sensors capture this energy connection, we just don't know how to describe it, and our left-brain-dominating culture has not even provided words to talk about "it" in a "respectable" way.[i]

---

[i] We do, however, have derogatory expressions – woo-woo, quackery, new agey, true-believer, kumbaya – that represent the softened version of the

In order to beam a positive presence, we need first to quiet down and connect with our deeper self, with our center. We need to create that positive presence first. The good news is that we don't have to "do" anything: We can just sit, taking a few minutes to just notice our presence, where we're sitting, how our feet are touching or resting, noticing our back, our head. We don't need to correct anything, just notice it, pushing aside for a moment the to-do list, and giving ourselves the brief experience that we're right where we need to be, now – that we don't have to be anything else, but just what we are. Feeling like a noodle in the soup of Being.

The links between the personal and people are becoming clearer. As Karen Armstrong observed, the sages of humanity have focused on how individuals act on the world. Is it with power over, or with compassion? They put morality in the center, and it didn't matter what people believed but *how they personally behaved.* Spirituality was to be seen in action, and to encounter "God," "Nirvana," "Brahman," or the "Way," individuals had to start within, transcending the self-centered interest, greed, aggression, and unkindness, and developing empathy and compassion. Benevolence could not stop with one's own people, but had to extend to the entire world. In Buddhist teachings, compassion is the road to enlightenment. Gandhi built his model on the foundation of an individual connected to others via service: to the family, the village, the district, the state, the nation, and the world community. As Gandhi explains: "Life is an oceanic circle whose center will be the individual."[175]

mental models that burned the witches a few centuries ago. The Double-Tongue dictionary, a lexicon of English slang, jargon, and new words defines *Woo-woo* as "concerned with emotions, mysticism, or spiritualism; other than rational or scientific; mysterious; *new agey.* But mostly the term is used for its emotive content and is an emotive synonym for such terms as *nonsense, irrational, nutter, nut,* or *crazy.*"

Exploring the impact of focusing on our thoughts and deeper self, on our personal dimension, has connected us with the people dimension. I can read this message now like a red thread throughout this book: from the beginning, in the interviews with business leaders who were touched in their heart and needed to "act"; in the unsustainable mindset that is personal yet that impacts us collectively; in the mind-change that begins with self, and equally expands the impact in ways we cannot imagine. And maybe even before the writing of this book: when I had my own personal collapse, as I realized that my current life was happy yet meaningless, when I felt the pain of the world deep in my heart and felt the urge to do something.

We shape reality and are shaped by others through thoughts, actions, and mere presence. The image that comes to my mind is that of the Möbius Strip, a geometric object that has curious characteristics. To experiment with it, take a strip of paper, do a half twist and tape the extremes together.

If an ant were to crawl along the length of the band, it would return to its starting point having traversed the entire length of the strip, meaning both sides of the original paper, without ever crossing an edge. Now imagine that you write "it's personal" on one side of the paper, and "it's people" on the other. You would be able to slide from one to the other seamlessly. Very much like what happens to us every day. My bracelet was not exactly like that, but I ended up learning what it meant.

Epilogue

The Earth has nurtured life throughout billions of years, with humanity evolving into where we stand today. We have to take the next step collectively, evolving our consciousness so as to return to a synergistic resonance with all that is. We have played the separateness game for a short time (what are a couple of millennia against the age of our planet!?) and we have been able to see that much of it didn't work – as shown by how we think of ourselves and of others, and how we relate to each other and to the Earth. We saw ourselves as on top of the world, and the pedestal is now crumbling as if struck by an earthquake. It's time to end the experiment and tap into the deeper wisdom we have not forgotten, because we're wired to keep this wisdom within us. What task could be more important?

Many mystics, scientists, and philosophers have explored the evolution of human consciousness, identifying phases, stages, orders of consciousness, and levels of evolution. What these models have in common is the expansion of awareness, the increasing integration of self with all that is, to a point where there is no distinction between the individual and the whole: we feel part of it. This may seem a distant scenario, almost a utopian one, especially when we are reading today's newspaper. However, in the simple statements of the business leaders I interviewed, I could find glimpses of understanding that we are all connected; I could hear comments about the blissful feeling when doing something for others in a selfless way. I found them sharing bits of wisdom that could have come from any of humanity's sages or tribal leaders. All throughout the books that informed my thinking and my writing, I have found fragments of this wisdom. In the insights of Manhattan MBA students, and in the candid comments of a third-world woman with a second grade instruction, I have found it there, too.

We know that every human-triggered change in our history began in the imagination of a single person. The need to share made it the imagination of two, and from there on the contagion of human passionate ideas spread and became shared reality. If this was the process of large revolutions that shaped history in the past millennia, think of the speed of consciousness evolution going viral in our times, when a Facebook post or a Twitter are the spark that overthrow decade-long dictators. We have history to prove that what seemed impossible happened – because some thought it was possible.

And then, so many of our history's largest changes were caused by anger, frustration, desperation, the desire of freedom or fairness. Now think how powerful positive emotions can be. Who doesn't yearn for happiness? Who is not intrigued by, and attracted, to those who are calm, joyful, those who flow through the challenges of life with the lightness of a feather?

When we're tapping in the dark, the tiniest light becomes our guide.

The strong, self-confident, autonomous, and self-empowered individual dominating the world with his will and thinking has brought us a model that went too far on the pendulum. We're learning *Systems 101* in an accelerated course in the everyday news: Yes, we're all connected. And with half a brain we can only go so far.

We may be finally getting back in touch with what we always knew. The age of the *Homo Spiritualis*[i] may be here. This is the time for Big Bang Being, and we each have some light to contribute ...

---

[i] I thank Chris Bache for this wonderful concept of *Homo Spiritualis*. So many things come to being when we learn to name them.

What does Big Bang Being mean for you?

I have said a lot. That's fine; I've chosen to be a coach for people who want to make a difference. So what will you do? Stay with the question, dream, plan, act, and then flow. And don't forget to bubble.

Appendix
The Sixteen Leaders

Name	Gender		Industrial area	Age	Position
	Male	Female			
Carl	x		Retail	75	CEO-Founder, medium-size U.S. MNC
Willie	x		Technology	70	Former VP Product Development, large U.S. MNC
Patrick	x		Technology	66	Former CEO, small U.S. MNC
Michael	x		Food	61	Chairman, large U.S. corporation
Harry	x		NGO	60	President-Founder-association of corporations, NGOs and government
Daniel	x		Household products	56	VP, medium-size U.S. corp.
Diego	x		Coffee	56	President-Founder, small U.S. corporation
Evan	x		Apparel	53	Director, medium-size U.S. corporation
Robert	x		Pharmaceutical	53	VP, large European MNC
Ronald	x		Restaurant	53	Global Sr. VP, large U.S. MNC
Pam		x	Apparel	53	former Director Global Product Design, large U.S. MNC
Connie		x	Retail	49	Director, Legal Affairs, large U.S. MNC
Barry	x		Coffee Coop	47	President, Founder small international Coop
Mark	x		Restaurant	45	Former President and Owner of large U.S. Franchises-in Europe
Suzanne		x	Food	39	VP, R&D, large European MNC
Craig	x		Food	37	VP, Investors Relations, large U.S. corporation

References

Aburdene, P. (2007). *Megatrends 2010: The rise of conscious capitalism.* Charlottesville, VA: Hampton Roads Publishing Company.

Adams, J. D. (2008). Six dimensions of mental models. In J. Wirtenberg, W. G. Russell & D. Lipsky (Eds.), *The sustainable enterprise fieldbook: When it all comes together* (pp. 60–70). Sheffield, UK: Greenleaf Publishing.

Angier, N. (July 23, 2002). "Why we're so nice: We're wired to cooperate." *New York Times.*

Antonites, A. J. (2004). *An action learning approach to entrepreneurial creativity, innovation and opportunity finding.* D.Com. dissertation, University of Pretoria, South Africa.

Armstrong, K. (2007). *The great transformation: The beginning of our religious traditions.* New York: Anchor Books.

Ashmos, D., & Duchon, P. (2000, June). Spirituality at work: A conceptualization and measure. *Journal of Management Inquiry,* Vol. 9 No. 2, pp. 134–146.

Bache, C. (2000). *Dark night, early dawn.* New York: State University of NY.

Bandura, A. (1986). *Social foundations of thought and action: A social cognitive theory.* Englewood Cliffs, NJ: Prentice-Hall.

Barlow, M. (2001, Summer). Water as commodity: The wrong prescription. *The Institute for Food and Development Policy,* Backgrounder, Vol. 7 No. 3.

Belk, R. (1988) Possessions and the extended self. *Journal of Consumer Research,* 15, pp. 139-168

Benyus, J. M. (2002). *Biomimicry: Innovation inspired by Nature.* New York: Perennial.

Block, P. (2009). *Community: The structure of belonging.* San Francisco: Berrett-Koehler Publishers.

Bohm, D., & Edwards, M. (1991). *Changing consciousness: Exploring the hidden source of the social, political and environmental crisis facing the world.* San Francisco: Harper.

Briggs, J., & Peat, F. D. (1999). *Seven life lessons of chaos.* New York: HarperCollins.

Capra, F. (1996). *The web of life.* New York: Anchor Books–Doubleday.

Capra, F. (2002). *The hidden connections.* New York: Anchor Books–Random House.

Capra, F. (2007). Life and leadership: A systems approach (Executive summary). Retrieved December 21, 2007, from www.frtijofcapra.net/management.html

Channon, J. (1992). Creating esprit de corps. In J. Renesch (Ed.), *New traditions in business* (pp. 53–66). San Francisco: Berrett-Koehler Publishers.

Cohen, A. (2011). *Evolutionary Enlightenment: A new path to spiritual awakening.* New York: SelectBooks Inc.

Cohen, B., & Greenfield, J. (1997). *Double dip: Lead with your values and make money, too.* New York: Simon & Schuster.

Connor, M. (2006, Fall). Interview published in *CRO* magazine, Fall 2006, pp. 12–17.

Cooperrider, D. (Ed.). (2004). *Constructive discourse and human organization.* Boston: Elsevier/JAI.

Daloz, L. A., Keen, C. H., Keen, J. P., & Parks, S. D. (1996). *Common Fire: Leading lives of commitment in a complex world.* Boston: Beacon Press.

Dawson, W. J. (2010). *The quest of the simple life.* Qontro Classic Books.

Delbecq, A. L. (2008). Spirituality and leadership effectiveness: Inner growth matters. In John D. Drake (Ed.), (2000) *Downshifting: How to work less and enjoy life more*, San Francisco: Berrett-Koehler Publishers.

Gallos, J. V. (Ed.), *Business leadership, A Jossey-Bass reader* (2nd ed.) (pp. 485–503). New York: John Wiley & Sons.

Ferkiss, V. (1993). *Nature, technology and society: Cultural roots of the current environmental crisis.* New York: New York University Press.

Francine, J. (2010). *The joy of less: A minimalist living guide: How to declutter, organize, and simplify your life.* Medford, NJ: Anja Press.

Gaukroger, S. (2006). *The emergence of a scientific culture: Science and the shaping of modernity.* Oxford: Oxford University Press.

Goleman, D. (1996). *Emotional Intelligence.* London: Bloomsbury Bantam Books.

Griffin, S. (1995). *The eros of every day.* New York: Anchor Books.

Gurven, M. (2004). To give or not to give: The behavioral ecology of human food transfers. In *Behavioral and Brain Sciences*, 27, pp. 543–583.

Harman, W. (1998). *Global mind change: The promise of the 21st century.* San Francisco: Berrett-Koehler Publishers.

Havel, V. (1998, November–December). Spirit of the Earth. *Resurgence.*

Hawken, P. (2007). *Blessed unrest: How the largest movement in the world came into being and why no one saw it coming.* New York: Penguin Books.

Hicks, D. A. (2003). *Religion and the workplace: Pluralism, spirituality, leadership.* New York: Cambridge University Press.

Holt, M. (2002, December). It's time to start the slow school movement. *Phi Delta Kappa*, Vol. 84 No. 4, pp. 264–271.

Hrdy, S. B. (2011). *Mothers and others: The evolutionary origins of mutual understanding.* Cambridge, MA: Harvard University Press.

Hughes, D. J. (1974). *Ecology in ancient civilizations.* Albuquerque: University of New Mexico Press.

Jackson, T. (2011). *Prosperity without growth: Economics for a finite planet.* London: Earthscan Dunstan House.

Johnson, B. (2000) *Polarity Management: Identifying and managing unsolvable problems.* Amherst, MA: HRD Press

Kabat-Zinn, J. (2005). *Wherever you go there you are: Mindfulness meditation in everyday life.* New York: Hyperion.

Kahane, A. (2011). *Power and love: A theory and practice of social change.* San Francisco: Berrett-Koehler Publishers.

Kegan, R. (1994*). In over our heads.* Cambridge, MA: Harvard University Press.

Keogh, M. (Ed.) (2011). *Hope beneath our feet: Restoring our place in the natural world.* Berkley, CA: North Atlantic Books.

Keogh, P. D., & Polonsky, M. J. (1998) Environmental commitment: a basis for environmental entrepreneurship? *Journal of Organizational Change Management*, Vol. 11 No. 1, pp. 38–49.

Kinsley, D. R. (1995). *Ecology and religion.* Upper Saddle River, New Jersey: Prentice Hall.

Kristof, N.C. After recess: Change the world. *New York Times*, February 4, 2012. www.nytimes.com/2012/02/05/opinion/sunday/kristof-after-recess-change-the-world.html

Laszlo, E. (1989). *The inner limits of Mankind.* London: Oneworld.

Laszlo, E. (2010). *Chaos Point 2012 and beyond.* Charlottesville, VA: Hampton Roads Publishing Company, Inc.

Laszlo. E. (2008). *Quantum shift in the global brain: How the new scientific reality can change us and our world.* Rochester, VT: Inner Traditions.

Leffer, N. (2006, April/May). The sustainable skyline. *Worthwhile*, 2, pp. 72–74.

Liebig, J. E. (1994). *Merchants of vision: People bringing new purpose and values to business.* San Francisco: Berrett-Koehler Publishers.

Lotspeich, C., & Larson, A. (2006, Spring). Systems innovation and entrepreneurship in the green building industry. *Batten Briefings.* University of Virginia, Darden School of Business.

McCullough, M. (2008). *Beyond revenge: The evolution of the forgiveness instinct.* San Francisco: Jossey Bass.

McGilchrist, I. (2009).*The Master and his emissary: The divided brain and the making of the Western world.* New Haven and London: Yale University Press.

McKibben, B. (2011). *Eaarth: Making a life on a tough new planet.* New York: St. Martin's Griffin.

Min Jiayin. (1995). *The chalice and the blade in Chinese culture: Gender relations and social models.* China Social Sciences Publishing House.

Mirvis, P. H. (1997). Soul work in organizations. *Organization Science,* Vol. 8 No. 2, p. 193.

Mitroff, I., & Denton, E. (1999). *A spiritual audit of corporate America: Multiple designs for fostering spirituality in the workplace.* San Francisco: Jossey-Bass.

Moore Lappé, F. (2011). *Ecomind: Changing the way we think, to create the world we want.* New York: Nation Books.

Morowitz, H. (1992). *Beginnings of cellular life.* Yale University Press.

Munju Ravindra (2011). Wonder: A practice for everyday life. In Martin Keogh (Ed.), *Hope beneath our feet: Restoring our place in the natural world* (p. 186). Berkeley, CA: North Atlantic Books.

Nair, C. (2011). *Consumptionomics: Asia's role in reshaping capitalism and saving the planet.* Singapore: John Wiley & Sons.

Neal, J. A. (2008a). *Leadership and spirituality in the workplace.* Retrieved July 15, 2009, www.judineal.com/pages/pubs/leadership.htm

Neal, J. A. (2008b). *Spirituality in the workplace: An emerging phenomenon.* Retrieved July 15, 2009, www.judineal.com/pages/pubs/phenomenon.htm

Norberg-Hodge, H. (1991) *Ancient futures: Lessons from Ladakh for a globalizing world.* San Francisco: Sierra Club Books.

Ornstein, R. (1997). *The right mind.* San Diego, CA: Harcourt Brace & Company.

Palmer, P. J. (2004). *The hidden wholeness: The journey toward an undivided life.* San Francisco: Jossey-Bass.

Menon, A., & Menon, A. (1997, January). Enviropreneurial marketing strategy: The emergence of corporate environmentalism as market strategy. *Journal of Marketing,* Vol. 61 No. 1, pp. 51–67.

Porter, T. (2008). Managerial applications of corporate social responsibility and systems thinking for achieving sustainability outcomes. *Systems Research and Behavioral Science,* Vol. 25 No. 3, p. 397. Retrieved July 27, 2009, from ABI/INFORM Global (Document ID: 1567392531).

Quinn, L., & Dalton, M. (2009). Leading for sustainability: Implementing the tasks of leadership. *Corporate Governance,* Vol. 9 No. 1, pp. 21–38.

Rimanoczy, I. B. (2010). Business leaders committing to and fostering sustainability initiatives, Doctoral Dissertation, Teachers College, Columbia University.

Rimanoczy, I., & Turner, E. (2008). *Action reflection learning: Solving real business problems by connecting earning with learning.* Palo Alto, CA: Davies-Black Publishing.

Rogers, M. E. (1994). Learning about global future: An exploration of learning processes and changes in adults. Unpublished doctoral dissertation. University of Toronto.

Russell P. (2000). *The global brain awakens: Our next evolutionary leap.* New York: Element Books.

Sachs, J. (2011). *The price of civilization: Reawakening American virtue and prosperity.* New York: Random House.

Schleiermacher, F. (1893). *On religion: Speeches to its cultured despisers.* London: Trubner & Co.

Schor, J. B. (2010). *Plenitude: The new economics of true wealth.* New York: The Penguin Press.

Senge, P., & Carstedt, G. (2001). Designing the next Industrial Revolution. *Sloan Management Review*, Vol. 42 No. 2, pp. 24–38.

Senge, P., Scharmer, C. O., Jaworski, J., & Flowers, B. S. (2005). *Presence: An exploration of profound change in people, organizations and society.* New York: Doubleday.

Shuman, M. (2012). *Local dollars, local sense: How to shift your money from Wall Street to Main Street and achieve real prosperity.* White River Junction, VT: Chelsea Green Publishing Company.

Speth, J. G. (2008). *The bridge at the edge of the world.* New Haven and London: Yale University Press.

Steffen, W., Sanderson, A., Tyson, P. D, Jäger, J., Matson, P. A., Moore III, B., Oldfield, F., Richardson, K., Schellnhuber, H. J., & Turner, B. L. (2004). *Global change and the earth system: A planet under pressure.* Berlin, Heidelberg, New York: R. J. Springer-Verlag.

Vaill, P. (1998). *Spirited leading and learning.* San Francisco: Jossey-Bass.

Visser, W. (2007). Corporate sustainability and the individual: A literature review. University of Cambridge Programme for Industry Research Paper Series, No. 1.

Visser, W., and Crane, A. (2010). Corporate sustainability and the individual: Understanding what drives sustainability professionals as change agents. Social Sciences Research Network (SSRN).

Walsh, R. (1999). *Essential spirituality: The 7 central practices to awaken heart and mind.* New York: John Wiley & Sons.

Zohar, D., and Marshall, I. (2000). *Spiritual intelligence: The ultimate intelligence.* New York: Bloomsbury Publishing.

Index

About the Author

Isabel Rimanoczy, Ed.D.
Isabel Rimanoczy is a Legacy Coach, who believes that we all have something amazing to give: We just need to connect with our deeper being to become aware of this. Once we find this deeper being, we can be intentional in making our mark, shaping the world we want to live in.

Isabel is a consultant to corporations and individuals who want to bring the soul to work, and through tailored workshops, webinars, and retreats she helps participants uncover their deeper selves and their purpose and convert them into actions. She uses art, poetry, storytelling, meditation, music, individual reflection exercises, and group dialogues to develop the right brain hemisphere to the level of the left one, creating a "super-learning" state.

Isabel is a frequent speaker and presenter at international conferences. She is a visiting professor at Fordham University, where she teaches a course on developing the sustainability mindset. She grew up in Argentina, where she earned her BA in Psychology at the University of Buenos Aires, as well as an MBA at the University of Palermo. She obtained her doctorate at Teachers College, Columbia University, New York. Isabel is the co-founder and director of *MINERVAS, Women Changing the World*, a nonprofit 501(c)3 organization that supports women making a difference.

Isabel's other published works are *Action Reflection Learning: Solving Real Business Problems by Connecting Learning with Earning* (2008) and *Minervas Circles of Dialogue* (2011). Her website is www.legacycoaching.net, where you can sign up to receive her famous Quote of the Day. For speaking engagements, custom designed retreats and legacy coaching contact *info@legacycoaching.net*

To stay connected with videos and stories related to the theme of this book, visit BigBangBeing.com

WOMEN CHANGING THE WORLD

www.minervas.org

Minervas: a Movement

The Minervas movement implies action, but is also more than action. It's the manifestation, through actions, of an outlook that we all, women and men, have buried in the depth of our soul. It is a perspective that views the world with compassion and empathy, seeks collaboration with others, and acknowledges with humility that we are part of all Nature. It is a wisdom that manifests itself in the voice of our intuition. It uses feelings as a guide for action and underscores that we all have a mission: a peacemaking responsibility with each other. And it all begins with yourself, giving yourself the permission to listen to your own voice, to stand up, and make your voice heard, in both words and actions.

Minervas, Women Changing the World was founded in 2009 and is registered in the U.S.A. as a 501 (c) (3) philanthropic organization.

Mission

Minervas seeks to create a new balance in the world by unleashing and integrating the feminine perspective into all we are and do. We develop women as conscious change agents through Circles of Dialogue and other processes that are scalable, thereby multiplying the impact as we change the world.

Vision

We envision a world in which women help restore balance and equanimity to society and the environment, by fully integrating yin and yang. It is a world ruled by love, compassion, peace and joy. A world, in which men and women collaborate, share, respect and recognize their human oneness with nature.

minervas.org

Facebook Minervas. Women Changing the World

www.facebook.com/lasMinervas

For information about workshops and other activities and events, contact us at: info@minervas.org

Endnotes

1 www.unpri.org
2 globalreporting.org
3 www.unprme.org
4 www.theoathproject.org
5 Quinn, L., and Dalton, M. (2009). Leading for sustainability: Implementing the tasks of leadership. *Corporate Governance*, Vol. 9 No. 1, pp. 21–38.
6 Neal, J. A. (2008a). *Leadership and spirituality in the workplace*. Retrieved July 15, 2009, www.judineal.com/pages/pubs/leadership.htm
7 Delbecq, A. L. (2008). Spirituality and leadership effectiveness: Inner growth matters. In J. Gallos, (Ed.), *Business leadership, A Jossey-Bass Reader* (2nd ed.) (pp. 485–503). New York: John Wiley & Sons, p. 485.
8 Hicks, D. A. (2003). *Religion and the workplace: Pluralism, spirituality, leadership*. New York: Cambridge University Press.
9 Personal communication, July 13, 2009.
10 See more about unfamiliar environments as a learning principle in Rimanoczy, I., & Turner, E. (2008). *Action Reflection Learning: Solving real business problems by connecting earning with learning*. Palo Alto, CA: Davies-Black Publishing.
11 Bandura, A. (1986). *Social foundations of thought and action: A social cognitive theory*. Englewood Cliffs, NJ: Prentice-Hall.
12 The No Impact Project is an international, environmental, nonprofit project, founded by Colin Beavan, in the spring of 2009, following the success of his blog, book, and film, which chronicle his family's year-long experiment living a zero-waste lifestyle in New York City. Central to his thesis is the notion that deep-seated individual behavior change leads to both cultural change and political engagement. The No Impact Project uses entertainment, education, and group action to engage new people in the quest for ways of living that connect individual happiness with service to community and habitat. noimpactproject.org
13 Cohen, A. (2011). *Evolutionary Enlightenment: A new path to spiritual awakening*. New York: SelectBooks Inc.
14 Some authors call this phenomenon "enviropreneurship": Keogh, Paul Douglas, & Polonsky, Michael Jay, (1998). Environmental commitment: A basis for environmental entrepreneurship? *Journal of Organizational Change Management*, Vol. 11 No. 1, pp. 38–49; and Menon, Ajay, and Menon, Anil (1997, January). Enviropreneurial marketing strategy: The emergence of corporate environmentalism as market strategy. *Journal of Marketing*, Vol. 61 No. 1, pp. 51–67.

[15] See Visser, W. (2007). Corporate sustainability and the individual: A literature review. University of Cambridge Programme for Industry Research Paper Series, No. 1. Also Visser, W., and Crane, A. (2010). Corporate sustainability and the individual: Understanding what drives sustainability professionals as change agents. Social Sciences Research Network (SSRN).

[16] Rogers, M. E. (1994). Learning about global future: An exploration of learning processes and changes in adults. Unpublished doctoral dissertation. University of Toronto.

[17] Goleman, D. (1996). *Emotional intelligence.* London: Bloomsbury Bantam Books.

[18] Adams, J. D. (2008). Six dimensions of mental models. In Wirtenberg, J., Russell, W. G., & Lipsky, D. (Eds.), *The sustainable enterprise fieldbook: When it all comes together* (pp. 60–70). Sheffield, UK: Greenleaf Publishing.

[19] Antonites, A. J. (2004). *An action learning approach to entrepreneurial creativity, innovation and opportunity finding.* D.Com. dissertation, University of Pretoria, South Africa.

[20] Cohen, B., & Greenfield, J. (1997). *Double dip: Lead with your values and make money, too.* New York: Simon & Schuster.

[21] Lotspeich, C., & Larson, A. (2006, Spring). Systems innovation and entrepreneurship in the green building industry. *Batten Briefings.* University of Virginia, Darden School of Business, p. 11

[22] Leffer, N. (2006, April/May). The sustainable skyline. *Worthwhile,* 2, pp. 72–74.

[23] Connor, M. (Fall 2006), Interview published in *CRO* magazine, pp. 12–17.

[24] *CRO* magazine, Fall 2006, p. 28

[25] Senge, P., & Carstedt, G. (2001). Designing the next Industrial Revolution. *Sloan Management Review,* Vol. 42 No. 2, pp. 24–38.

[26] Capra, F. (2007). Life and leadership: A systems approach (Executive summary). Retrieved December 21, 2007, www.frtijofcapra.net/management.html

[27] Capra, F. (1996). *The web of life.* New York: Anchor Books-Doubleday, p. 28.

[28] Capra, F. (2002). *The hidden connections.* New York: Anchor Books–Random House, p. 230.

[29] Benyus, J. M. (2002). *Biomimicry: Innovation inspired by Nature.* New York: Perennial.

[30] Morowitz, H. (1992). *Beginnings of cellular life.* Yale University Press.

[31] Capra, F. (2002). *The hidden connections.* New York: Anchor Books, Random House.

[32] Daloz, L. A., Keen, C. H., Keen, J. P., & Parks, S. D. (1996). *Common fire: Leading lives of commitment in a complex world.* Boston: Beacon Press, p. 202.

[33] Bohm, D., & Edwards, M. (1991). *Changing consciousness: Exploring the hidden source of the social, political and environmental crisis facing the world* (p. 6). San Francisco: Harper, p. 6.

[34] Senge, P., Scharmer, C. O., Jaworski, J., & Flowers, B. S. (2005). *Presence: An exploration of profound change in people, organizations and society.* New York: Doubleday, p. 190.

_hor, J. B. (2010). *Plenitude: The new economics of true wealth*. New York: The Penguin Press, p. 168.

[36] Nair, C. (2011). *Consumptionomics: Asia's role in reshaping capitalism and saving the planet*. Singapore: John Wiley & Sons.

[37] Daloz et al. (1996), op. cit., p. 204.

[38] Hawken, P. (2007). *Blessed Unrest: How the largest movement in the world came into being and why no one saw it coming*. New York: Penguin Books.

[39] Kegan, R. (1994). *In over our heads*. Cambridge: Harvard University Press, p. 92.

[40] Capra, F. (1996), op. cit., p. 299.

[41] Cooperrider, D. (Ed.) (2004). *Constructive discourse and human organization*. Boston: Elsevier/JAI.

[42] Porter, T. (2008). Managerial applications of corporate social responsibility and systems thinking for achieving sustainability outcomes. *Systems Research and Behavioral Science*, Vol. 25 No. 3, p. 397. Retrieved July 27, 2009, from ABI/INFORM Global (Document ID: 1567392531).

[43] Adams, J. D. (2008), op. cit.

[44] Russell P. (2000). *The global brain awakens: Our next evolutionary leap*. New York: Element Books.

[45] Harman, W. (1998). *Global mind change: The promise of the 21st century*. San Francisco: Berrett-Koehler Publishers.

[46] Neal, J. A. (2008b). *Spirituality in the workplace: An emerging phenomenon*. Retrieved July 15, 2009, www.judineal.com/pages/pubs/phenomenon.htm

[47] Vaill, P. (1998). *Spirited leading and learning*. San Francisco: Jossey-Bass, p. 218.

[48] Palmer, P. J. (2004). *The hidden wholeness: The journey toward an undivided life*. San Francisco: Jossey-Bass.

[49] Mirvis, P. H. (1997). "Soul work" in organizations. *Organization Science*, Vol. 8 No. 2, p. 193.

[50] Mitroff, I., & Denton, E. (1999). *A spiritual audit of corporate America: Multiple designs for fostering spirituality in the workplace*. San Francisco: Jossey-Bass. p. xv–xvii.

[51] Ashmos, D., & Duchon, P. (2000, June). Spirituality at work: A conceptualization and measure. *Journal of Management Inquiry*, Vol. 9 No. 2, pp. 134–146.

[52] Neal, J. A. (2008b), op. cit.

[53] Liebig J. E. (1994). *Merchants of vision: People bringing new purpose and values to business*. San Francisco: Berrett-Koehler Publishers.

[54] Channon, J. (1992). Creating esprit de corps. In J. Renesch (Ed.), *New traditions in business* (pp. 53–66). San Francisco: Berrett-Koehler Publishers, p. 58.

[55] Aburdene, P. (2007). *Megatrends 2010: The rise of conscious capitalism*. Charlottesville, VA: Hampton Roads Publishing Company.

[56] Zohar, D., & Marshall, I. (2000). *Spiritual intelligence: The ultimate intelligence*. New York: Bloomsbury Publishing, p. 267.

[57] Adams, J. D. (2008), op. cit., p. 63.

[58] Russell, P. (2000), op. cit.

[59] cities.media.mit.edu/pdf/Mobility_on_Demand_ShanghaiCaseStudy.pdf

[60] With permission of the authors, from Steffen, W., Sanderson, A., Tyson, P.D., Jäger, J., Matson, P.A., Moore III, B., Oldfield, F., Richardson, K., Schellnhuber, H.J., Turner, B.L., & Wasson, R.J. (2004). *Global Change and the Earth System: A Planet Under Pressure*. Berlin, Heidelberg, New York: Springer-Verlag. First Fig: Sources: U.S. Bureau of the Census (2000) International database; Nordhaus (1997) In: *The economics of new goods*. University of Chicago Press; World Bank (2002) Data and statistics; World Commission on Dams (2000) The report of the World Commission on Dams; Shiklomanov (1990) Global water resources; International Fertilizer Industry Association (2002) Fertilizer indicators; UN Centre for Human Settlements (2001); The state of the world's cities (2001); Pulp and Paper International (1993) PPI's international fact and price book; McDonald's (2002) www.mcdonalds.com; UNEP (2000) Global environmental outlook 2000; Canning (2001) A database of world infrastructure stocks, 1950–95 World Bank; World Tourism Organization (2001) Tourism industry trends.

[61] McKibben, B. (2011). *Eaarth: Making a life on a tough new planet*. New York: St. Martin's Griffin, p. 4.

[62] Russell, P. (2000), op. cit., p. 94.

[63] World Bank, World Databank. Retrieved August 11, 2010, data.worldbank.org

[64] Sachs, J. (2011). *The price of civilization: Reawakening American virtue and prosperity*. New York: Random House, p. 137.

[65] McKibben, B. (2011), op. cit., p. 47.

[66] Speth, J. G. (2008). *The bridge at the edge of the world*. New Haven and London: Yale University Press. New York: Penguin Press, p. 7.

[67] Retrieved July 24, 2012, co2now.org

[68] Nair, C. (2011), op. cit., p. 30.

[69] Retrieved June 1, 2009, www.time.com/time/health/article/0,8599,1902070,00.html

[70] Ferkiss, V. (1993). *Nature, technology and society: Cultural roots of the current environmental crisis*. New York: New York University Press, p. 2.

[71] Hughes, D. J. (1974). *Ecology in ancient civilizations*. Albuquerque: University of New Mexico Press, p. 32.

[72] Nair, C. (2011), op. cit., p. 14.

[73] Chen, Sh., and Ravallion, M. (2008). The developing world is poorer than we thought, but no less successful in the fight against poverty, World Bank, August 2008.

[74] World Bank Development Indicators, 2008.

[75] Barlow, M., (2001, Summer) Water as commodity: The wrong prescription. *The Institute for Food and Development Policy*, Backgrounder, Vol. 7 No. 3.

[76] 1999 *Human Development Report*, United Nations Development Programme, p. 38.

[77] Sachs, J. (2011), op. cit., p. 135.

[78] Nair, C. (2011), op. cit., p. 39.

[79] minerals.usgs.gov/granted.html#future

[80] Nair, C. (2011), op. cit., p. 44

Water: A shared responsibility. The United Nations World Water Development Report 2, Paris/New York: UNESCO/Berghahn Books, 2006, p. 134.

[82] Griffin, S. (1995) *The eros of every day*. New York: Anchor Books, p. 75.

[83] Russell, P. (2000), op. cit., p. 89

[84] McKibben, B. (2011), op. cit., p. 133.

[85] Briggs, J., and Peat, F. D. (1999). *Seven life lessons of chaos*. New York: HarperCollins, p. 62.

[86] Kinsley, D. R. (1995). *Ecology and religion*. Upper Saddle River, NJ: Prentice Hall, p. 211.

[87] Sachs, J. (2011), op. cit., p. 150.

[88] Sachs, J. (2011), op. cit., p. 155.

[89] Ferkiss, V. (1993), op. cit, p. 83.

[90] Griffin, S. (1995), op. cit., p. 65.

[91] McKibben , B. (2011), op. cit., p. 148

[92] Schleiermacher, F. (1893). *On religion: Speeches to its cultured despisers*. London: Trubner & Co.

[93] Briggs and Peat (1999), op. cit., p. 150.

[94] Briggs and Peat (1999), op. cit., p. 90.

[95] Harman, W. (1998), op. cit., p. 11.

[96] McGilchrist, I. (2009). *The master and his emissary: The divided brain and the making of the western world*. New Haven and London: Yale University Press, p. 166.

[97] Gaukroger, S. (2006). *The emergence of a scientific culture: Science and the shaping of modernity*. Oxford: Oxford University Press.

[98] McGilchrist, I. (2009), op. cit., p. 6.

[99] Retrieved April 5 2012, www.nationmaster.com/graph/med_mob_pho-media-mobile-phones

[100] Henry J. Kaiser Family Foundation, Food for thought: Television food advertising to children in the United States, March 2007, p. 57, quoted by Jeffrey D. Sachs, op. cit., p. 139.

[101] Source: Data from World Values Survey Databank and the RTL Group, cited by Sachs, op. cit., p. 140.

[102] Sachs, J. (2011), op. cit., p. 143.

[103] McKibben, B. (2011), op. cit., p. 135.

[104] Nair, op. cit., cites Eric Randolph, Maoist Insurgency Trips up rising India, YaleGlobal, July 29, 2010.

[105] Sachs, J. (2011), op. cit., p. 98.

[106] Jackson, T. (2011). *Prosperity without growth: Economics for a finite planet*. London: Earthscan Dunstan House.

[107] Nair, C. (2011), op. cit., p. 87.

[108] Laszlo, E. (2010). *Chaos Point 2012 and beyond*. Charlottesville, VA: Hampton Roads Publishing Company, Inc., p. 40.

[109] Moore Lappé, F. (2011). *Ecomind: Changing the way we think, to create the world we want*. New York: Nation Books, p. 36.

[110] Schor, J. B. (2010), op. cit., p. 171.

[111] Shuman, M. (2012) *Local dollars, local sense: How to shift your money from Wall Street to Main Street and achieve real prosperity*. White River Junction, VT: Chelsea Green Publishing Company.

[112] Speth, J. G. (2008), op. cit., p. 121.

[113] Jackson, T. (2011). op. cit., p. 32.

[114] Belk, Russell (1988) Possessions and the extended self. *Journal of Consumer Research*, 15, pp. 139-168

[115] Jackson, T. (2011), op. cit., p. 101.

[116] Jackson, T. (2011), op. cit., p. 130.

[117] Sachs, J. (2011), op. cit., p. 151.

[118] Ravindra, Munju (2011). Wonder: A practice for everyday life. In Keogh, Martin (Ed.), *Hope beneath our feet: Restoring our place in the natural world*. Berkley, CA: North Atlantic Books, p. 186.

[119] Laszlo, E. (2010), op. cit., p. 25.

[120] Havel, V. (1998, November–December) Spirit of the Earth, *Resurgence*, 30. Quoted in Speth, op. cit., p. 200.

[121] ivoh.org/about-images-voices-hope

[122] Kristof, N.C. (2012). After recess: Change the world. *New York Times*, February 4, 2012. www.nytimes.com/2012/02/05/opinion/sunday/kristof-after-recess-change-the-world.html

[123] Norberg-Hodge, H. (1991). *Ancient futures: Lessons from Ladakh for a globalizing world*. San Francisco: Sierra Club Books.

[124] Ornstein, R. (1997). *The right mind*. San Diego, CA: Harcourt Brace & Company.

[125] McGilchrist, I. (2009), op. cit., p. 207.

[126] McGilchrist, I. (2009), op. cit., p. 3.

[127] McGilchrist, I. (2009), op. cit., p. 6.

[128] McGilchrist, I. (2009), op. cit., p. 137.

[129] McGilchrist, I. (2009), op. cit., p. 174.

[130] McGilchrist, I. (2009), op. cit., p. 166.

[131] Griffin, S. (1995), op. cit. p. 64.

[132] Griffin, S. (1995), op. cit. p. 64.

[133] Laszlo, E. (2010), op. cit., p. 60.

[134] Laszlo, E. (2010), op. cit., p. 84.

[135] Briggs and Peat (1999), op. cit, p. 123.

[136] Laszlo, E. (2010), op. cit., p. 39.

[137] Laszlo. E. (2008) *Quantum shift in the global brain: How the new scientific reality can change us and our world*. Rochester, VT: Inner Traditions, p. 33.

[138] Kinsley, D. R. (1995), op. cit., p. 174.

[139] Laszlo, E. (1989). *The inner limits of Mankind*. London: Oneworld, p. 109.

[140] Kinsley, D. R. (1995), op. cit., p. 175.

[141] Laszlo, E. (1989), op. cit., p. 109.

[142] Block, P. (2009). *Community: The structure of belonging*. San Francisco: Berrett-Koehler Publishers, p. 2.

[143] Russell, P. (2000), op. cit., p. 89.

[144] McCullough, M. (2008). *Beyond Revenge: The evolution of the forgiveness instinct*. San Francisco: Jossey Bass.

[145] Griffin, S. (1995), op. cit., p. 142.

[146] Griffin, S. (1995), op. cit., p. 144.

[147] Eisler, R., UN Speech, September 16, 2009, New York. The real wealth of nations: From global warming to global partnership.

Min Jiayin (1995). *The chalice and the blade in Chinese culture: Gender relations and social models.* China Social Sciences Publishing House.

[149] Gurven, M. (2004). To give or not to give: The behavioral ecology of human food transfers. *Behavioral and Brain Sciences* 27, pp. 543–583.

[150] Hrdy, Sarah Blaffer (2011). *Mothers and others: The evolutionary origins of mutual understanding.* Cambridge, MA: Harvard University Press.

[151] Briggs and Peat (1999), op. cit., p. 61.

[152] Capra, F. (1996), op. cit., p. 301.

[153] Harman, W. (1998), op. cit., p. 156.

[154] Laszlo, E. (2010), op. cit., p. 133.

[155] Kahane, A. (2011). *Power and love: A theory and practice of social change.* San Francisco: Berrett-Koehler Publishers, p. 36.

[156] Angier, N. (2002, July 23). Why we're so nice: We're wired to cooperate. *New York Times.*

[157] McGilchrist, I. (2009), op. cit., p. 124.

[158] Block, P. (2009), op. cit., p. 75.

[159] Holt, M. (2002, December). It's time to start the slow school movement. *Phi Delta Kappa,* Vol. 84 No. 4, pp. 264–271.

[160] Quoted in Howard W. French, More sunshine for Japan's overworked students. *New York Times,* February 25, 2001, p. 18.

[161] Also see Ghazi, Polly (2004). *Downshifting: A guide to happier simpler living;* Drake, John D. (2000). *Downshifting: How to work less and enjoy life more.* San Francisco: Berrett-Koehler Publishers; Jay, Francine (2010). *The joy of less: A minimalist living guide: How to declutter, organize, and simplify your life.* Medford, NJ: Anja Press; Dawson, William J. (2010). *The quest of the simple life.* Qontro Classic Books.

[162] Walsh, R. (1999). *Essential spirituality: The 7 central practices to awaken heart and mind.* New York: John Wiley & Sons, p. 7.

[163] Armstrong, K. (2007). *The great transformation: The beginning of our religious traditions.* New York: Anchor Books, p. Xvi.

[164] Zohar, D., and Marshall, I. (2000). *Spiritual intelligence: The ultimate intelligence.* New York: Bloomsbury Publishing, p. 23.

[165] Zohar & Marshall, op. cit., p. 20.

[166] Harman, W. (1998), op. cit., p. xviii.

[167] Laszlo. E. (2008), op. cit., p. 78.

[168] Gilligan, C. (1982). *In a different voice: Psychological theory and women's development.* Cambridge, MA: Harvard University Press.

[169] Johnson, B. (1996). *Polarity management: Identifying and managing unsolvable problems.*

[170] Bache, C. (2000). *Dark night, early dawn.* New York: State University of NY, p. 209.

[171] Russell, P. (2000), op. cit., p. 82.

[172] Bache, C. (2000), op. cit., p. 178.

[173] Laszlo, E. (2010), op. cit., p. 84.

[174] Kabat-Zinn, J. (2005). *Wherever you go there you are: Mindfulness meditation in everyday life.* New York: Hyperion.

[175] Keogh, M. (Ed.) (2011). *Hope beneath our feet: Restoring our place in the natural world.* Berkley, CA: North Atlantic Books, p. 64.